SOUL
FRIEND

NEW REVISED EDITION

SOUL FRIEND

SPIRITUAL DIRECTION IN THE MODERN WORLD

Kenneth Leech

Foreword By
George Carey, Archbishop of Canterbury

MOREHOUSE PUBLISHING

Morehouse Publishing
P.O. Box 1321
Harrisburg, PA 17105

Morehouse Publishing is a division of The Morehouse Group.

This edition published in 1994 by Darton, Longman, and Todd, Ltd., 1 Spencer Court, 140–142 Wandsworth High Street, London SW18 4JJ, U.K. Reprinted 1996, 1998, 2000. First published in Great Britain in 1977 by Sheldon Press, Marylebone Road, London NW1 4DU, U.K.

Cover design by Wesley Hoke.

Library of Congress Cataloging-in-Publication Data
Leech, Kenneth.
    Soul friend : spiritual direction in the modern world / Kenneth Leech ; foreword by the Archbishop of Canterbury.
        p. cm.
    Includes bibliographical references and index.
    ISBN 0-8192-1888-X (alk. paper)
        1. Spiritual direction. I. Title.

BV5053 .L435 2001
253.5'3—dc21
                                                                    2001030136

Printed in the United States of America

    02 03 04 05 06 07 08 09   10 9 8 7 6 5 4 3 2

'Anyone without a soul friend
is a body without a head.'
CELTIC SAYING

Contents

Foreword

When it was first published, *Soul Friend* opened a door for me, and for many of my generation. It was a door through which we could walk and discover more of the richness of Christian spirituality. My predecessor, Michael Ramsey, was quite right when he said of it: 'Here at last we have a work on the cure of souls which understands the trends of the present day and at the same time draws upon the deep tradition of Christian spirituality in the work of counsellor, confessor and spiritual director.'

Since then, of course, 'spirituality' has become a buzz word within a wide variety of Christian traditions. Spiritual directors are to be found not just in the Catholic wing but amongst Evangelicals and Charismatics as well. I welcome many of the developments within the field of spiritual direction, but, like Kenneth Leech, I am increasingly worried by the individualistic nature of some of them and also by the sense of superior exclusiveness encouraged by a few practitioners. There are plenty of examples from the past – from the Letters to the Corinthians onwards – of those who wish to set themselves up as a 'spiritual' élite. Such groupings have, without exception, brought damage to the Church of God.

How refreshing then that *Soul Friend* places spiritual development firmly within the corporate and sacramental life of the Church. The growth of an individual's relationship with God cannot be set apart from their relationship with their fellow Christians. It is my hope that this new edition will bring to another generation a wealth of fresh insights similar to those which were shared by my own.

+ George Cantuar

Notes to the revised edition

So much has happened since 1977 that I was tempted to embark on a major rewriting of much of the text. Yet it seemed important to revise the book in such a way that it was recognizably the same book. And in fact, as I read it, I realized that the main body of the work has survived and needs no major change. So I have concentrated on four areas.

First, I have tried to remove sexist language. However, it is important that we honestly recognize both the sexism within the Christian tradition and the cultural conditioning in the use of language. I have therefore retained the original language of all citations. I have also avoided the cumbersome usage of 'him or her' and have alternated the use of masculine and feminine forms, unless the chronology of the context demands otherwise. Because the ordination of women to the priesthood is a fact in many parts of the Anglican Communion, though not yet in the Roman and Orthodox churches, I have also used 'she' and 'her' in reference to priestly ministry.

Secondly, I have added a new Introduction, though I have kept virtually all the material which was in the original Introduction.

Thirdly, I have added small amounts of material to the text, and have corrected one or two minor historical errors. I have also expanded several footnotes to take account of recent developments.

Finally, I have greatly expanded the bibliography. Even so, there is much material which I have had to omit, but I hope that I have included most of the significant works which have appeared in this field since 1977.

I am grateful for help and suggestions in revising the book to Jan Baltz, Janet Batsleer, the Revd Martin Dudley, the Revd Tilden Edwards, the Revd David Goodacre, Margaret Hebblethwaite, Sister Isobel Mary SLG, the Revd Dr Margaret Guenther, the Revd Paul James, Fr David Lonsdale SJ, Sara Maitland, and Dr Gerald May; to Fr Simon Tugwell OP, and Fr Richard Woods OP, for helping me correct some historical errors about the early Dominicans; and to the Revd Winston Crum, formerly of Seabury-Western

Seminary, Evanston, for inviting me to speak to his students about a possible revision of the book many years before I would otherwise have thought about it.

Introduction to the revised edition

It is over fifteen years since I wrote the first edition of this book. First published in Britain in 1977, it had grown out of a School of Prayer for Anglican ordinands which I led at St Augustine's College, Canterbury, during the years 1971 to 1974, when I was tutor and chaplain there. During one session of the School we devoted most of the time to a course on spiritual direction, and the papers which were given during this course were enlarged and expanded to form the heart of the present book.

In my Introduction to the first edition I explained the aims and limitations of the study. It is not an original work so much as an attempt to bring together in an accessible form an accumulated body of wisdom and guidance from the Christian spiritual tradition. It is therefore a compendium of resources which may serve to introduce people to the rich and diverse world of Christian spirituality. It is certainly not meant to be a 'popular' handbook or a 'practical guide' to the work of spiritual direction. I stressed in 1977 that I had grave doubts about whether it was possible to produce such a book, and that, if it were, it would be a dangerous enterprise. Still less would I be competent to produce such a guide even if it were desirable. I believed then, and believe even more strongly now, that the ministry of spiritual direction cannot be learnt from books, but only from personal experience in prayer and pastoral care. It is not true to say that spiritual directors are born and not made; but they are always miracles of grace, charismatic persons in the true sense of that abused word. The purpose of this study is to try to provide some nourishment for this important ministry by drawing on the teachings of the great spiritual guides and to try to help those who are themselves seeking direction on the spiritual way, and who wish to know more about the Christian tradition of prayer.

When I wrote the book, it was common to find writers lamenting the decline of the priest as pastor and speaking of a 'crisis of identity'. For example, it was claimed that 'the ordained man is no longer wanted, as he was a few years ago, in helping people with their interpersonal relationships'. The priest therefore is reduced to either searching around frantically for a new role, or dealing 'almost exclusively with that remnant, continually getting smaller, who faithfully attend public worship'.[1] Claims that the priest ministered almost entirely to churchgoers were made by supposedly well-informed persons. Thus a parish priest, ordained many years ago and now dead, claimed in 1976 that 'today the clergy have become practically confined to ministering to a dwindling remnant of churchgoers'.[2] From my experience, I did not believe these claims were true. On the contrary, the picture which I saw, as a parish priest in the East End of London, was of a society in which more and more people were looking for some sense of spiritual direction, and the problem of priests and others was how to meet that need adequately without being overwhelmed. I found myself in strong agreement with the view of Martin Thornton that 'spiritual direction is our greatest pastoral need today'. Writing over thirty years ago, Thornton predicted 'the beginning of a religious revival of a deep and subtle type', and he went on to contrast the approach of the spiritual guide with that of evangelists, 'youth experts', preachers, and church organizers. 'The former group are concerned with how a demand for their ministrations can be created; the latter with how the growing demand for guidance can be met'.[3] This was certainly to oversimplify the picture and to overstate the case, but it seemed to me to contain an important element of truth. The 'crisis of identity' among many priests had occurred at the very time that thousands of people were seeking spiritual guidance and could not find it. I wondered if perhaps the reason that many clergy felt underemployed was that what they had to offer was not what was needed.

My own experience was that lack of work was emphatically not the problem that those who took spiritual guidance seriously were likely to encounter. On the contrary, they were likely to become overburdened very quickly. It seemed essential to communicate to people that guidance of individuals in the spiritual life was at the heart of the Christian religion. It was not the preserve of a small group of experts based on religious orders or therapy groups. Union with God is not a peripheral area for the Christian, and it is union with God which is the central concern of spiritual direction. The church seemed to be in desperate need of spiritual guides, men and women who were steeped in prayer and in the Spirit, and who could therefore be bearers of the Spirit to our age. I therefore wrote *Soul Friend* in the hope that it would be of some help to those who might be called to this ministry.

The book was welcomed with great enthusiasm, and was widely seen as filling a major gap. Archbishop Michael Ramsey, who spoke at the press launch, said: 'At last we have a work on the cure of souls which understands the trends of the present day and at the same time draws upon the deep tradition of Christian spirituality in the work of counsellor, confessor and spiritual director'.[4] Martin Thornton, whose writings had influenced me a good deal in my early years of ministry, said that 'the book should be bought, read, re-read, and constantly referred to by every serious pastor, whether priest or layman . . . For the sake of the church and the world, please buy it'.[5] In the United States, Henri Nouwen saw it as having 'given us new access to one of the most important areas of Christian ministry' and claimed that it 'reclaims the centrality of spiritual direction in ministry'.[6] The book sold way beyond my expectations. Having written it with young, mainly male, ordinands of the Church of England in mind, I soon realized that most of those who read it were none of these! At the time of publication, and for some time afterwards, it was the only modern book available on the British and American markets about the ministry of spiritual direction. It still sells, to an audience quite different to the one I anticipated.

In 1977 I specifically rejected the idea that it should be seen as a guidebook, a 'how to do it', and I expressed grave doubts as to whether such a book were possible or desirable.[7] I also strongly emphasized my belief that spiritual direction was part of the ordinary ministry of the church, not a specialist field reserved for experts. Now, in 1994, where are we? Spiritual direction is certainly 'in' again with a vengeance. There are workshops, institutes, cassettes, courses, books galore. Everywhere, and in all traditions, there is a concern with the 'inner life' and with personal guidance. Many positive and creative developments have occurred. Writers like Gordon Jeff in Britain and William Barry and Alan Jones in the USA have produced popular books aimed at a much wider market than mine was. Institutes such as Shalem in Washington DC or Stillpoint in Nashville, and networks such as SPIDIR in South London, have grown up to train people, mainly lay women and men, as spiritual directors. There has been considerable attention to the role of women, expressed in books by Kathleen Fischer and Margaret Guenther among others. And, of course, there has been the remarkable revival of interest in and practice of Ignatian retreats. All this has been exciting, healthy, positive, hopeful.

Yet there are aspects of this growth which worry me. I am worried, first, that spiritual direction is being seen as more important than it is. It is, after all, one ministry among others. Directors play an important but quite a lowly and limited function within the wider context of pastoral care and theological formation. I detect now a tendency in some quarters to make the spiritual director more important than she or he is, in a way which is at variance with the mainstream of Christian tradition. Dom Jean Leclercq once said that it is necessary to have a spiritual director but it is not necessary to make use of that person.[8] I am not sure that direction is necessary for all people at all times. And so I look with some alarm at what seems to be excessive reliance on direction, involving in some cases monthly or even weekly sessions. In particular, some people within liberal Protestant traditions, having been over-wary in the past of 'priestcraft' and of individuals who 'stand between the soul and God', seem to have swung to this extreme position uncritically.

One result of this over-reliance is that some spiritual directors seem to have little time to do anything else. Margaret Guenther, in her excellent recent book *Holy Listening*, contrasts the spiritual director who has time, with the plight of the 'tightly scheduled parish clergy'.[9] But isn't this tight scheduling part of the problem? Nobody would claim that parish clergy were the *only* people who should be doing spiritual direction, but surely they should see it as part of their ministry. Neither the tight scheduling which makes such work impossible, nor the heavy concentration of such ministry in the hands of a few overburdened 'specialists', seems healthy.

I am worried also that this ministry is being professionalized and seen as a specialist ministry in a way which is potentially extremely dangerous. I understand that there is now an international organization of spiritual directors with headquarters in the USA. There – and here maybe – some spiritual directors charge fees for their services, something which would have horrified the saints in all ages. People are being 'accredited' with certificates, diplomas and doctorates in spiritual direction by the many institutes and departments which have sprung up. Now, of course, like St Teresa of Avila, I prefer learned guides to incompetents. But I am not at all happy with the captivity of some approaches to direction to the professional model which has done so much damage to pastoral ministry in other fields, and to unexamined concepts of 'training' with all their ideological assumptions. I stand by my insistence in 1977 that spiritual direction is not essentially a ministry for specialists and professionals, but part of the ordinary pastoral ministry of every parish and every Christian community. Even more so do I stand by my suggestion that the role of 'training' is extremely limited, and that this ministry is essentially a by-product of a life of prayer and growth in holiness. Part of our task is to discover, help and affirm the work of direction which is already being done by unknown people who do not write books or run courses.

A whole chapter of *Soul Friend* is devoted to trying to clarify the differences between spiritual direction, counselling and psycho-therapy, recognizing the significant areas of overlap. One psy-chiatrist whom I consulted about the revision said: 'Please do not alter anything there, or blur the distinctions'. Yet I am increasingly worried not only by the tendency in some quarters to blur the distinctions and to assimilate direction into a therapeutic model (Rieff's 'triumph of the therapeutic'[10] in a new spiritual format) but also by the uncritical and simplistic adaptation of certain quasi-therapeutic tools. The most obvious example of this is the use of the Myers-Briggs Type Indicator. This grid of sixteen personality types, based on a rather questionable theory of temperament, has rapidly become *de fide* in parts of the spirituality circuit. I do not entirely dismiss Myers-Briggs' simplification of Jung's fairly complex work on personality types, but there is no doubt that in some quarters there has been a further process of over-simplifi-cation and even trivialization.[11] There are other examples of the way in which methods and techniques, in themselves helpful, have become part of a cult. For example, I am entirely in favour of people keeping journals, and have done so myself for many years, but the way in which Progoff's 'intensive journal' method has been taken up by some people so that the whole of spiritual formation is reduced to it – when did 'journal' become a verb? – is alarming.[12] 'Salvation by technique' will be an increasing problem in our tech-nocratic age.

I am worried, finally, because much spiritual direction assumes a view of spirituality which is not wholesome and only tenuously Christian, and which reflects the individualism and privatization of religion in the West rather than any embodiment in a corporate tradition. I have warned for many years of the dangers of a new gnosticism. Now Christopher Lasch claims that gnosticism is 'the characteristic form of contemporary spirituality',[13] and I find myself agreeing with him. Nor is this gnostic illuminism only a problem outside the church. Much current Christian writing on spiritual direction, as on spirituality as a whole, has lost its roots in Scripture and tradition and has colluded with the current culture of contentment and narcissism. Consumer capitalism is only too good at co-opting such approaches to spirituality.

So my concerns about much of what currently passes for 'spirituality' remain and grow stronger by the hour. I am horrified at the way in which a lowly and humble ministry has been institutionalized and privatized, and, for all the talk of its 'social implications', de-politicized. I am sorry if I have unwittingly contributed to this false inwardness, and to the compartmentalization of consciousness of which it is a part. As a priest in the USA said to me after I had spoken at a conference on racial harassment and the resurgence of fascism: 'You must often get confused with the other Kenneth Leech who writes books on spirituality'.

Within classical Christian understanding, spiritual direction is a personal ministry which takes place within a corporate framework, a framework of sacrament, discipleship and social action. It takes place within a context of theological reflection and social struggle. Only within such a context can it make sense and make progress. It is because I see a loss of such a context that I remain, and become increasingly, worried. Of course this does not mean that I am not concerned with helping non-Christians. Most of my work has always been, and still is, with non-Christians and people outside the churches, and my ministry of spiritual direction began here. My emphasis on the Christian community as the locus for direction is not intended to restrict it to the church, still less to priests, but to attack the trend to privatization and gnosticism. The spiritual needs of the present day cry out for a strong and deeply rooted Christian community. The ministry of spiritual direction grows from a life of prayer, discipleship and the struggle for holiness. It is a by-product of that life, and only makes sense with it. I have revised this book, which I began to write twenty years ago, both out of a commitment to the deepening of spiritual life, and out of a concern that this ministry is in danger of being trivialized, professionalized and enclosed within an élitist and inward-looking enclave. Spiritual direction must be reclaimed in the service of the Kingdom of God.

1
Spirituality and the present climate

> Can you see any hope for this homicidal, neurologically crippled species other than a mass religious ecstatic convulsion?
>
> TIMOTHY LEARY[1]

> In 1963 the mere mention of the God concept was good for a laugh. By 1965 it was many people's most serious concern.
>
> JEFF NUTTALL[2]

THE 'SPIRITUAL QUEST OF YOUTH'

There is a serious danger at present in some writing and thinking around the area of youth and spirituality that the 'spiritual quest of youth' will be exaggerated and distorted to such an extent that the more widespread phenomenon of extreme conservatism in social attitudes will continue to spread unchecked. To some extent indeed the latter can be seen as a reaction against the former: the revolt of many of the young both against western materialism and against the prevailing political malaise has provoked many adults to a defensive and reactionary posture. But to an even greater extent, the present climate represents the *persistence* of a tradition which never died out among the young. Most young people never revolted, never protested, and never undertook any spiritual pilgrimage. They remained, like their parents, conventional and conservative.

In an earlier study,[3] I attempted to describe some of the characteristics of the 'youth culture' of the 1960s with specific reference to its search for a spirituality. I was criticized by a number of reviewers for doing what I specifically denied that I was doing: describing the movements of youth in that period in exclusively 'religious' categories, and generalizing on the basis of a small minority of young people in central London. It is essential therefore to recog-

nize the wider context and to define one's limits. I do not believe
that the movements associated with the 'counter-culture' and the
'radicalization of youth', which have now been described in a
number of studies, have so far affected modern society to more
than a marginal extent. The impact on the big cities, with their
concentration of journals, meetings and access to the media, can
help to promote exaggeration. But the fact is that the cultural
trends which I and others have described represent significant
minority movements. As one sociologist noted: 'Life in Burslem,
Tadcaster and Crewe was not greatly affected.'[4]

At the same time, the movements are more significant and their
influence more subtle than is often appreciated. Moreover, the
interest of young and not so young in spirituality never was confined, and is not confined today, to the 'counter-culture' even in its
widest connotations. It is a phenomenon which still awaits
adequate research and documentation. For me, it marked the starting point in my ministry of taking personal spiritual guidance
seriously, and led me to re-examine my own inner life and inner
resources. I found that the demands made upon me required more
than personal planning or sociological skills, and that I was being
led to a deeper exploration of the most neglected area of clergy
training, ascetical and spiritual theology.

During the 1960s it was frequently being argued that the future
of humanity was 'non-religious', that society was secularized, and
that the church's mission must be based on that assumption.

> We came increasingly to believe that all this was true. Even our
> religious establishments, our various Vaticans came to believe
> that it was true. They have been operating, more or less, on this
> assumption ever since. This assumption is not true: it has been
> discredited not by theologians but by events. In fact we were
> entering—not a secularized age, as we thought—we were enter-
> ing an age of incredible religiosity.[5]

The view that society was increasingly and inevitably 'religionless'
was severely criticized by the American sociologist Andrew Greeley.
Arguing that 'the basic human religious needs and the basic
religious functions have not changed very notably since the late Ice
Age', Greeley concluded:

> I do not believe that religion is in a state of collapse and none
> of the empirical data that I have available lead me to believe

that it is ... The religious crises of the intellectual community by no means reflect the religious situation of the mass of the people. 'Western man', 'modern man', 'technological man', 'secular man' are to be found, for the most part, only on university campuses, and increasingly only among senior faculty members, as the students engage in witchcraft, astrology and other bizarre cultic practices.[6]

By 1968 it was clear in many sections of modern life that there was a renewed interest in 'spiritual' issues.

It was a confused and bizarre interest which many who worked with young people encountered. There were those who used LSD and other psychedelic drugs and immediately sought guidance, both from other trippers and from those outside the drug cultures altogether, about further explorations of consciousness. The writings of Alan Watts and Ronald Laing became very popular. Both were concerned with the breaking down of the barriers by which the ego, the transitory waking self, prevented the experience of transcendence. For many young people, it seems that LSD initially helped this process, but they wanted to move on from this experience. They described their need in openly spiritual terms, so that even the Interim Report of the Canadian Government's Commission was led to comment on the degree of interest in religion among drug takers.[7] These young searchers looked wherever they felt their need might be met—meditation schools, paperback mysticism, Yoga, even the church. But the church seemed ill-prepared to meet that need.

These young people were not restricted to any one social class or cultural group. Not all among them were drug users, and most of them were not 'hippies'. They were a very mixed group. What they did seem to have in common was a search for meaning in their lives, and by this they meant an *inner* meaning, a spiritual meaning. Ronald Laing referred to their search as a quest for transcendence of the ego, for 'meta-egoic' experience.

People who explore states of ego-loss, or are precipitated into them willy-nilly, search for references: maps of the worlds within worlds, of meta-egoic space and time. Most people involved in this don't refer to the Christian tradition for their terms of reference. They go not to the Bible but to the Tibetan Book of the Dead, the biography of Milarepa, the Tao Te Ching, the Secret of the Golden Flower, to the Buddhists, Zen, Tibetan and other schools, the Taoists, the Sufis, the Hindus. Such texts that seem able to speak to the condition of these meta-egoic ego-loss experiences, over barriers of egoic-time, space and cultural conditions.[8]

It was this quest for transcendence and ego-loss which was very frequently associated with the use of psychedelics, and by 1967 the psychedelic movement had grown into a mass culture, concentrated particularly in the Haight-Ashbury district of San Francisco. In Britain, London's streets became familiar with the surface features of psychedelia. Beneath the surface, a new spirituality seemed to be emerging.

The place of LSD and other chemicals in this emergence should not be exaggerated, but it was and is of great importance. It was not a question of the simple causal link: psychedelic drugs merely opening up the consciousness and leading directly to spirituality. It was rather a resurgence of spirituality which for a time used the only resources which were available in a technological and materialistic culture—chemicals. In one sense the psychedelic movement was simply the application of the highly respectable 'Better living through chemistry' thesis to the realm of the spirit. Or, as Meher Baba put it in 1968, 'God in a Pill'.[9] Soon after the early work with Leary on psychedelic drugs, his colleague Richard Alpert sought out a guru in India who told him,

> LSD is like a Christ coming to America in the Kali Yuga. America is a most materialistic country, and they wanted their Avatar in the form of a material. The young people wanted their Avatar in the form of a material. And so they got LSD. If they had not tasted of such things, how will they know?—how will they know?[10]

Alpert, even though he ceased to use drugs, continues to hold that when used under reasonably conscious conditions, these agents have enabled some people to break out of their limited perceptual vantage points and understand alternative possibilities of reality.[11] Less positively, and perhaps more cynically, Theodore Roszak commented in 1968:

> The gadget happy American has always been a figure of fun because of his facile assumption that there exists a technological solution to every human problem. It only took the great psychedelic crusade to perfect the absurdity by proclaiming that personal

salvation and the social revolution can be packed into a capsule.[12]

The basic thesis of the psychedelic movement was expressed by Timothy Leary in the early days of his drug experiments. The human brain, he argued, was 'capable of limitless new dimensions of awareness and knowledge', but 'you have to go out of your mind to use your head; that you have to pass beyond everything in order to become acquainted with the new areas of consciousness'. Jerry Garcia of the Grateful Dead noted, 'Acid has changed consciousness entirely. The U.S. has changed in the last few years and it's because that whole first psychedelic thing meant, "Here's this new consciousness, this new freedom, and it's here in yourself." ' Michael Hollingshead, the Englishman who first introduced Leary to LSD, has documented in great detail the way in which the drug search assumed spiritual dimensions and a theological language. In his book *The Man Who Turned on the World*, he claims that

> we are seeing a change in the nature of western man due to a shift in emphasis away from a theological revelation to an ontologist mysticism, that is, authority of a Divine Person to the more individually 'free' belief in absolute Nature. In either approach to God, we are reminded that we are summoned to a deeper spiritual awareness, far beyond the level of subject-object.[13]

Many years earlier, Aldous Huxley had written of 'the chemical conditions of transcendental experience',[14] while in the nineteenth century both Benjamin Blood and William James were concerned with the issues of drugs and mysticism.[15] Indeed, the link between drug use and the attainment of spiritual status is extremely ancient.[16]

The pharmacology of LSD and the historical course of the psychedelic movement have been discussed elsewhere, and ought not to detain us here. The important point is that to make the drug the centre of attention is a mistake. The most that any drug can do is to accentuate or suppress functions in behaviour which already exist. Drugs cannot in principle introduce anything new into the mind or into behaviour. So it was soon rediscovered that the entire range of 'drug effects' could be produced without the use of drugs, by traditional methods of consciousness change—meditation, sensory deprivation, fasting, chanting, Yoga, dancing, and so on. Moreover, these 'natural', non-chemical methods might enable the state of enriched consciousness to be continuous and lasting. So out of the psychedelic movement grew an interest in non-chemical approaches, in methods of self-exploration and enriching of consciousness by natural means. Hence we have seen through the late 1960s and 1970s the blossoming of a wide range of spiritual movements and groups whose aim is to raise the level of consciousness.

For it has been a central assumption of this new spiritual quest that the West is suffering from severe spiritual deprivation, what Roszak calls 'a diminished mode of consciousness'.[17] It was this point which Laing made so powerfully in his best-selling work *The Politics of Experience and the Bird of Paradise*, which first appeared in 1967.

> We live in a secular world. To adapt to this world the child abdicates its ecstasy . . . Having lost our experience of the Spirit, we are expected to have faith. But this faith comes to be a belief in a reality which is not evident. There is a prophecy in Amos that there will be a time when there will be a famine in the land, not a famine for bread, nor a thirst for water, but of *hearing* the words of the Lord. That time has now come to pass. It is the present age.[18]

Laing ironically was assuming the mantle of the theologian at precisely the time that many theologians were writing as though they were psychiatrists! Others were to make the same point. 'We are heading into a profoundly religious age', wrote McLuhan in 1968,[19] while the economist E. F. Schumacher strongly attacked the autonomy of economics and urged the recovery of spirituality. 'The guidance we need for this work cannot be found in science or technology, the value of which utterly depends on the ends they serve: but it can still be found in the traditional wisdom of mankind.'[20]

The particular form of the 'traditional wisdom of mankind' which was being rediscovered and re-experienced in the 1960s was eastern rather than western, Hindu rather than Christian, non-rational rather than rational, occult rather than prophetic, and emotional rather than intellectual. Charles Reich referred to it as 'the new consciousness', and said that 'the extraordinary thing about this new consciousness is that it has emerged out of the wasteland of the corporate state, like flowers pushing up through the concrete pavement'.[21] Monica Furlong saw it as a revival of the ancient theme of spiritual journey.

> The return to primitive forms of journey such as witchcraft and astrology; the new found interest in meditation and in contemplative forms of experience; the adoption of eastern forms of religion, particularly Buddhism, Zen Buddhism and Vedantism; the attempt to understand something new about the meaning of the group, by group dynamics and new forms of communal living; the turning to drugs, especially LSD and cannabis, in an attempt to learn something new about the self and its meaning; the expression and sharing of some of this ferment of thought in pop music and musicals like *Hair*; all of these seem to me to be attempts to set out upon, or talk about, an inner journey.[22]

It is significant too that Hermann Hesse's novels became popular in this period, for in *Siddhartha* Hesse uses the account of one of Buddha's journeys as a way of recounting his own quest for spiritual direction.

In this quest, journey or search, we can identify three central themes which seem to be present in most of the forms which the journey takes, though they are not all present together at the same time. The first is a disenchantment with, or lack of interest in, the conventional, established religions of the West, particularly institutional Christianity. The second is a desire for transcendence, for deeper ways of experiencing reality. The third is a concern for peace, for justice, for human liberation and human fulfilment, combined with a disillusionment with mainstream political solutions. Some of these themes in contemporary spirituality will need more detailed examination.

THE JOURNEY INWARDS

In Hesse's *Siddhartha*, the young son of a Brahman priest discovers that, while he can make other people happy, he is not himself truly at peace. He has contemplated, meditated, and used the great Om mantra, but in spite of all his efforts, he remains empty, 'his intellect ... not satisfied, his soul ... not at peace, his heart ... not still'. He needs to replace intellectual knowledge by direct experience, to find the reality within his own self. 'One must find the source within one's own self.' So Siddhartha goes off into the forest with his friend and confidant Govinda in search of an authentic spirituality. After some years of ascetical discipline, he still finds that the ego is present, he is still not at peace. So he goes in search of a Buddha, and Govinda becomes the Buddha's disciple. Siddhartha, however, chooses 'to leave all doctrines and all teachers and to reach the goal alone—or die'.[23] In his search, he 'has discovered the comforting secret that a teacher is unnecessary'.[24] He moves on to a city where a beautiful courtesan Kamala instructs him in the art of love, but he later leaves the city for the forest. He thinks of suicide but is deterred by the distant sound of the Om mantra from his past, and he goes to sleep. He wakes to find Govinda, now a monk. Siddhartha, however, realizes that he has, through his struggles, become free of his ego-self, and he remains by the river, learning from its voices. He has attained Buddhahood.

The whole book, of course, needs to be read. It is hardly surprising that Hesse began to assume the status of a cult figure at the point in the 1960s when many young people found themselves undertaking precisely this journey—a spiritual pilgrimage, without a teacher, free from the forms and structures of the past, a quest for the Self beyond the self. Siddhartha's pilgrimage is in fact Hesse's own. 'All these stories dealt with me, reflected my own path, my own secret dreams and wishes, my own bitter anguish.'[25] They reflected the path, the dreams and the anguish of many.

Leaving drugs behind, many young people came to feel that the journey might best be pursued through meditation. Meditation schools, groups and cults, mainly Hindu in orientation, now flourish in many places, as well as occult movements, and the more traditional disciplines of Zen and Sufi mysticism. Nor has this revival of exploration of the eastern traditions affected only the young, or the ex-drug user. Some of these movements now include many middle-aged and elderly disciples as well as many young people who have never used drugs. The eastern schools which exist in Britain fall into three main groups, according to their origins in Hindu, Buddhist or Islamic traditions. Hinduism assumes many forms. Its scriptures are the Vedas, and its disciples are often linked together in ashrams, or community houses. The most important and best-known of the Hindu sacred texts is the Bhagavad-Gita, and this now sells widely in Britain in the translation by A. C. Bhaktivedanta Swami, the founder of the Krishna Consciousness movement. The Yoga Sutras of Patanjali also come out of the Hindu tradition and are one of the essential texts for practising contemplation through Yoga. Yoga and Vedanta in fact are the two major schools which grew out of the Hindu literature, and movements derived from both schools are popular at the present time. Yoga is widely taught and practised in London and other centres, although the most popular form is a very westernized version of Hatha Yoga, propagated for health purposes, from which most of the contemplative core has been removed. Sometimes there may be a simple form of meditation offered, but the basic appeal is that of physical fitness and agility. But there are schools which go much deeper, and a visit to most large bookstores will introduce the inquirer to the literature of a wide variety of such schools.

The Vedanta schools have grown up largely as a result of the activity of the Ramakrishna Society and other more recent groups. They use mantras, symbols, vocal prayer, and silence. Some of the Buddhist schools have been established in Britain for many years. The Buddhist Society of London was formed over sixty years ago, but recently there has been a revived interest in Buddhism, and since the invasion of Tibet by the Chinese, Tibetan monks have established centres in the West. The two movements of Islamic origin which exist here are the Sufis and Subud. Sufism is the mystical movement within Islam, and a large and flourishing Sufi movement grew up in Britain around Pir Vilayat Inyat Khan. As well as these, there is a growing number of movements which are syncretistic and have mixed together elements from East and West as well as from various religious traditions. It is these 'independent' schools which have attracted most attention and gained large followings among the young.

Within this wide range, there are, of course, distinct movements which have different appeals. The Divine Light Mission, for example, tended to appeal to rather simple-minded youth in much the same way as some of the Christian revivalist groups appeal. Indeed, the atmosphere and style of the Mission was well within the revivalist tradition. In July 1973 at Alexandra Palace, Blue Aquarius played to some 8,000 people at an event which *The Sunday Times* music critic called 'the fastest harnessing of contemporary musical idiom to a religious cause since the Salvation Army'.[26] The language of the songs was a kind of psychedelic Moody and Sankey.

> The Lord of the Universe has come to us this day,
> And he will turn you on.

Who will save the world?
The living God will save the world.
What does he give?
Love, Light and Peace.
Who is Guru Maharaj Ji?
The Saviour of Mankind[27]

The Mission offered 'knowledge'. The first English girl to receive
the knowledge described it in 1972 as 'knowledge of one's own
true self, the true nature of one's soul'.[28] But knowledge of self was
also seen as knowledge of God. 'All I ask is your love, all I ask is
your trust, and what I will give you is a sure peace that will never
die . . . I can show you that God exists.' The Mission, before it ran
into internal difficulties in 1974, was claiming over 60,000 followers in the United Kingdom. It was a successful movement
because it stressed access to knowledge of the inner world, the
attainment of peace and certainty in a world of doubt and confusion ('Never leave room for doubt in your mind'), direct experience of God within, and the use of guaranteed methods. A
spokesman for the Mission claimed in 1973:

> The 'knowledge' of Guru Maharaj Ji is of simple and gentle inner
> meditation, peacefully bestowed and peacefully practised . . . Old
> ladies, children, housewives and business men—ordinary people
> with no time for the outlandish or esoteric—have received it
> and practise it daily, becoming more peaceful, tolerant and
> understanding, and loving the Guru who has taught them—at
> no cost whatsoever—the means to be so.[29]

This pattern—inner peace, certainty, direct experience, and guaranteed methods—is one which is repeated in many other movements
and cults. While the Divine Light Mission has now receded, many
parallel movements, offering an almost identical path, remain, and
new ones arise from time to time.

A different kind of movement which has gained very large numbers of disciples is Transcendental Meditation (TM) as taught by
Maharishi Mahesh Yogi and his Spiritual Regeneration Movement.
There is now a substantial scientific literature dealing with the
effects of the twice-daily periods of twenty minutes which form
the staple diet of the TM practitioners. The Maharishi's movement
is extremely well-organized, and courses in the Science of Creative
Intelligence have been sold to numerous educational institutions.

It is claimed that the stress and anxiety which are at the root of human distress can be relieved through meditation. The initiate is given a secret mantra, that is, an unintelligible sacred phrase which is personal to each initiate, and he is taught how to repeat it to himself until the mind is stilled and consciousness is raised beyond the waking state. Transcendental consciousness, according to Maharishi, is a fourth major state of consciousness, as natural as the other three physiologically defined states of wakefulness, dreaming, and deep sleep. No particular belief is required, no profession of faith, no renunciation, no commitment. TM is seen as a purely natural technique which can be learned.

> Transcendental Meditation (TM) is a natural technique which allows the conscious mind to experience systematically finer states of thought until it arrives at the finest state of thought and transcends it, arriving at the source of thought, the state of pure intelligence.[30]

The movement claims that the origins of TM lie in the ancient Vedic traditions. A great deal of emphasis is placed on its potential as 'an effective non-chemical alternative to drug abuse for many people'.[31] The State of Michigan Governor's Office of Drug Abuse made TM into 'a necessary ingredient to every drug abuse education effort'.[32] The Maharishi has offered to reduce the urban crime rate fairly quickly. Experiments have shown, he claims, that twelve US cities in which TM was practised by one per cent of the population showed a six per cent decrease in crime, while twelve cities with few meditators showed a nine per cent increase.[33] Not content with these efforts, he has said that he can solve the problems of the world in one generation,[34] and both the US Army and sections of big business have found TM useful in solving their own problems. So it was interesting to note that while the early disciples of Maharishi were long-haired hippies, the present generation are more likely to be short-haired professionals. It is, claimed Maharishi in 1974, 'the influence of the knowledge'.[35] The Maharishi's World Plan, launched in 1972, includes not only the development of the full potential of the individual, but also intelligent use of the environment, improvement of government activities, fulfilment of economic aspirations, and achievement of the spiritual goals of humankind in this generation.

Both the Divine Light Mission and TM are examples of movements with roots in India which have become 'westernized' and

'secularized' to a high degree, and have incorporated the technological, cultural and financial approaches of western society. There
are now many westernized gurus, westernized cults and groups,
many of which represent a curious mingling of eastern spiritual
traditions and western superstitions. The interest in the occult, for
example, has been a major influence on some schools and individuals. Others have not looked to religious categories at all, but
to the current vogue in 'group' experience, seeing the group as the
vehicle for expansion of consciousness. So we have witnessed a
considerable upsurge of the 'growth industry': the world of growth
groups, encounter, sensitivity and other kinds of group, Primal
Therapy, Gestalt workshops, body awareness, and so on. The
interest in self-awareness and self-exploration does not necessarily
assume a specifically religious form, nor does the interest in meditation always lead towards religious belief of any kind.

What is abundantly clear, however, is that many people are
seeking an inner experience of disclosure which they have been
denied in our materialistic culture. It is the experience of being
more awake—or, in some cases, more asleep! To some, relaxation
and release from tension is the primary aim, but this is only a
preliminary to wakefulness, according to many meditation
teachers. One excellent account of the purpose of meditation is
The Miracle of Being Awake, 'a manual on meditation for the use
of young activists', written by the Vietnamese Buddhist Nhat Hanh.

> When we sit in mindfulness, both our body and mind can be at
> peace and total relaxation. But this state of peace and relaxation
> differs fundamentally from the lazy, semi-conscious state of mind
> that one gets while resting and dozing. Sitting in such lazy self-
> consciousness, far from being mindfulness, is like sitting in a
> dark cave. In mindfulness we are not only restful and happy but
> alert and awake. Meditation is not evasion: it is a serene encoun-
> ter with reality.

Meditation is a concentration in the present, a consciousness of
one's presence and of the present reality, the practice of mindfulness
second by second—while washing the dishes, while making tea,
while bathing. Mindfulness is the opposite of machine thinking.
Nothing is done mechanically. So Nhat Hanh stresses correct
breathing as the natural and effective tool to prevent dispersion of
thoughts and maintain mindfulness, 'the bridge which connects life
to consciousness, which unites one's body to one's thought'.[36] The

aim then is unification, the attainment of inner wakefulness and awareness in the midst of daily life. This is what Maharishi Mahesh Yogi calls 'transcendental consciousness', and he claims that, with practice, it becomes possible for such transcendental consciousness and the life of daily activity to coexist. To this state of awareness he then gives the name 'cosmic consciousness', and he sees it as the normal result of continued meditation. Moreover, he says:

> Cosmic consciousness develops into God consciousness through devotion, the most highly refined type of action, which unites in the light of God the two separate aspects of cosmic consciousness, the Self and activity.[37]

The critical issue, of course, is whether through meditation one *is* increasing wakefulness, or inducing sleep. Writing of TM, one British physician summarizes the available research: 'The neurophysiological state of people during meditation is one of alert relaxation'.[38] But it is obvious that some forms of meditation can lead to a dulling or clouding of consciousness, and not to insight or sharpening of perception. Meditation can be a drug of sedation, a consciousness constrictor, a means of avoiding the impact of reality. One can see both kinds of motivation at work in the current revival of meditation. It is worth noting that Maharishi Mahesh Yogi lays considerable stress on the necessity of personal guidance in order that deceptions and false paths may be avoided.

> The practice of Transcendental Meditation has to be imparted by personal instruction. It cannot be imparted through a book, because the teacher must not only show the aspirant how to experience the subtle states of thinking, but should also be responsible for checking his experience as he proceeds on that path ... The practice of Transcendental Meditation must always be taught by expert masters of meditation who have been trained to impart it accurately as well as to check experience.[39]

We shall need to refer later to the dangers of false paths in meditation and prayer. But it is important to take seriously the positive aspects of the current search. What are individuals who meditate seeking? The answers most frequently given include 'a greater awareness of their inner self'[40] or 'the exploration of inner space, of love, tenderness, togetherness, wholeness, the total environment of man'.[41] F. C. Happold argued that 'our age is one of those *leap-epochs* in the history of mankind in which consciousness is passing into a new level of awareness and insight, in which the only acceptable religion is likely to be a mystical one'.[42] Writing in similar vein, Edgar Mitchell, the sixth astronaut to walk on the moon, stressed the importance of this shift in consciousness.

> I believe that civilization is in a critical state, and mankind is at an evolutionary crossroad. On the one hand, problems and conflicts have arisen which are global in scale and have brought society to a condition of escalating planetary crises. On the other hand, man's potential for creative change, fulfilment and benevolent control of his environment have never been greater. I believe that both problems and personalities are ultimately a function of human consciousness—i.e. there will never be a better world until there are better people in it. The most effective and enduring way to resolve the problems and to realize the potentialities is through the enlightenment of individuals. I believe that man's consciousness is *the* critical factor in the future we will build for ourselves.[43]

William Johnston, the Jesuit authority on Zen, agrees, and he relates the issue to the failure of the church.

> If institutional religion has somehow failed those in search of meditation, this is partly because it has been unable to keep pace with the sudden evolutionary leap in consciousness that has characterized the last decade. We are now faced with a new man, a more mystical man, and it is on the mystical dimension of religion that we must focus our attention.[44]

In other words, it is the shallow naivety of conventional Christianity which has made it unable to cope with and respond to the demands of this new interest in consciousness. On the other hand, the eastern traditions seemed to offer some guidelines and methods. The interest in Zen, popularized by Alan Watts, is closely connected to the fact that Zen is believed not to involve intellectual beliefs, in particular in 'a God', and that it lays its emphasis on life now, rather than on history or doctrine. It is an attempt to find the centre of personality elsewhere than in the brain, and to escape from the limitations of subject and object. This is why the so-called atheism of Zen and of all forms of Buddhism is so attractive. Zen in fact is a form of meditation without an object, and its aim is to achieve awareness of 'pure being'. In the words of one famous Zen verse, it is a tradition which does not depend on words and letters but on 'a direct pointing at the soul of man, seeing into one's own nature, and the attainment of Buddhahood'.[45]

This attainment, this awareness of one's true nature, is realized *now* and *here*. It is the immediacy and the present moment which is so important. There is no need to bother with doctrinal formulations about the past, or with the prospects of the future. It is NOW.

> This is your own time, this spot where you sit is your own spot. It is on this very spot and in this very moment that you become a Buddha, and certainly not beneath some Bodhi tree off in some distant life.[46]

THE RETURN OF JESUS AND THE SPIRIT

The 'Jesus movement' was a name given originally to an upsurge of enthusiasm for Jesus which occurred in America at the end of the 1960s, and which, for the most part, was outside the boundaries of the institutional church. In Britain, the movement has been markedly different, more restrained, more church-based, probably much more conventional. Some of its features are nevertheless the same. Much of the early writing on the Jesus movement was very superficial. Since the famous article 'The new rebel cry—"Jesus is coming!" ' which appeared in *Time* in June 1971, and the tremendous coverage which followed it, media interest in the phenomenon has subsided. But much of this early concern was with Jesus stickers and Jesus T-shirts, and was deplored by many within the movement. Jim Palosari of the Jesus Family described these phenomena as part of the infantile stage of the movement. It is essential then to distinguish a number of different and conflicting elements within the Jesus movement, or movements, for there are several of them. First, there is the phenomenon of the evangelical Christian group which has simply 'gone trendy'. We may call this a 'Jesus movement' in some sense, but it is a fundamentally different kind of growth to the spontaneous upsurge from the counter-culture which has often been described. Whatever may have been the case in the United States, it is clear that in Britain, many of the Jesus papers and Jesus stickers, and much of the apparatus of the 'Jesus movement' have actually emanated from well-established, financially stable and highly reputable evangelical firms and organizations. In no sense can they be seen as a part of the counter-culture, but at best as part of a crusade or mission to young people. Then, secondly, there are groups of young people who stand broadly within the evangelical churches and who have been affected by the Charismatic renewal. They may well coexist alongside the evangelical churches, though their relationship to them will often be flexible and at times uneasy. Take, for example, the Jesus Family, once based at Rochdale and Manchester, with close links with the local Christians of the Baptist church. This group was a direct descendant of the American Jesus group which staged the Lonesome Stone tour in Britain some years ago. The Family were critical of the mainstream churches, but they worked alongside them, relating on the one hand to young people in the churches, and on the other, to unattached youth through their rock group the Mighty Fliers. Thirdly, there is the Children of God, a more extreme sectarian group, which sees most other Christian groups as allied with Mammon. The Children of God claimed in 1975 that between 1971–5 they had gained 240,578 converts. They are a modern messianic and millenarian group, holding strongly to the view that 'Jesus is coming soon', and seeing evidences of the imminence of the eschaton in the events of the Middle East. They support Colonel Gaddafy, are highly critical of the American system, of the churches, and of all other Jesus people whom they see as 'a bunch of system kids and church kids with long hair'.[47]

But in spite of these important variations, it is possible to discern some common elements in the 'Jesus revolution', which throw light on the appeal and attraction of these groups. They are a reaction against the vague liberalism of the 1960s when people spoke gleefully of the 'end of ideology' and saw dogma and polemics as belonging to the pre-ecumenical age. Against such vagueness, the Jesus people point 'One Way'. They are literalist in their approach to the Bible, again a reaction against the tendency in much western Christianity to study the text of Scripture but neglect its message. They are almost all associated with, and influenced by, neo-Pentecostalism, a witness to their need for direct experience of God and for the freedom of the Spirit to praise him. They hold rigid views in most cases about non-marital sex, homosexuality, and many of the 'progressive' attitudes in the contemporary West, which they are inclined to attribute to the work of demons. They are marked most of all by a strong sense of personal relationship to Jesus, and are dominated by hope of his future return. 'Jesus is coming soon' reads one of the most popular Jesus stickers. Consequently, they tend to have little or no interest in the political struggles of humanity. In one detailed analysis of political self-characterization, the American sociologist James T. Richardson studied a large Jesus commune in the United States. The results were very revealing.[48]

Political self-characterization	Before entering	After	Change
Conservative	8	6	−25%
Moderate	6	5	−17%
Liberal	19	1	−95%
Radical	23	3	−87%
Nothing/Don't Care	27	71	+163%

The Jesus movements certainly indicate that some young people are demanding a change—a change in the understanding of Christianity which dominated much of the thinking in the West in recent years, and of a return to an older revivalist, adventist and more personal understanding of the gospel.

While there is no evidence that a Jesus movement on American lines has taken root elsewhere, except among a small minority, the Charismatic renewal, or neo-Pentecostalism, has been a significant influence in many areas, and its influence is still growing. Of making books about the Charismatic movement there seems to be no end, and it is difficult to summarize the movement adequately in a short space. Clearly there *is* a movement, an organized movement with its theologians and its popular writers, its organs of communication and expression, its own language and methods, and so on. Some people have been anxious to stress that it is an 'experience' and not a 'movement', but both need to be taken into account.

What characterizes Pentecostalism, whether in its classical or its newer forms, is a high doctrine of the gifts of the Spirit, in particular those of speaking in tongues and healing. The 'baptism in the Holy Spirit' which is normally manifested in tongues is seen as a distinct stage in Christian experience, different from and subsequent to conversion. It is 'a second encounter with God, in which the Christian begins to receive the supernatural power of the Holy Spirit into his life . . . This second experience . . . is given for the purpose of equipping the Christian with God's power for service'.[49] The history of the recent revival of Pentecostalism is now fully documented, and scholars have turned their attention to the underlying theology of the movement.

For our purpose, what is important to notice is that, since the spread of the 'Charismatic experience' has occurred within traditionally non-Pentecostal churches, particularly the Roman Catholic, the theological interpretations of the experience are now varied. Some would question the use of the term 'baptism in the Spirit' altogether, claiming that one can be baptized only once. But what is shared is an experience of the Holy Spirit's power and it is this which is the binding force of the movement. Not all Charismatics, for example, insist that 'tongues' are a necessary element in the 'baptism in the Spirit'. Francis Sullivan, sj, defines this experience as 'a religious experience which initiates a decisively new sense of the powerful presence and working of God in one's life, which working usually involves one or more charismatic gifts'.[50]

With the spread of this movement, we have seen such effects as an increase in spontaneous prayer groups, the production of new hymns, songs, choruses, and expressions of praise, the use of tongues in both public and private prayer, the practice of laying on of hands and of healing ministries and exorcisms, and so on. The most characteristic feature of the Charismatic renewal is the prayer meeting, while in the Roman Communion the movement has led to a reassessment of sacramental confession and of popular participation in the liturgy. More will be said in Chapter Four about the characteristics of Pentecostal spirituality.

The Charismatic renewal is primarily what the name indicates—a renewal movement—and only indirectly an evangelistic one. It is a movement aimed at the renewal of the churches, and not directly at unbelievers, although it was inevitable that renewal would lead to an increased awareness and sense of evangelism among those Christians affected by it, and in fact it has done so. The movement in Britain has so far probably remained strongest among the middle-class and middle-aged. Some observers feel that it is a response to an inability to cope on the part of many Christians, a new discovery of hope at a time of disillusionment and fear and failure. Others, particularly in South Africa, have suggested that the movement is a way of evading difficulties of Christian responsibility by taking refuge in inner experiences of warmth and the accompanying jargon which reinforces the solidarity of the in-group. Certainly, there is a good deal of evidence of escapism, sentimentalism and Gnostic trends in the Charismatic movement. The movement can very quickly cease to respond to what Cardinal Suenens called 'the principle of surprise in the church', and come to represent instead the ritualized form (tongues) and the ceremonial gesture (clapping), in Max Weber's phrase 'the routinization of charisma'.[51] Michael Harper, one of the leaders of the organized movement in Britain and internationally, has admitted that 'the pentecostal position is particularly open or prone to gnostic deviations',[52] though he was thinking particularly of the danger of élitist and sectarian attitudes. Equally dangerous is the Gnostic withdrawal from the material world and its neglect of serious attention to the world's needs. It is, of course, claimed from time to time that the Charismatic movement has radical consequences for society, but the evidence to the contrary is much stronger in the West. The Charismatic movement seems frequently to lead to a social attitude which is escapist, non-prophetic and sentimental, while its most progressive posture is one of reformism. The opposite trend seems to occur in the form which the movement has taken in Latin America, especially in Chile and Cuba, where there is a much deeper involvement in class struggle and political action. It remains to be seen whether the movement elsewhere will be 'radicalized'. Meanwhile, the conclusion contained in the Statement of the Theological Basis of the Catholic Charismatic Renewal, issued at Rome in 1973, remains true: 'In some cases, there is real social engagement, but the involvement is superficial in that it does not touch the structures of oppression and injustice'.[53]

LET THE OPPRESSED GO FREE

The radical Christian movements in Britain and America have, on the whole, run along quite different lines from those taken by the Pentecostalists, and they represent another key element in the current spiritual climate. The term 'liberation theology' was at first used very specifically about theological developments in Latin America as described in the work of theologians such as Alves, Gutierez and Bonino, but it has come to be used more widely to describe those movements in the West which are concerned with human liberation as an essential dimension of Christian theology. Thus the American feminist theologian Rosemary Ruether in her study *Liberation Theology* (1972) examined monasticism, celibacy, anti-Semitism, women's liberation, ecology, black theology and socialism as well as the Latin American movements. The word 'liberation' has become a key concept not only in Christian discussions of the gospel and human oppression, but also in that range of movements which have appeared since the 1960s outside, and to a large degree hostile to, the church—women's liberation, gay liberation, black liberation, and so on. Many of these groups see the movement against oppression as involving of necessity a break with the Christian tradition which is identified with a white male capitalist order. As the slogan on the wall expressed it, 'God is not dead. She is black.'

In Britain, the understanding of Christianity as a message of liberation for the oppressed is seen in the Student Christian Movement and is expressed in its journal *Movement*. Early *Movement* pamphlets included *The Politics of Bible Study, The Eye of the Storm* (on mysticism and spirituality), *Cuba Now! Signs of the Kingdom, Towards a Theology of Gay Liberation*, and *For the Banished Children of Eve* (an introduction to feminist theology). In 1973 the SCM brought together some 350 young Christians for a conference at Huddersfield called 'The Seeds of Liberation'. In a report of this happening later, one of those who was present wrote that 'the re-examination required was not so much a cerebral critique of theology or politics but a flesh and blood discovery of spiritual roots'. He went on: 'A new term has entered the vocabulary of politically radical Christians in Britain—spirituality.'[54] In Europe, it is Taizé which provides a focal point for thousands of young people who look for 'a springtime of the church'. From this community in the Burgundy hills of France, an Easter message in 1970 proclaimed to all who would listen that 'the Risen Christ comes to quicken a festival in the innermost heart of man. He is preparing for us a springtime of the church: a church devoid of means of power, ready to share with all, a place of visible communion for all humanity.' Four years later, on 1 September 1974, Taizé opened its Council of Youth with a Letter to the People of God.

Church, what do you say of your future?

Are you going to give up the means of power, the compromises with political and financial power?

Are you going to surrender your privileges, stop capitalizing? Are you at least going to become 'a universal community of sharing', a community finally reconciled, a place of communion and friendship for the whole of humanity?

In each locality and over the whole world, are you in this way going to become the seeds of a society without class and where none have privileges, without domination of one person by another, of one people by another?

Church, what do you say of your future?

Are you going to become the 'people of the beatitudes', having no security other than Christ, a people poor, contemplative, creating peace, bearing joy and a liberating festival for mankind, ready even to be persecuted for justice?

Fine words, and many no doubt pay lip service to them, or are drawn by their attractiveness as jargon. But they typify a kind of position which is being taken up by young Christians within, and affected by, the Third World, who seek a spirituality of liberation which 'will centre on a conversion to the neighbour, the oppressed person, the exploited social class, the despised race, the dominated country'.[55] The Manifesto of the Young Church of Chile, which was nailed to the doors of Santiago Cathedral on 11 August 1968, expresses the theme more strongly.

> ... we want once again to become the church of the people, as in the Gospel, living with the same poverty, simplicity and struggle: That is why we say: *No* to a church that is enslaved to the structures of social compromise, *Yes* to a church that is free to serve all men ... *No* to a church which compromises with power and wealth, *Yes* to a church which is prepared to be poor in the name of its faith in man and in Jesus Christ ... *No* to the established disorder, *Yes* to the struggle for a new society which will give human beings back their dignity and make love a possibility.[56]

It is a message which certainly strikes chords in the hearts of many young Christians all over the world who are not interested in a church which merely seeks to recreate the old orders of the past.

The understanding of the gospel as a message of human liberation has affected sections of the evangelical world as well as theological radicals. Thus the Lausanne World Conference on Evangelism in August 1974 included a significant number who held that the gospel 'is good news of liberation, of restoration, of wholeness, of salvation that is personal, social, global and cosmic'.[57] So there has grown up, especially in the Third World and in the United States, a new evangelical radicalism which is highly critical of the tendencies within the evangelical tradition which lead to conservatism and to support of established social structures. However, the theologies of liberation have mainly drawn support from sources and traditions other than the conservative evangelical. An important factor in the growth of a 'revolutionary theology' in Latin America was Pope Paul's encyclical *Populorum Progressio* which the *Wall Street Journal* denounced as 'souped up Marxism'. The significance of this encyclical was that it initiated a process of Christian-Marxist dialogue in Latin America which was essentially different from the old style of a debate between friendly intellectuals. In the Third World context, the relationship of Christianity to Marxism became an issue not of intellectual debate but of theological practice within a revolutionary situation. Theology begins from the concrete situation, the process of change in Latin America. 'Even a blind man can see that Latin America moves irreversibly towards some form of socialism', said Bishop Antulio Parrilla Bonilla of Puerto Rico.[58] So many Latin American Christians, Roman Catholic and Protestant, have seen their commitment to the gospel as involving a commitment to socialism. In April 1972 four hundred Latin American Christians met at Santiago and inaugurated the movement Christians for Socialism. They defined themselves as 'Christians who, starting from the processes of liberation which our Latin American countries are undergoing, and from our concrete and active involvement in the building of a socialist society, think out our faith and re-examine our attitude of love for the oppressed'.[59]

Meanwhile, in the 'developed' western countries, there has emerged a complex range of radical theologies, and of radical Christian movements in search of a theology. The SCM in Britain, the now defunct Free Church of Berkeley in California whose liturgy *The Covenant of Peace* became the model for many 'liberated churches', the radical groups who gathered around the Berrigan brothers, the influence of Harvey Cox, James Cone, John Robinson and other writers, the *Catholic Worker* and its anarchist tradition, the *Slant* group and the various strands of thinking within the Dominican order, the radical voices in the World Council of Churches—all these have contributed to the formation of a style of Christianity which places the struggle for justice, peace and freedom at the centre of its concern.

In the United States, two specific areas in which radical Christians have been led to question fundamental assumptions within the old Christian Leftist groupings have been those of black theology and of feminism. The leading exponent of black theology in the USA has been James Cone of Union Theological Seminary in New York. Cone argues that black power is in no sense the antithesis of Christianity, but is Christ's message to modern America. If Christ is present among the oppressed, then he must be working through the black power struggle, for 'black rebellion is a manifestation of God himself actively involved in the present day affairs of men for the purpose of liberating a people'. The purpose of black theology, in Cone's view, is to analyse the black person's condition in the light of revelation, in order to create a new understanding of black dignity, and provide the necessary soul among black people to destroy racism. Black theology is a street theology, an active theology, a proletarian theology, a theology for the oppressed. For 'being black in America has very little to do with skin colour. To be black means that your soul, your mind and your body are where the dispossessed are'.[60]

The movement of feminist theology is equally concerned to set Christianity free from enslavement to historical stereotypes of male and female. To some feminist theologians, notably Mary Daly, traditional Christianity is irredeemably patriarchal, sexist and chauvinist. 'The idea of salvation uniquely by a male saviour perpetuates the problem of patriarchal oppression'.[61] So affected by male domination is traditional Christianity that women can only withdraw from it into a post-Christian movement. Others, such as Rosemary Ruether, are very critical of the misogynism within Catholic tradition, but see its roots not in the teaching of Jesus but rather in the male's fear of his own sexuality. So women always become Eve, the eternal temptress, the symbol of defilement, the carnal set over against male spirituality. Today, says the feminist theology, the experience of God can no longer be mediated through the masculine language of the churches.

> Only when men and women are peers in the church can we create human relationships that express authentic communication and exorcise the evil spirits of injustice and dehumanization that turn women and all oppressed people into fantasized symbols of the negative self.[62]

Ruether makes a close link between the oppression of women and of the natural order. The mentality that regards the natural environment as an object of domination drew upon images and attitudes based on male domination of women. She links the two demands of the feminist and ecological movements as part of one struggle for socialism. Both demand a radical restructuring of the social and economic system.

Liberation theology is still in process of change. One of its fundamental convictions is that God is in the future, drawing us to realize new truths, dream new dreams, and to be set free from the thought-forms of the past which enslave us. It is a theology of continuous development and struggle, of permanent revolution. It is a theology too of salvation for the created order as well as for humanity, an attempt to rediscover the idea of the universe as sacramental.

> One feels, wherever one turns in this strange late time, that beneath the flamboyance and antinomianism which are every-where rampant, the prompting passion by which men are today coming more and more to be most deeply moved is a great need—in the absence of God—to find the world in which we dwell to be, nevertheless, in some sort truly a sacramental econ-omy where to be 'with it' is to be 'with' a sacred reality. We are, it would seem, a people whose most imperious desire is to win the assurance that Moses was given near Mount Sinai that the place whereon we stand is holy ground.[63]

Since the 1970s there have been significant shifts in Christian consciousness. During these years the search for a greater integra-tion between spirituality and social and political struggle has been strengthened in many different traditions—the new breed of evan-gelicals in the cities, the politically committed Roman Catholic feminists in the USA and in Britain, the liberation theologians of Central and South America, and many others. The struggle for an authentic, nourishing spirituality which will support and strengthen social and political action is a continuing one.

During the years of Ronald Reagan in the USA and Margaret Thatcher in Britain, the churches were affected by the prevailing mood of enterprise, individualism and consumerism, though some of them also offered resistance to it and critique of it. As the New Right, in its different forms, gained significant ground, much of the interest in 'spirituality' has moved into the area of personal growth and concern with the interior life of the individual. There have been clear signs, in many parts of the church and outside the church, of a culture of false inwardness, the religious correlate of the culture of narcissism. There is a real danger that 'spirituality' will be more and more 'commodified', absorbed into the market world of consumerism, and a central task of spiritual discernment will be to disentangle the values of the gospel from those of the dominant culture.

THE CHURCH AND ITS SPIRITUALITY
The preceding sections have attempted to describe some of the movements which are contributing to the contemporary spiritual climate. There are conflicting trends, and they are to some extent reflected in the course of events within the church in Britain where we can see these three broad movements in operation. First, there is a search for the inner world, for meditation, silence and contemplative prayer. Secondly, there is a sense of the need for power, for direct experience of the Spirit, and for personal love of Jesus. Thirdly, there is an increasing sense of the need to see the search for justice as an integral element in the gospel. Certainly a contemporary spirituality which does not include these elements will be inadequate. But to what extent have these movements affected the church's understanding?

Has the inward quest, for example, been taken seriously within the church as a whole? It is striking that it was at a period when the prevalent tendency within mainstream Christianity was towards 'involvement' and social action that many of the young turned to the eastern teachers. It is still common to find people who are surprised to know that meditation and mystical prayer are part of the Christian tradition at all. During the 1960s many clergy were finding the traditional practices of meditation extremely difficult, and were seeking a style of spirituality whose key themes were relevance, involvement, encounter. It was this unease and this search which John Robinson articulated in *Honest to God* (1963), where he sought to express a non-religious understanding of prayer. Robinson was particularly concerned that 'traditional spirituality' had seen prayer as a form of withdrawal, a disengagement from living. He wrote:

> It is certainly not that disengagement is unnecessary but that the pentecostal point, as it were, is in the engagement. . . . But to open oneself *unconditionally* in love *is* to be with him in the presence of God, and that is the heart of intercession. To pray for another is to expose both oneself and him to the common ground of our being; it is to see one's concern for him in terms

of *ultimate* concern, to let God into the relationship. Intercession is to *be with* another at that depth, whether in silence or compassion or action. It may consist simply in listening when we take the otherness of the other person most seriously ... There is an inescapable dialectic of engagement and withdrawal. But much depends on which we regard as primary.[64]

In 1967 Douglas Rhymes in an important book, *Prayer in the Secular City*, a study which is still valuable today, attempted to develop Robinson's ideas in relation to the prayer life of modern men and women, defining prayer as 'the in-Christness which lights up all our actions in daily living from within'.[65] Later Robinson himself was to develop his ideas in *Exploration into God* (1967). Others too made the quest for a 'secular spirituality' their central concern.

But the Christianity of the secular city seemed to have little to offer to those seekers who were turning to TM and to Buddhism. They felt that the various forms of Christianity which they had encountered were lacking in depth and were ill-fitted to help them in the journey they wished to undertake. Certainly the great Christian mystics were not at their most popular during the '60s, but towards the end of that decade there began to emerge a revived interest in prayer, contemplation and mysticism within the Christian tradition. The writings of Anthony Bloom, and later those of René Voillaume, Simon Tugwell, Monica Furlong and others began to introduce many people to contemplative prayer. Many came to realize the truth in Archbishop Michael Ramsey's words:

> Mystical experience is given to some. But contemplation is for all Christians ... [Prayer] is a rhythmic movement of our personality into the eternity and peace of God and no less into the turmoil of the world for whose sake as for ours we are seeking God. If this is the heart of prayer, then the contemplative part of it will be large. And a church which starves itself and its members in the contemplative life deserves whatever spiritual leanness it may experience.[66]

The Christian mystics themselves began to be reissued in paperback format. *The Cloud of Unknowing* became extremely popular, and the works of St John of the Cross appeared in paperback in the United States. In addition, Christians began to turn to the eastern traditions of Yoga and Zen and the meditation schools to find there new insights and new light for their path. So Déchanet spoke of a 'Christian Yoga', as had Jack Winslow in India many years before, Aelred Graham of 'Zen Catholicism', and William Johnston of 'Christian Zen'. Herbert Slade began to use the Yoga Sutras of Patanjali in the service of Christian contemplation, while the late Abhishiktananda adapted the Hindu Prayer of the Name in a Christian way. Others have explored TM as a form of Christian prayer.[67]

Clearly, spiritual direction is urgently needed in order to give orientation to this inner search. How can the transition from drugs to meditation be best aided, and the pitfalls avoided? How can people who believe they have experienced God on LSD be helped to interpret and evaluate that experience? How can the 'dabbler' who moves from one eastern method or technique to another be helped to attain stability and sobriety of spirit? What resources are available for those who are finding through Yoga and Zen valuable insights into spirituality? What can be learned from movements such as TM, and are there dangers here which need to be recognized? What techniques can aid the growth of Christian prayer? Spiritual direction is vital, but it cannot exist unless there is a close acquaintance with the contemporary context of the inner quest.

What then of the Jesus and Charismatic movements? What have been the positive spiritual effects on the church of these movements? Taking them together, we can identify a series of major consequences which have resulted in some areas: the increase in direct, simple testimony to God's power, a deeper sense of God's presence and power in prayer, a sense of the Bible having 'come alive', a greater degree of warmth in fellowship within Christian communities, a deeper appreciation of the variety of spiritual gifts, not only that of 'tongues', and frequently profound character changes in individual Christians. There is no question that these are results which can and do enrich the Body of Christ. In the experience of 'baptism in the Spirit', there is a liberation of the personality in the praise and service of God, and it is this liberation which often finds its expression in the gift of tongues. For many, the Charismatic experience may represent the beginnings of contemplative prayer. Joan Massingberd Ford, an American Roman Catholic writer, suggests that it is 'a touch—but not the state—of infused contemplation'.[68] Therefore careful and informed spiritual direction is essential if the Charismatic movement is to make progress. The movement needs to create within it a network of spiritual guides who can help individuals through peak experiences and enable them to cope with the inevitable experience of darkness for which traditional Pentecostal spirituality may leave them unprepared.

Radical Christians, involved deeply in social issues and political struggles, are in very grave danger of losing contact with their spiritual roots. The great spiritual director Evelyn Underhill saw the dangers of 'shallow activism' over fifty years ago.

> A shallow religiousness, the tendency to be content with a bright ethical piety wrongly called practical Christianity . . . seems to be one of the defects of institutional religion at the present time . . . and that is a type of religion which does not wear well. It does little for the soul in those awful moments when the pain and mystery of life are most deeply felt.[69]

She went on to say that 'there is a definite trend in the direction of religion of this shallow social type'.[70] The linking of contemplation and action is one of the essential aims of spiritual guidance. But it is necessary to allow the turmoil and ferment of the contemporary struggles to shake the spiritual patterns in which we are frequently imprisoned or protected. Authentic spiritual direction must include preparation for threats to spiritual security, for inner disturbances of spirit, for confrontations with new knowledge and new visions. A spirituality of liberation must be open to such dangers and risks: a closed spirituality must be a spirituality of oppression and ultimately of death. How are we to allow ourselves to be open to the destructive and healing impact of the black revolutionary, of the urban guerrilla, of the sexual liberationist, of the voices of the poor of the earth? What kind of spiritual direction is needed to prevent Christian asceticism and Christian contemplation from becoming both a façade and a diversion, or, in Berrigan's words, 'a guard between themselves and the horror around them'?[71] Direction involves listening, exposure, nakedness of spirit before the storm and the fire.

This is the framework within which spiritual direction is needed. Those who are exploring the world of meditation and silence need such personal guidance. Those who, through the Charismatic renewal, have come to a deeper experience of the Spirit's power need personal guidance in order that they can make progress and not become fixated at a particular stage in Christian experience. Personal guidance is necessary so that the radical movements of

Christian discipleship will be helped to relate the inner and outer worlds in a spiritual direction which takes account of the movement towards human liberation in our time. Never was spiritual direction more urgently called for than in the present climate of soul searching.

2

Spiritual direction in the Christian tradition

So the spiritual father forms a living bond with the tradition.

ANDRÉ LOUF[1]

For the avoidance of error, have someone to advise you—a spiritual father or confessor, a brother of like mind; and make known to him all that happens to you in the work of prayer.

THEOPHAN THE RECLUSE[2]

THE BEGINNINGS OF SPIRITUAL DIRECTION
The term 'spiritual direction' is usually applied to the cure of souls when it involves the specific needs of one individual. Max Thurian's definition is a useful starting point. 'Spiritual direction, or the cure of souls, is a seeking after the leading of the Holy Spirit in a given psychological and spiritual situation'.[3] Here the stress is on *seeking*, and the seeking is mutual. The director, and the person who is being directed, are both seekers: they are both parts of a spiritual direction, a current of spirituality, a divine-human process of relationship. 'Spirituality' and 'spiritual life' are not religious departments, walled-off areas of life. Rather the spiritual life is the life of the whole person directed towards God.

Nevertheless, the work of direction involves skill and training. So Martin Thornton related the work of ascetical theology to that of the director.

Ascetical theology is the practical doctrine of prayer, its techniques, methods and the disciplines which help to support and nurture it. Spiritual direction is its application by one skilled in this doctrine to the personal needs of individual people.[4]

Thornton saw direction as the primary concern of the Christian priest or minister. They are essentially involved in acquiring expert-

ise in the life of prayer and in ascetical theology. Archbishop
Ramsey similarly placed this ministry very high in the priest's
priorities.

> Amid the spiritual hunger of our times, when many whose souls
> are starved by activism are seeking guidance in the contemplation
> of God, a terrible judgement rests upon the priest who is unable
> to give help or guidance because he has ceased to be a man of
> prayer himself.[5]

Thornton related the loss of understanding of priesthood to the
prevalence of amateurism and incompetence in the things of
the Spirit.

> One calls in a plumber because he understands plumbing, not
> because of his wide experience of life, and one is coached by a
> golf professional *because* he is *not* a weekend amateur. One is
> suspicious of a doctor who has read no medical book for twenty
> years and knows nothing of modern drugs, and I suspect that
> intelligent modern Christians are getting suspicious of clergy who
> are for ever engaged in something other than prayer, learning and
> such like professional occupations ... It is *because* a priest has
> time for prayer, study and reflection that his guidance of those
> in the world's hurly burly is likely to be worth having.[6]

Similarly, I believe that prayer, study and ascetical theology are
vital to the ministry of any priest, and that without these disciplines, pastoral work is bound to wither or become superficial.
Spiritual direction therefore is not a fringe activity, a 'specialized'
form of ministry (though there will be specialists here as in other
areas), but it is an integral part of the ordinary pastoral work to
which every priest is called. To suggest this is to suggest that every
priest in fact is called to be a theologian.

The gulf between 'academic' theology and the exercise of pastoral care and spiritual guidance has been disastrous for all concerned. We are often told that the gulf is exaggerated, or that it
does not exist at all, but these assurances are unconvincing. The
study of theology, or at least of Christian theology, cannot survive
in a healthy state apart from the life of prayer and the search for
holiness. The theologian is essentially a person of prayer. As Evagrius expressed it, 'A theologian is one whose prayer is true. If you
truly pray, you are a theologian'.[7] Or St John Climacus, 'The
climax of purity is the beginning of theology'.[8] Indeed, the entire

spiritual tradition of the Christian East rejects the idea of a 'detached' theology. Theology is an encounter with the living God, not an uncommitted academic exercise. This encounter cannot survive if its only *locus* is the lecture theatre or the library. It needs the nourishment of sacramental worship, of solitude, of pastoral care and the cure of souls. Theology must arise out of and be constantly related to a living situation. Again, in eastern orthodox thought all theology is mystical.

> There is therefore no Christian mysticism without theology; but above all, there is no theology without mysticism . . . It is an existential attitude which involves the whole man: there is no theology apart from experience; it is necessary to change, to become a new man. To know God one must draw near to him. No one who does not follow the path of union with God can be a theologian. The way of the knowledge of God is necessarily the way of deification.[9]

In our western tradition, St Francis de Sales used the term 'mystical theology' as a synonym for prayer.[10] Karl Barth, who is generally seen as one of the theologians most hostile to mysticism, emphasized in his *Evangelical Theology* that 'the first and basic act of theological work is prayer'. He continued, 'Theological work does not merely begin with prayer and is not merely accompanied by it; in its totality it is peculiar and characteristic of theology that it can be performed only in the act of prayer.'[11] There is then the closest possible link between doctrine and spirituality. Spirituality is applied doctrine: false spirituality is applied false doctrine. But the doctrine is not always fully conscious. For example, Martin Thornton pointed to the fact that much devotion to Christ suffers from a lack of humanity, and this leads to restrictive tension and to some form of Manicheism. 'The proper spiritual guidance in this case is the application of anti-Apollinarian doctrine, and the more we read Gregory of Nazianzen the more competent we shall be. But we also need the example of St Bernard to show us how to apply it.'[12] So there should be no conflict between theology and spirituality, still less should theology be seen as a mere theoretical framework for spiritual life. Rather, all theology is contemplative, a concentrated looking upon God as revealed in Christ, and manifested in lives which are hidden with Christ in God.

Christian mystical theology finds its roots in Scripture. The traditional 'Three Ways' (purgation, illumination, union) are not alien mystical forms imposed artificially on the gospel, but they arise out of the very features of the gospel message—repentance, life in the Spirit, and perfection. The motion of spiritual progress is an essential element in the biblical revelation, for its concern is with the progress of a people, progress marked by sin and repentance, by wilderness and exile, by conflict and struggle. It is a progress which includes the illumination of the Spirit, the prophetic vision, and it culminates in the Incarnation. The Christian life is described in the New Testament as progress: putting one's hand to the plough and not looking back (Luke 9:62), enduring to the end (Matthew 24:12, 13), preparing for a race or conflict (1 Corinthians 9:24–6). There is the clear call to perfection, to holiness, to fullness of life in Christ. The call to be perfect (*teleios*) (Philippians 3:15) is variously translated as a call to spiritual maturity (RSV and NEB) and to spiritual adulthood (J. B. Phillips). It is this process of spiritual maturing which is the purpose of spiritual direction. Again, the themes of pastoral care and *cura animarum* also derive their dual emphasis from Scripture. In Latin, *cura* primarily means *care*, but it can also mean *healing*, and in Scripture the recurring symbol of the Shepherd holds together these two themes. The Shepherd is one who feeds and nourishes the flock, makes the weak strong, seeks the lost, cares for the sick, and bandages the wounded (Ezekiel 34:3–4; 15–16). This Shepherd image recurs frequently in the history of the cure of souls. In Ezekiel, the Shepherd is concerned not only with healing (34:16) but also with the achievement of harmony and of *shalom*, peace (34:24). And in the New Testament, there is a bringing together of the themes of the wounded healer, the slain lamb, the stricken shepherd, and the guide who nourishes the flock.

The priest who is a spiritual guide is thus concerned with the encounter with God, the process by which the human community and the individual human being are made one with the divine. The shepherd is involved with the flock, and this social dimension of spirituality is of crucial importance. Christians are not seeking a solitary walk with God, a private mystical trip, a flight of the alone to the Alone. They are involved in a corporate search for humanity, renewal, the Kingdom of God, the transfigured cosmos, the Body of Christ. It is within the context of the flock or the Body that all mystical theology is practised, and there are very serious hazards and dangers when the spiritual quest occurs outside that framework. That is not, of course, to deny the fact of spirituality outside the confines of the church. But the great teachers of the spiritual life in almost all traditions are one in warning of the dangers of the spiritual ego-trip, the search for enlightenment which ignores the common life, the human community, the demands of justice and peace. In the fourteenth century, Ruysbroeck had harsh words to say about such seekers. Whereas 'the enlightened loving man flows out to all men in charity in heaven and on earth . . . these men go their own way'.[13] On the other hand, the spiritual masters stress that 'Christian perfection is perfect justice, and perfect justice is perfect charity . . . If the perfecting of our spiritual life be nothing else than growth in justice and charity, then its essential law will be progress'.[14]

So it is within the common life of the flock and of the Body that the work of spiritual theology takes place. We can define ascetical theology as that activity within the Body of Christ which seeks to find out and to use the methods, techniques and principles which will aid the growth of the life of prayer. In the process, it will also find out those which hinder this growth. The word ascetic derives from the Greek *askein*, to prepare by work, to make oneself fit through exercises, to train. Asceticism then is spiritual training, taking up the cross and following Christ (Mark 8:34). The purpose of such training is the development of Christ in us, and an increased co-operation with the Holy Spirit. Ascetical theology has been termed the treatment of 'the exercises required of aspirants to perfection'.[15] But it is not a department of theology so much as 'Christian doctrine interpreted and applied by a teacher of prayer, together with the mental and physical disciplines which nurture and support it'.[16] There is a vital link between what happened at Bethlehem and Calvary and what happens to me now, for dogma and spirituality are one. As St Simeon the New Theologian wrote in the eleventh century:

> The ineffable birth of the Word in the flesh from his mother is one thing, his spiritual birth in us another. For the first, in giving birth to the Son and Word of God, gave birth to the mystery of the re-forming of the human race, and the salvation of the whole world—Jesus Christ our Lord and God who reunited to him what had been separated and took away the sin of the world; while the second in giving birth in the Holy Spirit to the word of the knowledge of God, continually accomplishes in our hearts the mystery of the renewal of human souls.[17]

It is with the mystery of the renewal of human souls that all true theology and all spiritual direction is concerned.

The idea of a personal guide in the inner life is not distinctively Christian. In primitive cultures, the witch doctor or *chimbuki* in South Africa and the *shaman* who figures in so many societies performed the role of spiritual guidance and of healing. The guide plays key roles in Hindu, Yoga and in Buddhism, as well as in the classical philosophical schools. In the latter, the *sage* is seen as one who, by wisdom, virtue and insight, improves and transforms the life of his disciple. Socrates, though he disclaimed the title of *didaskalos*, and Pythagoras were sages of this type. Socrates certainly saw himself as a *iatros tes psuches*, a soul healer. The master/disciple relationship was a preparation for a higher life which might be one dedicated to politics or philosophy. The relationship was voluntary and unpaid, but the disciple was expected to submit to tests from time to time. Epicurus held that there were some who reached truth alone, while others needed a guide, and some would need special training and discipline. The Epicureans, although they were atheists, laid great stress on the 'health of our soul'. The Stoics taught systematic examination of conscience and meditation.

But closer to the Christian concept of the spiritual director is that of the *guru* in Hinduism. The term is increasingly used today, but it is often 'being used lightly if not sacrilegiously'.[18] In Hindu spirituality the *guru* is not a teacher, master or leader. 'No, the *guru* is none of these, not a master, not a teacher, not a leader. The *guru* is the light, a divine manifestation'.[19] The *guru*'s role is said to be like that of the sun—to be, to illumine. Hindu literature gives great prominence to the *guru*. Many early texts describe him as a man of great virtue and enlightenment. So one Hindu catechism notes:

> Pride and arrogance suit no one: constancy, humanity, sweetness, compassion, truth, love of one's neighbour, conjugal fidelity, goodness, amiability, cleanliness are all qualities that distinguish really virtuous people. He who possesses all these ten qualities is a true *guru*.[20]

In the Institutes of Vishnu, it is said that 'a man has three *atigurus*, his father, his mother, and his spiritual teacher'.[21] Krishna is, of course, the 'guru of gurus'. Many writers have claimed that the dominance of the *guru* constitutes a fundamental weakness in Hindu spirituality.

There are many other instances of spiritual guidance among the eastern traditions—the mendicant ascetics (*bhikkus*) of Buddhism, the sages of China, and the *murshid* (the one who guides aright) in Sufism. Spiritual direction among the Sufis was well-established by the tenth century. Al-Hujwiri's book *The Unveiling of the Unveiled* in the eleventh century explains the relationship of the disciple to the guide, and stresses the skill of the *murshid* in ministering to his spiritual needs. Al-Ghazzali in the late eleventh century recommended the consultation of a *shaikh* or director, and his *Examination of the Wonders of the Heart* contained detailed instructions on examination of conscience. Today, the Sufi leader Pir Vilayat Inyat Khan sees the guide as one who accompanies the disciple on the path. 'The disciple is like a grain of sand in the heart of the *murshid*, the teacher, who transforms it into a pearl'.[22]

In the Jewish tradition, the sense of relationship to Yahweh meant that the need for a personal guide was considerably lessened. For Yahweh himself was guide and director (Psalm 73:24; Wisdom 7:15), his word was the lantern of the soul (Psalm 119:105). Nevertheless there were spiritual guides—prophets, priests and wise men. Jeremiah significantly notes, 'The Law shall not perish from the priest, nor counsel from the wise, nor the Word from the prophets' (Jeremiah 18:18, RSV). Jeremiah also indicates that there were schools of wise men in Edom (49:7), as there were in Egypt and among the Babylonians, and there are references to some early Israelite wise men in 1 Kings (4:31) and 1 Chronicles (26:14). In the classic definition of priesthood in Deuteronomy 33:8–10, in addition to the offering of sacrifice, there were two other functions: the ability to give oracles (Thummim and Urim), and the teaching of precepts (*mishpatim*) and law (*toroth*). The competence in these areas was taken for granted and was an essential part of priestly work. 'The priest shall not be lacking in guidance (*torah*)' (Jeremiah 18:18), as one translation renders the passage cited above. 'You have rejected knowledge, and I will reject you from serving me as priest' (Hosea 4:6). Guidance was therefore a key idea in the priesthood, but it was not restricted to priests. Ecclesiasticus has a famous passage on the importance of the physician (38:1–15) and he urges his readers to seek guidance from godly men (6:34–6; 37:7–15). In later times, the rabbis became spiritual guides. Thus before the Day of Atonement, penitence and oral confession were urged in late pre-Christian Judaism. Later, in the Hasidic communities, the Zaddik was a spiritual leader and helper who guided his disciple in the knowledge of God.

In early Christianity, references to personal relationship with a priest are sometimes related specifically to the need for penance and restoration to fellowship within the Christian community. But there are some more general references in the early Fathers to the need of spiritual guidance. Thus St Basil (330–79) tells his readers to find a man 'who may serve you as a very sure guide in the work of leading a holy life', one who knows 'the straight road to God', and he warns that 'to believe that one does not need counsel is great pride'.[23] St Gregory Nazianzen (330–87) also saw direction as 'the greatest of all sciences'.[24] St Jerome (340–420) advised his friend Rusticus not to set out on an unknown way without a guide, and Jerome himself wrote a number of letters of direction. St Augustine (354–430) emphasizes that 'no one can walk without a guide'. But for more detailed indication of the growth of spiritual direction in this early period, one must turn to the Desert Fathers of the East.

THE DESERT FATHERS AND THE EASTERN TRADITION

The first sign of spiritual direction within the Christian tradition on any sizeable scale can be seen in the Desert Fathers in Egypt, Syria and Palestine in the fourth and fifth centuries. Disciples would seek out the advice and guidance of these holy men and women, the *abbas* and *ammas* of the desert. They looked to them for holiness and purity of heart more than for teaching, and the central concept was that of spiritual fatherhood. By the fourth century, the term *pneumatikos pater* was well established in patristic writing. The disciples also looked to these men and women for *discretion*. This virtue was seen as the essential feature of the true spiritual master from the time of St Anthony the Great onwards. The spiritual director was not simply someone who taught a spiritual technique, but he was a father who helped to shape the inner life of his children through his prayer, concern and pastoral care. One sees the place of the spiritual father clearly in the Apophthegmata or Sayings of the Desert Fathers. Here one meets the figure of the *abba*, the charismatic holy man of the wilderness, and the sayings of these men contain answers to practical problems and difficulties. Thus one saying, attributed to St Anthony, says, 'I know of monks who fell after much toil and lapsed into madness, because they trusted in their own work'. He goes on, 'If he is able to, a monk ought to tell his elders confidently how many steps he takes, and how many drops of water he drinks in his cell, in case he is in error about it'.[25] Another brother confessed to an elder:

In my cell I do all that one is counselled to do there, and I find no consolation from God. The elder said: 'This happens to you because you want your own will to be fulfilled.' The brother said, 'What then do you order me to do, father?' The elder said, 'Go attach yourself to a man who fears God, humble yourself before him, give up your will to him, and then you will receive consolation from God.'[26]

Even in this early period, the discernment of spirits (*diakrisis*) is seen as a crucial element in spiritual direction. The stories of the Desert Fathers abound with illustrations of ascetics who went to ridiculous extremes, and became spiritual casualties through lack of such discernment. The eastern monks emphasized the dangers of travelling without a guide. But there is no notion of blind obedience or domination, for the spiritual fathers were to teach by example first, and only secondarily by word.

A brother asked Abba Poemén, 'Some brothers live with me: do you want me to be in charge of them?' The old man said to him, 'No, just work first and foremost, and if they want to live like you, they will see to it themselves.' The brother said to him, 'But it is they themselves, father, who want me to be in charge of them.' The old man said to him, 'No, be their example, not their legislator.'[27]

In the tradition of desert spirituality, two individuals stand out as teachers and guides: Evagrius and Cassian. Evagrius Ponticus (345–99) has been called the 'father of our literature of spirituality',[28] and it has been claimed that he 'called forth a real spiritual mutation'.[29] He was widely sought out as a spiritual director, according to Palladius, because of his gifts of 'knowledge and wisdom, and the discernment of spirits', the fruits of asceticism and purity of heart.[30] In the early days of his move to the desert, Evagrius visited an old Desert Father, perhaps Macarius of Egypt, and asked him, 'Tell me some piece of advice by which I might be able to save my soul.' The reply was, 'If you wish to save your soul, do not speak before you are asked a question.'[31] The reply was very much within the stream of desert spirituality with its emphasis on solitude and silence. Evagrius was referred to in his later years as 'that man of understanding'.[32] He was the first important writer to emerge from the desert monastic movement, and he was the first to present the desert teaching on prayer in a systematized form. It is in Evagrius that we find the eight categories of evil thoughts which formed the basis of the seven deadly sins and of later developments in self-examination. It is in his work also that we find a detailed treatment of the conflict with evil thoughts and with 'demons'.

John Cassian (360–435), the disciple of Evagrius, lived for a few years in a monastery in Bethlehem, and then left for the Egyptian desert. Out of his time in Egypt came his twenty-four *Conferences*, reports of discourses given by hermits in various parts of the desert. The tradition of conferences, or extended discourses on spiritual problems, dates from the Rule of Pachomius, and by the end of the fourth century it was the standard method of spiritual direction. In Cassian's monastery at Marseilles we see a pattern of life based on the Eucharist, the Divine Office and confession with direction. There was at least a six-fold Office, and it is possible that the office of Lauds or Morning Prayer was invented at the Bethlehem monastery. There was as yet no system of private penance, but there were two ideas which later became fused, that of unceasing repentance, and that of the pouring out of one's thoughts and temptations to an experienced senior brother.

From Cassian's *Conferences* we read of Abba Moses to whom, because of his practice of virtue and contemplative prayer, others went to ask him 'to give us words which would help us in our spiritual progress. We had heard of his inflexible rule never to give instruction in the spiritual life except to persons who sought it in faith and heartfelt contrition.'[33] To such seekers, the wise old monk spoke of the monastic life, of purity of heart, and of the knowledge of God. He spoke to them of the control of thoughts, and of *discretion*, the greatest gift of God's grace. He stressed 'the importance of disclosing thoughts to the elders and receiving discretion from them'.[34] Similarly Abba Isaac spoke to them of unceasing prayer, and of the types of prayer, using the Lord's Prayer as a model.

These holy men spoke of prayer out of the depths of their own life and experience. Their dialogues indicate what it was that their disciples sought from them. As Germanus said to Abba Isaac, 'We want you to show us material for this recollectedness by which God is conceived in the mind and the conception is retained permanently.' Isaac went on to reveal what he called 'the formula for contemplation' and said that 'the formula was given to us by a few of the oldest fathers who remained. They did not communicate it except to a very few who were athirst for the new way.' The formula in fact consisted of the constant use of 'O God, make speed to save me: O Lord, make haste to help me.'[35] Isaac recommended its use at all times and in all moods and conditions. Already we see the origins of 'spiritual exercises' which were to play a central part in spiritual guidance.

THE 'SPIRITUAL FATHER' IN THE EASTERN ORTHODOX TRADITION

St Mark the Ascetic, one of the Egyptian fathers who died at the beginning of the fifth century, told the monk Nicholas that those who were to follow Christ should 'question other servants of God . . . in order to know how and where to direct [their] steps, and not walk in the dark without a bright lamp'. Another eastern guide of the seventh century, St Dorotheos, in his *Directions on Spiritual Training*, wrote:

> No men are more unfortunate or nearer perdition than those who have no teachers on the way of God. For what does it mean that where no guidance is, the people fall like leaves? A leaf is at first green, flourishing, beautiful, then it gradually withers, falls, and is finally trampled underfoot. So it is with the man who has no guide.

So he advises his disciples to seek counsel from 'one we trust'. Again, St Isaac the Syrian in the late sixth century urged:

> Confide your thoughts to a man who, though he lack learning, has studied the work in practice. Therefore follow the advice of a man who has himself experienced all, and knows how to judge patiently what needs discrimination in your case, and can point out what is truly useful for you.[36]

St John Climacus in the seventh century insisted that beginners who wished to leave Egypt for the Promised Land must find another Moses as a guide, while the advanced must deliver the care of their souls to a man who is the representative of a Master.[37] Similarly, Anastasius the Sinaite in the eighth century advised confession to 'spiritual men who have experience of souls'. Those following the spiritual way should 'find a spiritual man, experienced and able to heal us'.[38]

The desert movement remained the source of spiritual nourishment for centuries to come, and it is from the eastern monks that we have received much of the material on spiritual direction in the medieval period. St Simeon the New Theologian in the eleventh century urged obedience to the spiritual father. 'To put everything in the hands of your spiritual father, as in the hand of God, is an act of perfect faith ... A man who has acquired active faith in his father in God when seeing him thinks he sees Christ himself'. Simeon says that a spiritual father should be 'an experienced teacher with knowledge of the passions', 'a saintly instructor free from passions'. St Gregory of Sinai in the fourteenth century held the view that 'it is impossible for anyone to learn by himself the art of virtue', and so he urged that those seeking growth in prayer should listen to those with experience. Also in the fourteenth century, the monks Callistus and Ignatius of Xanthopoulos urged the disciple to 'spare no effort in trying to find a teacher and guide ... a man bearing the Spirit within him, leading a life corresponding to his words, lofty in vision of mind, humble in thought of himself, of good disposition in everything, and generally such as a teacher of Christ should be'. They go on:

> Having found such a man, cleave to him with body and spirit like a devoted son to his father and from then onwards obey all his commands implicitly, accord with him in everything, and see him not as a mere man, but as Christ himself ... Is it therefore possible to think that a man leads a Divine life, in accordance with the Word of God, if he lives without a guide, pandering to himself and obeying his own self-will?[39]

In the seventh century the Jesus prayer had become established on Mount Sinai, and by the eighth century Mount Athos incorporated the Sinai type of spirituality into its own. By the fifteenth century, the Jesus Prayer and the spiritual direction which was associated with it had spread to Russia. In the use of the Jesus Prayer, spiritual direction was very strongly emphasized. In particular, the writers stressed that the breathing exercises—the so-called 'physical method'—must not be practised by anyone who is not under the close guidance of a director. If such a director is not available, the prayer should be said without the physical techniques, although even then the Orthodox guides insist that all who practise the Jesus Prayer in any form must be regular at the Euchar-ist, frequent penitents and communicants. So Theophan the Recluse (1815–94), writing of verbal and silent prayer, warned, 'How important it is to have experienced instructions here, and how very

harmful it can be to guide and direct oneself.' On the Jesus Prayer
he laid down the general principles of spiritual direction as followed by all the eastern teachers:

> The various methods described by the Fathers (sitting down,
> making prostrations, and the other techniques used when per-
> forming the prayer) are not suitable for everyone: indeed without
> a personal director they are actually dangerous. . . .
>
> For the avoidance of errors, have someone to advise you—a
> spiritual father or confessor, a brother of like mind; and make
> known to him all that happens to you in the work of prayer.

On the directions given in the *Philokalia* regarding the use of the
Jesus Prayer, Theophan wrote:

> These directions should be followed under the eye of a teacher
> who knows the correct way of performing the Prayer. But if
> anyone tries to practise it by himself merely from descriptions
> in books, he cannot escape illusion. In any description only an
> external outline of the work is given: a book cannot provide all
> the detailed advice which is supplied by the *staretz* who under-
> stands the inner state that should accompany the Prayer, and so
> can watch over the beginner and give him the further guidance
> that he needs.

Theophan warned of the danger of self-deception through the sense
of inner warmth, and particularly of the danger of over-concern
with the physical exercises. An essential part of the director's work
was to discern the true motives of the heart. For 'it is better to
have a guide whom we meet personally and who can see our face
and hear our voice; for these two things reveal what is within'. He
recognized that 'it is precisely during this period of practising inner
prayer that people who lack a skilful hand to guide them are mostly
liable to go astray'.[40]

In Russia the great spiritual guides were the *startsy*, and the
spiritual guide himself was called *starchestvo*. *Staretz* (plural
startsy) is simply the Russian for 'old man', and to become a *staretz*
is seen as the culmination of a long life of simplicity and humility,
a life devoted to the acquiring of the Holy Spirit. One of the earliest
Russian *startsy* to be recorded was Nilus of Sora (1453–1508),
who had spent several years on Mount Athos. In the seventeenth
and eighteenth centuries, a number of Russian spiritual guides are
worth noticing. Bishop Dmitri of Rostov (1651–1709) was a good

example of Russian pastoral episcopacy, 'a living symbol of the good shepherd, and an example of episcopal life that was typically eastern—that is to say, one in which the administrator gave place to the spiritual director'.[41] Or there was Nicodemus the Hagiorite (1748–1809), who was responsible for the *Philokalia* (1782), a compilation of passages from the Greek Fathers centred on the Jesus Prayer, and also adapted various western spiritual exercises for eastern use. The two best examples of this activity are his *Spiritual Exercises*, based on Ignatius, and his *Unseen Warfare*, based on Scupoli. In the eighteenth century also Paissi Velichkovski (1722–94) revived the tradition of direction based on the Jesus Prayer. He settled in Moldavia, but after his death his spiritual influence became concentrated on the monastery of Optino near Kozelsk in Central Russia. Macarius (1788–1860), the second great *staretz* of Optino, has left us his *Letters to Lay People*, published in Moscow some twenty years after his death. Like all the great guides before him, he stresses the need to follow 'the guidance of a wise man experienced in the fight'.

> As to those who are happy without seeking spiritual direction and quite blissful without bothering much about the deeper Christian life—the life of the mind and heart—theirs is the peace of this world, not the peace of our Master. Whenever we set out firmly to tread the inner path, a storm of temptations and persecutions always assails us. It is because of the dark host that spiritual direction is profitable, nay necessary to us whether we retire to a monastery or continue to live in the world.[42]

In the nineteenth century, there were three other outstanding Russian *startsy*—St Seraphim of Sarov, Father John of Kronstadt, and the Staretz Amvrosy. St Seraphim (1759–1833) was certainly the greatest and the most legendary of Russian directors. He saw the aim of the Christian life to be 'the acquiring of the Holy Spirit'. Spiritual direction was a relationship of life shared in the Spirit, a sharing in glory, as one of the most famous stories of the saint brings out.

> 'We are both together, son, in the Spirit of God! Why lookest thou not on me?' The disciple answered, 'I cannot look, father, because lightning flashes from your eyes. Your face is brighter than the sun and my eyes ache in pain!' Father Seraphim said, 'Fear not, my son, you too have become as bright as I. You too

are now in the fulness of God's Spirit; otherwise you would not be able to look on me as I am.'[43]

Father John (1829–1908) was a different kind of figure, perhaps the best example in the Russian tradition of the spiritual guide who was an ordinary parish priest. His 'specific role was that of a *praying priest*',[44] and he has been compared to the Curé d'Ars in the West. Father John's view of priesthood was expressed in these words:

A priest is a spiritual physician. Show your wounds to him without shame, sincerely, openly, trusting and confiding in him as his son: for the confessor is your spiritual father and mother: for Christ's love is higher than any natural love. He must give an answer to God for you.[45]

Amvrosy, or Alexander Mikhailovich Grenkov (1812–91), was the disciple of Macarius, inherited his ministry of direction after the latter's death in 1860, and remained as spiritual director to the Optino monastery for about thirty years. Both Dostoyevsky and Solovyev visited Amvrosy, and he was certainly one of the physical models for Zossima in *The Brothers Karamazov*. Tolstoy also visited Amvrosy in 1877 and later in 1881, when he noted that 'when one talks with such a man, one feels the nearness of God'.[46] Amvrosy became widely known as a healer, and his letters of direction deal with a wide range of questions concerning fasting and asceticism.

The spiritual father then as seen in the eastern Orthodox tradition seems to have three principal features. First, he is a man of insight and discernment (*diakrisis*). He is able to see into the heart of another, a gift which is the fruit of prayer and ascetic struggle. Secondly, he is a man with the ability to love others and to make the sufferings of others his own. 'A *staretz*', wrote Dostoyevsky, 'is one who takes your soul and your will into his soul and his will.' In the words which he puts in the mouth of Zossima, 'There is only one way of salvation, and that is to make yourself responsible for all men's sins . . . To make yourself responsible in all sincerity for everything and for everyone.' That is to say, the work of the *staretz* is to share the passion and death of Christ. Thirdly, he is one with the power to transform the cosmos by the intensity of his love. Again, Zossima expressed this idea very powerfully.

At some ideas you stand perplexed, especially at the sight of men's sin, uncertain whether to combat it by force or by humble love. Always decide, 'I will combat it by humble love.' If you make up your mind about that once and for all, you can conquer the whole world. Loving humbly is a terrible force: it is the strongest of all things and there is nothing like it.[47]

PRE-REFORMATION DEVELOPMENTS IN THE WEST

In the thinking about the cure of souls in the West, St Gregory the Great (540–604) holds an important place. He devoted an entire volume (Book Three) of his *Pastoral Rule* to the theme 'Sermons should be of many different kinds', and he went on to apply this principle to some thirty-five types of listener! Addressing the clergy, in the first two books particularly, Gregory made the famous observation that 'the art of ruling souls is the art of arts' (*Ars est artium regimen animarum*).[48] He emphasizes three essential interior dispositions in the pastor and guide of souls: zeal for right conduct and discipline; love, learning, patience, pity, and a desire to adapt to all and condescend to all; and humility, the guarantee of purity of intention. Gregory referred to 'the priestly heart' as a heart which was attached only to the search for God and the good of the neighbour, and he extolled the virtue of discretion which was made up of discernment, moderation and confession.[49]

While Gregory was writing, the Celtic Church in Britain was being nurtured by such saints as Patrick and Columba and their followers. In the Celtic tradition we meet the figure of the 'soul-friend' who seems to have existed before the arrival of Christianity. The Irish word *anmchara* has also been rendered as 'spiritual guide' or 'spiritual director'. Certainly, every Celtic chief had his counsellor or druid at his court, and his ministry included incantations, fortune-telling and spells. When St Columba arrived in Iona, he appears to have expelled the two druids who purported to be bishops. However, the Celtic church saints inherited much of the pastoral status and functions of these old druids. 'The cleric supplants the druid as the king's chief adviser, under the title *anmchara*, soul-friend.'[50] The position of soul-friend was voluntary, and Columba refused to become the soul-friend of Donnan of Eig. But it was seen as necessary for everyone to possess a soul-friend, and the saying 'Anyone without a soul-friend is a body without a head' (attributed both to Brigit and to Comgall) became an established Celtic proverb. St Columba had as his soul-friend in Ireland St Laisren. Some soul-friends were women, such as Brigit, or Ita of

Cluain Credill, who was Brendan's confessor. Columbanus confessed to a woman, but later he reverted to priests. But the soul-
friend was essentially a counsellor and guide, and the office was
not seen in specifically sacramental terms. Often the soul-friend
was a layman or laywoman. Similarly in the East the monastic
absolution, which included absolution by lay brothers, was not
suppressed until western scholastic sacramental teaching made its
influence felt at the eastern negotiations with the West at the
Council of Lyons in 1274.

In the Celtic church, which became increasingly monastic in
structure, centres such as Iona and Lindisfarne seem to have
become bases for spiritual direction, and it has been suggested that
there was a close connection between the Celtic spirituality and
the eastern desert movement. Certainly the *anmchara* (Welsh
periglow) is similar to the Greek *syncellus*, the one who shares the
cell. *The Rule for Monks* written by St Columbanus contained a
chapter which is not found in the Benedictine or other rules,
entitled 'On Discretion'. Discretion, that quality which was valued
so highly by the Desert Fathers, was described as 'a moderating
science', a gift by which God gives the light of discernment.
Another key element in the Celtic understanding of direction was
the stress they placed on the mutuality of priest and penitent.
Thus the First Capitulary of Theodulf noted that 'the confession
which we make to the priests brings us this support, that we wash
away the stains of our sins when we receive at their hands salutary
counsel, the very wholesome exchange, observances of penance, or
the exchange of prayers.'[51]

Later western monasticism was shaped by the Rule of St
Benedict. Chapter 46 of the Rule instructs those who offend to
manifest their guilt to the Abbot or 'the spiritual seniors who know
how to deal with their own wounds and not to disclose or publish
those of others'. This regulation had nothing to do with sacramental confession, but rather with a relationship of disciple to a master.
Indeed, St Benedict presupposes such a relationship for all his
monks, since most of those who entered monasteries could not
read, and all education was centred around a kind of apprenticeship to a master. On the other hand, the term *pater spiritualis* only
occurs once in Benedict, in connection with obtaining permission
for Lenten penances. Here the term clearly means the superior. The
entire monastic family was seen as 'a school for the service of the
Lord', and the monks were described as 'disciples who should

listen'. The Abbot was expected to 'understand also what a difficult and arduous task he has undertaken: ruling souls and adapting himself to a variety of characters'.[52]

Outside the monasteries, there is evidence of the existence of groups of penitents and oblates from the seventh and eighth centuries onwards. Jonas of Orleans' *De Institutione Laicali* (on lay training) from the ninth century is one of a number of works which were attempting to provide guidance for the spiritual lives of lay people. Jonas stresses the value of regular self-examination and confession. About the same period, Prudentius, the Bishop of Troyes, produced his *Breviary of the Psalter*, an abridged version for use by a rich lady while travelling. Also during the Carolingian period, confraternities of clergy grew up in the urban areas with the main purpose of providing material and spiritual support. Lay manuals and penitentials continued to appear, though the latter tended to become less concerned with 'sin lists' and more with motives and interior responsibility. There was a desire for Bibles and liturgical books. 'Many desire to pray well', wrote Charlemagne in an encyclical of 789, 'but because of faulty books, they pray badly.'[53] Alcuin's Bible was one of the responses to this need, and there were also commentaries and devotional collections.

Alcuin (735–804) was also a strong advocate of frequent confession and direction. Thus he wrote:

> Come then, O penitent, confess thine own sins, lay bare by confession the secret of thine iniquity. Known unto God are those things which thou hast wrought in secret, which if the tongue have not spoken, yet the conscience will not be able to conceal. Tell thy sins by confession before thou feel the anger of the Judge ... Accordingly, my dearest son, listen to the remedy of confession. Lay open your wounds in confession that the medicaments of healing may be able to take effect in you.

Elsewhere he wrote: 'Diligently purge the slightest soils of words and thoughts ... before a faithful and prudent confessor, according to thy conscience, so that nothing remains.'[54]

In the eleventh century, the growth of lay brotherhoods meant that more lay people received personal spiritual guidance from monks. The *Regularis Concordia*, drawn up about 965, rules that all monks should confess each Sunday to the 'spiritual father', the abbot or his representative. In some cases there was daily confession to a priest of one's choice. '*Accedit ad sacerdotem ad*

quem potissimum volvent', wrote Ulrich of Cluny.[55] St Anselm
(1033–1109) was famed as a wise director, and his biographer
Eadmer notes that 'illumined by the searching light of an inner
wisdom, and guided by a discriminating reason, he could analyse
characters of every age and sex with such an accuracy that when
he came to speak you perceived that he had lifted a curtain and
was showing each one his own heart'.[56]

In the contemplative community at Clairvaux, there was an
institution called 'confession' which was not the sacrament of penance as we know it, but the manifestation of conscience to a
spiritual guide. Frequently in the writing of St Bernard, *confessio*
refers not to the confession of sin, but to the confession of praise,
or to the conversation or spiritual colloquy. St Bernard refers to
'spiritual brothers', a term similar to the *spirituales seniores* of the
Benedictines. Bernard speaks particularly of the monk Humbert
from whom many received spiritual direction.

> What a counsellor! How honest and discreet! I could appreciate
> it all the more since I had more often the opportunity of placing
> my head on his breast. But I am not the only one who knew
> him in this way; you were able to know him as well as I. Who
> is there who, in the number and strength of his temptations, did
> not learn the source and remedy from his mouth? He knew so
> well how to penetrate into the corners of a sick conscience that
> he who went to confess to him might have believed that he had
> seen everything, been present at everything.[57]

St Bernard wrote to the parents of one of his young monks: 'I will
be for him both a mother and a father, both a brother and a sister.
I will make the crooked path straight for him, and the rough places
smooth. I will temper and arrange all things that his soul may
advance and his body not suffer.'[58] He urged those who were
novices in the religious life to have a guide to lead and encourage
them. Without such direction they were likely to lack discretion,
to give themselves up to excesses of devotion, and to injure their
health. Again one sees the strong emphasis on discretion: '*discretio,
mater virtutum est et consummatio perfectionis*'.[59]

Within the early Cistercian tradition, the importance of obedience to a guide comes out in the writing of William of Saint Thierry.

> A humble and loving submission to authority brings peace to
> the soul. It brings security to blind faith, until such time as the

Holy Spirit comes, giving understanding of what the ear has heard . . . But if we neglect to depend on authority at the beginning of our life of faith, we inevitably take the wrong road, being guided by our unaided reason . . . These are but the first stages in our apprenticeship to the love of Christ.[60]

Yet the relationship of disciple to spiritual father was often a relationship which was filled with tenderness and mutual love. This is manifested with particular clarity in Aelred of Rievaulx, of whom it has been said that 'the greater part of his writings forms the diary of a spiritual director'.[61] His *Pastoral Prayer* is a striking example of spiritual fatherhood expressed in intercession. Novices would visit Aelred frequently for spiritual dialogues, and his *Mirror of Charity* and *Spiritual Friendship* describe some of these dialogues. In the *Pastoral Prayer* Aelred prays:

Grant me to accommodate myself to the character, ways, disposition, gifts, shortcomings of each: to do as circumstances demand, and as you see best . . . You know, Lord, my intention is not so much to be their superior as to lovingly help them and humbly serve them, to be, at their side, one of them . . . Grant them, Lord, the grace to ever think and feel towards me your servant and theirs, for your sake, as best serves their spiritual welfare. Let them love and fear me, but only so far as you see is for their good.[62]

It is in Aelred also that the importance of *friendship* is emphasized most strongly. 'To live without friends', he says, 'is to live like a beast.'[63] Thomas Merton has said that 'the thing that is most characteristic of Aelred's monastic theology is its emphasis on friendship'.[64] His friend and disciple Yvo rendered the Johannine verse 'God is friendship', a paraphrase which met with Aelred's approval. For him, spiritual friendship was the way to God. 'Friendship is like a step to raise us to the love and knowledge of God . . . friendship lies close to perfection.'[65]

More books and manuals of lay directions appeared in the twelfth century. Peter of Blois produced his *Treatise on Sacramental Confession* towards the end of the century. Confraternities of the Blessed Sacrament for lay people started to appear, although communions remained infrequent. On the other hand, confessions of devotion began to increase. During the thirteenth century in England, the solitaries became spiritual directors, and this process

continued in the fourteenth century. The *Ancrene Riwle*, a late
twelfth century manual for anchoresses, has been seen as 'the
first masterpiece of religious guidance, unrivalled for almost two
centuries afterwards'.[66] Another major development which had
profound effects on spirituality was the spread of the Franciscan
and Dominican movements. With both groups there was a strong
emphasis on prophetic preaching and apostolic ministry. The most
significant spiritual writer of the Franciscan movement was St
Bonaventure (1221–74), whose work *De Triplici Via* is the first
detailed treatment of the three-fold path in the life of prayer.
Bonaventure emphasizes regular examination of conscience and
frequent confession, though he does not seem to regard frequent
meetings with a spiritual director as necessary except in the early
stages of growth. Later it should be replaced by the gift of discretion. It is with the Dominicans, however, that spiritual direction
becomes directed more towards the laity, though at first they tried
to avoid long-term commitments to the care of individuals. However, they directed their preaching and teaching to the new urban
classes, and, in Germany in particular, to sectarian groups such as
the Beguines, Beghards and Fraticelli. By the thirteenth century
laymen were themselves acting as directors as in the early monastic
movement. The Dominicans moved into the area of spiritual direction with great seriousness. In 1220, in the Prologue of the Primitive Constitutions, dispensations were allowed for study, preaching
or the good of souls, for the Order was instituted 'for preaching and
the salvation of souls'. In 1215 the Fourth Lateran Council established the rule of obligatory annual confession and communion,
and recognized the possibility of confessors and directors other
than one's parish priest. On 4 February 1221, Pope Honorius II
commended the Order of Preachers to all the prelates of Christendom, and 'he exhorted them also to confide to them the ministry
of confession'.[67]

The ideal of spiritual direction among the Dominicans was laid
down by Paul of Hungary in his *Summa Magistri Pauli* of c.1220.

Let him be inclined to correct kindly and to bear the weight
himself. He must be gentle and affectionate, merciful to the faults
of others. He shall act with discernment in different cases. Let
him aid his penitent with prayer, alms, and other good works.
He is to help him by calming his fears, consoling him, giving
him back hope, and, if need be, by reproving him. Let him show

compassion in his words and teach by his deeds. Let him take part in the sorrow, if he wishes to share in the joy. He must inculcate perseverance.[68]

Long before the end of the thirteenth century, spiritual direction was also being given by Dominicans to women religious. There was an increase in summas and penitentials. The *Manuel des péchés*, written in Anglo-Norman around 1260, appeared in an English adaptation by Robert Mannyng under the title *Handlying Synne* in 1303. Also in 1260 the Brethren of the Free Spirit were condemned for teaching that one should not ask counsel from learned men *sive de devotione sive de aliis*.

In the fourteenth century writers there are numerous references to spiritual direction and guidance. It is possible that Walter Hilton wrote *The Scale of Perfection* with spiritual directors in mind.[69] Certainly in his letter to Adam Horsley he wrote:

> I speak of those seculars who do not fear to set out on the way of the spiritual life without a director or capable guide, whether a man or a book, obeying their own impulses . . . If not even the least of the arts can be learned without some teacher and instructor, how much more difficult it is to acquire the Art of Arts, the perfect service of God in the spiritual life, without a guide.[70]

Hilton stresses the need for discretion and discernment of spirits in the contemplative life, and he urges recourse to a director especially in the early stages. On the continent, Gerard Groot, the founder of the *devotio moderna*, stressed the importance of obedience to a guide, and so did his disciple Gerard Zerbolt in his *The Spiritual Ascent*. Out of this school came Thomas à Kempis, whose *Imitation of Christ* became one of the most popular and most widely used spiritual guide books in western Christianity. It urged its readers to 'take counsel with a wise and conscientious man. Seek the advice of your betters in preference to following your own inclinations'.[71] Thomas warned that the devil was displeased by a humble confession. John Gerson, author of *On Mystical Theology*, was widely used as a director, and he also wrote *De probatione spirituum*, on spiritual discernment, and *De arte audiendi confessiones*, 'on the art of hearing confessions'.

Again, in the Dominican tradition, St Catherine of Siena (1347–80) became spiritual director to a circle of friends, her *bella brigada*, and she wrote numerous letters of guidance. St Vincent

Ferrer (1346–1419) in his *Treatise on the Spiritual Life* emphasized that 'a person who has a director by whom he allows himself to be guided, whom he obeys in all his actions, great and small, will more easily and quickly arrive at perfection than he ever could by himself'. But, he added, 'unfortunately, it must be admitted that nowadays scarcely anyone is to be found capable of directing others in the way of perfection'.[72] Tauler (1300–61), however, warned that certain directors were like hunting dogs that ate the hare instead of bringing it to their master.

The literature of pastoral care generally reached a peak in the fourteenth century. The starting point in many respects was the Lateran Council of 1215 and in particular the decree *Omnis utriusque sexus* which established the rule of annual confession and communion. If this rule was to be taken seriously, there was a desperate need for manuals of guidance for the clergy. So 'the correct use of the sacrament of penance is a theme which dominates or underlies most of the religious literature of the thirteenth and fourteenth centuries'.[73] The pastoral role of the priest in the confessional was closely related to that exercised in preaching. So the *Oculus sacerdotis* noted: 'But if the priest, on account of the shortness of time and the multitude of penitents, cannot explain such matters to each one individually, then he ought to preach them publicly at the beginning of Lent'.[74] Several thirteenth-century bishops issued directives on hearing confessions. Alexander of Stavensby, the Bishop of Lichfield, in his Constitutions (1224–37) provided general regulations, while Walter Cantilupe, the Bishop of Hereford, mentioned a treatise on confession which all priests were to possess and use. Robert Grosseteste, Bishop of Lincoln, wrote several treatises on the subject, and Archbishop Pecham in 1281 issued an elaborate code. Among the manuals, the *Oculus sacerdotis* attributed to William of Pagula, Vicar of Winkfield, near Windsor, from 1314, is a manual for confessors (Part One), a programme of instruction for parishioners (Part Two), and a course on the sacraments (Part Three). The *Cilium Oculi*, whose date and authorship are unknown, seems to be intended as a supplement to the earlier work, while the *Regimen Animarum* of about 1343 deals primarily with pastoral care. The *Memoriale Presbiterorum* of about 1344 includes sections on confession, as does the *Pupilla Oculi* (about 1385). John Mirk's *Manuale Sacerdotis* of about 1400 concerned itself with the priest's life and spirituality. Other volumes, following the *Manuel des péchés*, aimed at guidance of lay people.

The fifteenth century saw an increase in manuals for the instruction of confessors and directors. A good example was the *Manipulus Curatorum* of Guy de Montrocher which distinguished the *confessio sacramentalis* of the ordinary pastor from the *confessio directiva* of the specialist. This specialist might come from afar, and he might be kept as a director. Thus the basis of the present concept was established by which parish priest and spiritual director may be two different people. Various fifteenth-century writers praised the virtue of regular direction, one of them being St Antonius, the 'father of counsels', who wrote:

> To assist at the love of God and devotion, to possess peace ...
> it is useful and necessary to have a spiritual guide to whom you
> can report at all times your conduct and your failings that he
> may help and counsel you and allow you to know your own
> state from hour to hour.[75]

Another protagonist of direction at this period was the Carthusian Denys of Ryckel, author of *De discretione et examinatione spirituum*.

THE WESTERN CATHOLIC TRADITION AFTER TRENT

After the Council of Trent, spiritual direction became both more widespread and more limited. It became more widespread in so far as the practice spread to include many lay men and women outside monasteries, and as the volumes written on the life of prayer increased in number. It was in the post-Tridentine period that the general framework of western spiritual direction was established, and this framework remained and dominated western Catholicism for over three hundred years. But there was also a severe narrowing of perspective. Spiritual direction became, to a very great extent, concerned with the treatment of scrupulosity, and with decisions about religious vocations. The reforming of the religious orders was, of course, a decisive factor in the shape that spiritual direction took after Trent. Habitual direction became a central element in monastic discipline. Manuals on direction increased in number, and there was an increased emphasis on the importance of mental prayer. The provision of a 'safe' method became a major concern of many spiritual guides who saw direction to involve the avoidance of heresy and of dubious forms of mysticism. So the spiritual director became not only the teacher of a method, but also the guardian of orthodoxy. For the Illuminati in 1623 had taught that there was no need of a director, and Michael Molinos the Quietist held that the idea of direction was ludicrous and novel. Again, after Trent, the spiritual director tended to become more specifically the director of conscience, one who settled *casus conscientiae*, special cases or problems. As Thomas Merton observed, 'this imposed rather unfortunate juridical limitations upon the traditional concept'.[76]

The western Catholic tradition after the Council of Trent included a number of outstanding spiritual directors, and some of the principal ones are worth examining.

i   St Ignatius Loyola (1495–1556)

In the *Spiritual Exercises* of St Ignatius, there is not only a clear and detailed view of the role of the director, but also the foundation for the development of a whole school of spiritual direction. The 'Ignatian retreat' has become an established form of spiritual discipline in the western church, and Pope Pius XI in his encyclical *Mens Nostra* of 20 December 1919 called the *Spiritual Exercises* 'the wisest and most comprehensive handbook of spiritual direction...the soundest guide to inner conversion and deep piety'.[77] One Jesuit writer of international repute has commented on the 'spreading desire to make the *Spiritual Exercises* under personal direction'.[78]

The *Spiritual Exercises* were first published in Rome in 1548 and they contain a variety of types of meditation and prayer. They are intended for use in times of retreat—on 25 July 1922 Pius XI made St Ignatius the patron saint of retreats—and they include a series of instructions intended primarily for directors as to their use. In fact, the whole volume is primarily a manual for directors, and is not intended for the retreatants themselves. The director is instructed to adapt the *Exercises* to the age, capacity, strength and disposition of the retreatant. The director's role is to stay in the background, to watch and encourage the retreatant and to allow God to work: 'he who gives the *Exercises* should not turn or incline himself to one side or the other, but keeping in the middle like a balance, should allow the Creator to work immediately with the creature, and the creature with its Creator and Lord'.[79] Throughout the work, the director is seen and described as the one who 'gives' the *Exercises*, and, indeed, there is a Directory, consisting of some forty chapters and giving instructions as to how such direction is to be exercised. The director is responsible for guiding the retreatants, determining the right length of time for each section, and questioning the retreatant where necessary. 'When he who gives the *Exercises* finds that the exercitant experiences no spiritual movements in his soul, such as consolations or desolations, nor is agitated by divers spirits, he ought to question him fully about the *Exercises* . . .' If the person is found to be desolate or tempted, the director is to be 'kind and gentle, encouraging and strengthening him for the future', and it is suggested that the director 'should be faithfully informed of the various agitations and thoughts which the different spirits excite in him; because, according to the greater or less profit he finds, his director may be able to give him some suitable spiritual exercises adapted to the needs of a soul thus agitated'.[80]

The *Exercises* include two lengthy sections containing guidance for spiritual directors: one on 'Rules for the Discernment of Spirits', that is, of 'the various movements excited in the soul', and the Directory, drawn up by several of the early Jesuits, as well as several short notes. The discernment of spirits is seen as a crucial part of spiritual direction. There are two sets of rules: one set deals with temptations and desolations, the other with distinguishing God-inspired thoughts and movements from the deceptions of the devil. The Directory is concerned with the preparation of retreatants, the manner of delivering the *Exercises*, and the procedure of Election. (An Election is an important, but not essential, element in an Ignatian retreat, and is a specific decision before God relating to one's vocation and state of life.) The director, who gives the *Exercises*, must be experienced in them and be skilled in giving them and explaining their method.

So the qualities of the good Ignatian director emerge clearly. Such a person

a should be 'well versed in spiritual things and especially in these *Exercises*';
b should be 'prudent and discrete, cautious and reserved . . . gentle', and preferably 'personally acceptable to the exercitant';
c should 'preserve the position and character of a master, as in truth he is';

    d   should not 'attribute anything to his own effort or skill' but
rather 'put great trust in God';

    e   should 'be very careful also not to add anything merely of
his own', and so 'let him endeavour only that the exercitant
may know how to seek the will of God';

    f   should 'take note of the exercitant' in order to provide the
best possible help;

    g   should have studied the *Exercises* thoroughly.[81]

Directors need to inquire of those under their care, Ignatius insists.
They must 'ask the exercitant how it has been with him since he
last saw him, and especially in his meditations, inquiring what
method he has pursued in them', and so on. They are instructed
also 'to prepare him for the test of desolation and aridity', exhort
to patience and stability, and 'be on his guard never to give the
exercitant any ground for suspecting that he has a poor opinion
of him'. In his actual delivery, the director is merely to introduce
the meditations, preferably in writing, and then to watch for signs
of over-strain 'by too violent an application to prayer'.[82] At the
close of the *Exercises*, the Director is to pursue the following
pattern:

    a   to urge the maintenance of regular daily meditation;

    b   daily examination of conscience; and

    c   weekly confession and communion;

    d   to suggest 'that he should choose some good confessor and
take him for his guide in this spiritual journey, treating with
him of everything that concerns his soul';

    e   to lead the person to the practice of spiritual reading and
fellowship with other Christians; and to

    f   daily growth in virtues.

Here then is a very thorough concept of direction, full of insight
and common sense, characterized by an insistence on method-
ology and stern discipline, and containing much that will be still
of value to the spiritual guide of today.

St Ignatius seems to have begun work as a spiritual director on
a small scale during his early period of recollection at Manresa
which followed soon after his conversion, but we have no knowledge of the method which he followed at this stage. After the
foundation of the Jesuits in 1541, direction centred around the
making of the *Spiritual Exercises*. Frequently the use of *methods*

has been seen as the characteristic feature of Ignatian spirituality. Even Pourrat sees the *Exercises* as the climax of 'the evolution of methodical prayer'.[83] But St Ignatius did not claim to have invented these methods. The method of imaginative contemplation which is described in the *Exercises* is also found in St Bonaventure's *De Triplici Via* and in Ramon Lull's *Art of Contemplation* in the thirteenth century, and earlier in the writings of Aelred of Rievaulx. Certainly Ignatius brought together a large number of exercises in a convenient framework of simplicity and intensive spiritual training. But to identify 'method' as the defining characteristic of the Ignatian way is, in de Guibert's words, like 'judging the type of locomotives by the colour they are painted'.[84] Rather the methods are utilized in the essential work of service through love, with a strong emphasis on the union of reason and the heart. These emphases—service, reason, love—are central to Ignatian spirituality.

Most of the spiritual direction given by the Jesuits was based on the confessional. Gabriel Hevenesi (1656–1715) heard 23,000 confessions in one year.[85] Many Jesuits spent most of their time as perpetual confessors, and it seems clear that most of these penitents were devout souls seeking direction. But another important aspect of Jesuit ministry was their preaching missions. It was Scaramelli's long experience of missions which led him to compile his Mystical and Ascetical Directories. Many followed the Ignatian style of direction including Alvarez de Paz, Robert Bellarmine, Alphonsus Rodriguez, Louis Lallemant, G. B. Scaramelli and J. N. Grou, who will be considered later.

ii Augustine Baker (1575–1641)

Augustine Baker, the English Benedictine, stressed the need for an 'external instructor and guide' for all those aspiring to perfection. While he held that Christians who were in a state of grace possessed sufficient internal light to direct them in the ordinary duties of a Christian life, in the avoidance of sin and the practice of goodness, yet, he argued, in the inner life, and particularly in growth towards contemplation, there was a danger of deception. It is at this point that grace directs the Christian to use the mediation of others. Yet according to Baker, direction is not a constant need. 'The necessity of an external instructor is generally only at the beginning of a contemplative course.'[86] The purpose of a director, according to

Baker, is 'to instruct the disciple in all the peculiar duties of an internal life'. What does this involve?

> ... to judge of her propension to contemplative ways, and that can at least teach her how she may fit herself with a degree of prayer proper for her; that knows all the degrees of internal prayer, and can determine how long she is to remain in such a degree, and when to change it for a higher; that can judge what employments &c. are helpful or hindering to her progress in internal ways; but especially that can teach her how to dispose herself to hearken to and follow God's internal teaching, and to stand in no more need of consulting her external director, &c.[87]

So the director's role can be summarized under four main functions:

a *evaluation* of the person's prayer-potential, and *guidance* in finding the right forms of prayer;
b *assessment* of the person's progress and help in evolving new ways of prayer;
c *identification* of aids and obstacles in the person's spiritual life;
d *enabling* the person to become more open to God and less dependent on the human director.

For the ministry of spiritual direction, Augustine Baker emphasizes three qualities: a good natural judgement, learning, and experience. Learning alone can be hazardous, and he warns against 'improper directors' whose learning can make them harmful to individuals who are on the way to contemplative prayer.

> The more learned that such improper directors are, the more incompetent are they for such an employment about souls whose profession is the aspiring to the prayer of contemplation; because if either they be ignorant of such prayer, or unwilling to acknowledge any prayer more perfect than that which themselves practise and teach others, their learning will make them both more able and forward to keep souls under a certain captivity, chained with methods and forms, the which, though very profitable, even to those souls in the beginning, yet afterward becomes very painful and even unsupportable to them living in solitude and a given abstraction of life.[88]

Baker, is, of course, writing of contemplatives, but his warning applies more generally to those who cause people to be slaves to

forms and methods which they have outgrown, and which the
Holy Spirit may be leading them to transcend. Clearly then
'the most fit directors are such as are versed in the ways that they
teach.' Baker insists that neither natural judgement, learning nor
experience all together are absolutely sufficient to qualify a person
to be a guide in the internal ways of the Spirit. Often, he says, 'an
actual supernatural illumination will be necessary.' Baker com-
plains that the office of spiritual director is 'invaded by persons
wholly unfitted for it'.[89]

The souls seeking a guide should 'avoid one of the like temper,
for passion which blinds the seeker will also blind the director'.[90]
Once a relationship is established, he recommends directors to
devote a reasonable amount of time at the beginning to getting
to know their disciples. After this, however, they should try to set
them on a spiritual path so that they will not need to have much
subsequent recourse to the director. He warns against the type of
directors who make their disciples excessively dependent on them.

> But it is too general a humour in directors nowadays to make
> themselves seem necessary unto their disciples, whom they
> endeavour to keep in a general continual dependence, to the
> great prejudice of their progress in spirit, beside many other
> inconveniences not needful to be mentioned particularly.[91]

Like St Ignatius, Father Baker stresses the importance of discernment of spirits. He is opposed to examination of disciples about
their internal exercises, believing that if things are going badly in
the inner life, it will become clear externally.

iii   St Francis de Sales (1567–1622)
St Francis de Sales is among the most insistent of all writers on the
necessity of direction. Pourrat observed: 'Before the *Introduction to
the Devout Life*, the universal need for direction had not been so
definitely stated. Nor was there anywhere to be found so complete
a teaching regarding it.'[92] Francis allows of no exception.

> And why should we wait to be masters of ourselves in that which
> concerns the spirit, since we are not so in what concerns the
> body. Do we not know that doctors when they are sick call other
> doctors to judge as to the remedies that are right for them?[93]

In *The Devout Life* he speaks of 'the necessity of a guide in order
to enter into and to make progress in devotion'. He goes on:

When you have found him, do not look on him as a mere man
nor trust in him as such nor in his human knowledge but in God
who will favour you and speak to you by means of this man,
putting into his heart and into his mouth whatever shall be
requisite for your happiness so that you ought to listen to him
as to an angel who comes down from heaven to conduct you
thither.[94]

Yet St Francis favours a relationship of friendship. The director is
to be a 'faithful friend', and there should exist 'a friendship . . .
wholly spiritual, sacred, holy and divine' between him and his
penitents.

St Francis summarizes the qualities of the director. 'He must be
full of charity, of knowledge, and of prudence; if one of these three
qualities is wanting in him, there is danger.'[95] He advised against
changing confessors.

Do not be too ready to change your confessor, but keep to the
same one; go to him regularly and confess your sins quite can-
didly and sincerely. Every month or so reveal your inclinations,
apart from any sin; the fact, for example, that you were troubled
by sadness, felt joyful and avaricious and so on.[96]

He suggests that the confessor should normally be the director
also. St Francis, however, did not restrict direction to the spoken
word, and he himself wrote many letters, all with his own hand.
In one of these, he defines his 'method, which is gentle, and allows
spiritual exercises to have their own gradual effect on souls'. But,
he says in one letter, there is a shortage of competent directors.

It is difficult . . . to find people of all-round discernment who
can see clearly to an equal degree in all matters: nor is it essential
to have people of this kind so as to be well directed, and there
is no harm, it seems to me, in gathering from many flowers the
honey which we cannot find in one alone.[97]

St Jane de Chantal, in her deposition for St Francis's canonization,
referred to the fact that 'he liked to leave great freedom to the
working of God's Spirit in souls'.[98] In a study of his method of
direction, Francis Vincent commented that he was not only one
of the princes of spiritual direction, but also one of the first theor-
eticians and one of the founders of the modern tradition.[99] Contemporary with, or immediately following, St Francis de Sales, the

French School included such figures as Berulle (1575–1629), De Condren (1585–1641), St Vincent de Paul (1576–1660), S. J. Olier (1608–57), Fénelon (1651–1715), and St Alphonsus Liguori (1691–1787). St Vincent saw direction as 'extremely useful', but where a director is not easily available, 'it is the Lord who takes the director's place and who in his goodness directs you'.[100] St Alphonsus saw the direction of the devout to be one of the most important duties of the confessor. He held that spiritual direction was to be concerned with mortification, reception of the sacraments, prayer, the practice of virtues, and sanctification of ordinary actions.

iv St Teresa (1515–82) and St John of the Cross (1543–91)
In the teaching of the great Carmelite saints, St Teresa and St John of the Cross, the spiritual director assumes a central role. In the beginnings of contemplative prayer, or the 'ligature' as Dom John Chapman called it, competent spiritual guidance is essential. 'At this time', says St John of the Cross, 'the soul must be led by a way totally opposed to the earlier one.'[101] He is emphatic that

> if there is no one who understands them at this time, they will turn back, leaving the proper road, and becoming weak, or at least failing to go forward ... imagining that this is the consequence of their negligence or sinfulness.[102]

The director of contemplatives needs experience. 'Besides being learned and discreet he must be experienced',[103] that is, he must himself have experiential knowledge of contemplative prayer. St Teresa says that it is better to have no director at all than a bad one at this stage. 'Let seculars give thanks to God that they can choose their own director, and let them not give up that precious liberty, but rather remain without one until they find the one whom the Lord will give.'[104]

Both saints devote a good deal of attention to the subject of incompetent directors. St John in particular laments the fact that many souls set out on the spiritual path but make no progress 'because they understand not themselves and lack competent and alert directors who will guide them to the summit'.[105] He particularly attacks those directors who are ignorant of contemplative prayer and who therefore urge their unfortunate disciples to greater efforts in meditation. 'They know no way with souls but to hammer

and batter them like a blacksmith.'[106] Such directors are harmful
and destructive, and St John is very hard on them.

> It may be that they err with good intention since they know no
> better. But there is still no excuse for the advice which they have
> the temerity to give when they do not know the first thing
> about the way and manner of spirit of the soul; knowing nothing,
> they meddle with their clumsy hands in things which they do
> not understand, instead of leaving it to someone who does
> understand.[107]

These directors are 'barriers and obstacles at the gate of heaven':
they 'hinder from entering those that ask counsel of them'.

More generally, both saints advise against over-rigid direction,
insisting that 'all do not travel by one road',[108] and that 'God leads
each one by a different way'.[109] St Teresa is critical of those directors who forbid, or disapprove of, reading during the life of prayer,
and says that she herself found it impossible for eighteen years to
pray without the help of a book.[110] She had particular problems
with her own spiritual directors. 'I could not find a director—I
mean a confessor who understood me—although I looked for one
for twenty years after the time I am talking of.'[111] It is very likely
that St Teresa was resisting her directors' insistence that she should
not try to meditate, and through her twenty years of struggle, she
rediscovered affective mental prayer. But she admits that 'I myself,
through not knowing what to do, have suffered much and lost a
great deal of time'.[112] Yet, in spite of all her criticisms of the
incompetent, St Teresa frequently insists that direction is necessary.

> My opinion has always been and always will be that every
> Christian should try to consult some learned person if he can,
> and the more learned the person the better. Those who walk in
> the way of prayer have the greater need of learning; and the
> more spiritual they are, the greater is their need.[113]

In the early stages of prayer, direction is particularly needed. 'The
beginner needs counsel to help him ascertain what benefits him
most. To this end a director is very necessary; but he must be a
man of experience.'[114] Again, St John says that it is God's will 'that
the government and direction of every man should be undertaken
by another man like himself'. It is through this relationship that
spiritual growth occurs. 'It is a difficult thing to explain how the

spirit of the disciple grows in conformity with that of his spiritual father in a hidden and secret way.'[115]

v J. P. de Caussade (1675–1751)

De Caussade has been viewed as one who saw direction as being more hindrance than help. Yet it is clear that he himself was a spiritual director and he wrote many letters of guidance. De Caussade seems, however, to be reacting against, and rejecting, an over-systematized and regimental style of direction. So he begins his best known work *Self-Abandonment to the Divine Providence*:

> God continues to speak today as he spoke in former times to our Fathers when there were no directors as at present, nor any regular method of direction. Then all spirituality was comprised in fidelity to the designs of God, for there was no regular system of guidance in the spiritual life to explain it in detail, nor so many instructions, precepts and examples as there are now. Doubtless our present difficulties render this necessary, but it was not so in the first ages when souls were more simple and straightforward.[116]

The book as a whole is one great plea for simplicity and for acceptance of 'the sacrament of the present moment'. De Caussade is very critical of interference with such simple followers by those who fail to understand the nature of their spirituality. 'Besides', he points out, 'these latter require less direction than others in consequence of having attained to this state with the help of very good directors.' He vigorously defends such souls, and says that they are always willing to be guided and they do ask for advice when they need it. But the essential point is that when they are deprived, 'they have recourse to the maxims supplied to them by their first directors'. As a result, 'they are always very well directed'.[117]

It is clear too from de Caussade's letters that he is not opposed to direction, and he was himself influenced by the Carmelite masters. He urges one nun 'not to trust to our own light in what regards ourselves but to allow our directors to guide our conscience'.[118] On the other hand, when another sister lost her spiritual director, he advised her to rejoice that she could now rely on God directly.[119] His general concern is that, through good direction in the early stages, the disciple is enabled to achieve interior direction and reliance on the direct influence of the Holy Spirit.

vi   J. N. Grou (1731–1803)

Jean Grou was the last of the great Jesuit writers on spiritual
direction before the period of the eighteenth and nineteenth centuries saw a general decline in the tradition. In his *Manual for
Interior Souls*, he devotes a valuable chapter to the question of
direction. He begins by relating direction closely to confession,
though regretting that 'there have always been very few confessors
who are directors at the same time'. Grou describes the purpose
of spiritual direction thus:

> To direct a soul is to lead it in the ways of God, it is to teach
> the soul to listen for the Divine inspiration, and to respond to
> it; it is to suggest to the soul the practice of all the virtues proper
> for its particular state; it is not only to preserve that soul in
> purity and innocence, but to make it advance in perfection: in a
> word, it is to contribute as much as possibly may be in raising
> that soul to the degree of sanctity which God has destined for it.

So the director needs to be 'the voice of God, the instrument of
Divine grace, the co-operator with the work of the Holy Spirit'.
He must be a man of prayer, considering only the glory of God
and the good of souls. So it is not surprising that 'true directors
are very rare'. Nevertheless, says Grou, 'the greatest mistake of all
is to wish to guide ourselves'. There are no exceptions if we seek
the path of perfection: 'We must take a director, that is, a guide,
to whom we can give an account of everything, and whom we can
obey as if he were God himself.'

Grou concludes the chapter with five rules for direction:

a   'for them not to meet except from necessity and then to
      speak only of the things of God';
b   mutual respect, courtesy and gravity;
c   never to conceal anything;
d   measureless obedience; and
e   'to look beyond the man, and only to see God in him; only
      to be attached to him for God's sake, and to be always ready
      even to give him up if God requires it'.[120]

After Grou, there was a dearth of writing on direction, indeed
in the whole area of serious work on spiritual theology. Trueman
Dicken has referred to 'the authentic tones of a spiritual theology
which had been silenced with the death of Jean Grou, and were
first heard again only in the writings of the Abbé Saudreau'.[121] In

fact, however, there is one work during the period between Grou and Saudreau which is important in the study of direction: F. W. Faber's *Growth in Holiness* (1854).

Faber had been one of the Tractarian leaders, but joined the Roman Communion in 1845. He refers to spiritual direction as 'the most vexed question of the whole spiritual life'. The religious orders are prone to exaggerate direction so that it becomes unreal to those in the world. Faber argues that the ancient writers are more balanced and sane. The director, says Faber, is not simply a 'spiritual counsellor'.

> The adjustment of domestic duties requires as much discernment as turning a point in mental prayer. The exactions of society are far more bewildering to see our way through than the uncertainties of a cloudy vocation. It is a marvel to me that persons should fancy that a director in purely spiritual things should be a person of higher attainments than one who is to guide us in spiritualizing worldly things.

The director therefore is concerned with worldly affairs. Faber actually asserts that 'spiritual direction is a witness against the world' and that the church is 'a divine conspiracy against the world'.[122]

Faber argues for the necessity of a director, basing his argument on the tradition, common sense, reason, the nature of the spiritual life, the nature of the director's office, and universality. 'The place which a spiritual director occupies in the ascetical system of the church is nothing more than an expression of her maternal common sense.'[123] The three departments of direction, according to Faber, are prayer, suffering and action, those areas in fact which are the favourite provinces of self-deceit.

The director in Faber's view is not a pioneer, but one whose role is 'to go behind and to watch God going before'. The Holy Spirit leads the penitents. The spiritual director, he insists, is not like a novice master in a community. 'He leads them by an acknowledged tradition and animates them with the definite fixed spirit of the order, and models them as a faithful copyist on their sainted founder. But this is not at all the function of a spiritual director.'[124] Rather he looks to God in the future, 'in the dimness ahead'. Faber warns against those directors who keep souls in bondage. 'Spiritual direction must be free as air and fresh as the morning sun', but it 'has a desperate proclivity to become tyrannical', and thus becomes an evil. Faber again stresses that 'the confounding of a spiritual director with a religious superior is fraught with specially pernicious consequences to our souls'.[125] So the relationship with a director is fundamentally different, and freedom of choice is essential. Faber points to the hazards of excess direction. 'The souls damaged by over-direction would fill a hospital in any large town.'[126]

Towards the end of the nineteenth century, Pope Leo XIII referred to the issue of direction in his *Testem Benevolentiae* of 22 January 1899. In attacking those who held that the guidance of the Holy Spirit was sufficient for a perfect Christian life, he claimed that those who sought perfection were more likely to go astray on their own, and were in more need than others of a spiritual guide. In fact, the Jesuits were continuing to direct souls through the confessional during the nineteenth century, and there were numerous collections of letters of direction by Jesuits in this period. From the nineteenth century also came a violent attack on direction by the French writer Jules Michelet in *La prêtre, la femme et la famille*, published in England in 1845 as *Spiritual Direction and Auricular Confession*. Direction, he argued, is tyranny. 'The patient and wary man ... day by day depriving you of a little of yourself ... this is a thing different from royalty, it is divinity. It is to be the God of another.'[127]

At the beginning of the twentieth century, direction was placed within a framework of spiritual theology in the two-volume work by the Abbé Saudreau, *The Degrees of the Spiritual Life: A Method of Directing Souls According to their Progress in Virtue* (1907). Saudreau began by explaining the importance of recognizing the *stages* of progress in spiritual life, quoting, among other authorities, the Articles of Issy drawn up by Bossuet, Fénelon and Tronson. Article 34 stressed that it is 'certain that beginners and perfect souls ought to be guided according to quite different rules'. Saudreau divides Christians into seven degrees: believing souls, good Christian souls, devout souls, fervent souls, perfect souls, heroic souls, and great saints. He believes that it is at the beginning of the second degree that the need of direction is felt, and he emphasizes four characteristics of such direction. First, it should be *paternal*, loving and gentle. He stresses gentleness, quoting St Alphonsus Liguori who was once asked what he considered the most important rule for spiritual directors. 'I have no doubt whatever as to that: the true characteristic of direction, and that which is most in conformity to the Spirit of God and of the Gospel is gentleness.'[128] Secondly, it should be *firm*. Thirdly, it should be *supernatural*. The director must deflect attention away from himself towards God. Fourthly, it should be *practical*. Attention in particular needs to be given to the discipline of prayer, the sanctification of common actions through recollection and rule of life, and renunciation, involving self-examination and mortification, and the frequent use of the sacraments. Saudreau discusses at length the ways in which individuals may be led to advance in mental prayer.

In the third degree, the devout, Saudreau is concerned with the development of the Illuminative Way and with growth in affective prayer, and the occurrence of delight and aridity. The director is urged to stress *recollection* and discipline, renunciation and humility, and to help the soul to move from meditation to affective prayer. These same principles apply, he says, to the fourth degree, the fervent.

The fifth and sixth degrees, in Saudreau's categories, fall within the unitive life, the prayer of contemplation. He stresses the importance of knowledge of the rules of the contemplative life, and draws attention to St Teresa's strictures on directors who hinder the progress of souls, cramping and tormenting them. Father Balthazar Alvarez speaks in the same way. 'Now no one has any right to interrupt this progress. Directors cannot, with a safe conscience, recall to an active state those whom God calls to repose: they would endanger by it both their souls and bodies.'[129] Saudreau therefore stresses the principles of direction of contemplatives, and the general outlines of contemplative prayer. As he moves to the final degrees, the heroic and the great saints, he stresses the fact that the soul by this stage is 'evidently under the constant influence and grace of and the continual direction, so to speak, of the Holy Spirit'. The role of the spiritual father should therefore be confined to enabling the soul to follow this divine directive and preventing it from going aside from it.[130]

During the same period as Saudreau, the Benedictine Dom Columba Marmion (1858–1923), the Abbot of Meredsous, became a spiritual guide of international repute, though he did not believe in too much direction.

What is necessary is that the director knows the soul *perfectly*, and that once done, he must indicate the way she is to follow, and

then leave her to the Holy Spirit. From time to time, at long
intervals, he must control her progress, and if anything out of
the common way should happen, he must know it, but in my
opinion, long and frequent letters of direction do more harm
than good.

In another letter he wrote: 'The Holy Ghost alone can form souls,
and the director has merely to point out to his spiritual child the
road by which God is leading her, give her some general rules for
her conduct, and control her progress, answer her difficulties, if
any, *at distant intervals*.'[131] Again, he explained his understanding
of the director's role in a letter to a nun:

> My part only consists in praying much for you, pointing out to
> you the pitfalls which even the best intentioned may encounter,
> advising you in difficult cases, and finally, in urging you to give
> yourself unreservedly to Jesus.

At a conference of nuns, he explained further:

> Most persons do not think of the Holy Spirit, and yet it is to
> him that God has confided the direction of souls. Many think a
> detailed direction is needed, they make endless analyses of soul,
> write pages upon pages, but the great Director of souls is the
> Holy Spirit. When the priest has been told all that he ought to
> be told, the necessary direction is given, and the shortest is often
> the best.[132]

The director, Marmion insisted, 'is not a fabricator of the conscience, but a guide, an enlightener, a helper'.[133] Excessive dependence on a director could easily become a substitute for personal
responsibility.

Saudreau's enormous work was followed by a series of Roman
studies on the spiritual life, all following the same general pattern,
the best known being A. Poulain, *The Graces of Interior Prayer*
(1907), Adolphe Tanquerey, *The Spiritual Life* (1923), the later
works by the Dominican R. Garrigou-Lagrange, *Christian Perfection and Contemplation* (1923) and *The Three Ages of the Interior
Life* (1947, 2 volumes), and Dom J-B. Chautard, *The Soul of the
Apostolate* (1946), a book often recommended by Pope Pius X.
There were also a number of works specifically on direction, such
as V. Raymond, *Spiritual Director and Physician* (1917) and later
C. H. Doyle, *Guidance in Spiritual Direction* (1950) and Robert

de Sinéty, *Psychopathologie et direction* (1934). In general, these works are at one in stressing the value of direction, though they vary in the degree of importance they attach to it. Thus Tanquerey speaks of 'the moral necessity of spiritual direction',[134] and he summarizes the duties of directors and of those under direction, quoting the usual western authorities. Garrigou-Lagrange devotes a chapter to the subject, and holds the view, with Tanquerey, that direction is not absolutely necessary, but that it is 'the normal means of spiritual progress'.[135] Chautard refers to members of religious orders who 'vegetate for lack of spiritual direction',[136] while A. Godinez in 1920 claimed that most of those called to contemplation failed to respond for lack of spiritual direction.[137] In his *Menti Nostrae* of 23 September 1950, Pope Pius XII argued that without spiritual direction, it is often very difficult to be duly responsive to the impulses of the Spirit, and he praised spiritual directors, stressing the particular importance of direction in the training of seminarians. One of the writers who was most insistent on the need for direction was the founder of the Little Brothers of Jesus, Charles de Foucauld. 'The soul's life depends on it: it is the one essential. If you have this, you can dispense with all the rest . . . It is the key to sanctification and the means of living in interior peace.'[138]

RECENT ROMAN CATHOLIC THINKING ON DIRECTION
Within the Roman communion, one of the best and most concise summaries of the tradition of spiritual direction, particularly oriented towards the Ignatian style, was written by Joseph de Guibert (died 1942), who was Professor of Ascetical and Mystical Theology at the Gregorian University in Rome. In his major work *The Theology of the Spiritual Life* (1956), which was edited from notes issued to his students, he devoted a lengthy chapter to the role of the director. De Guibert distinguished three types of direction: sacramental, pastoral and spiritual. Sacramental direction is the advice or instruction given during the sacrament of Penance, in order to ensure the valid and fruitful reception of the sacrament. Pastoral direction is that given in the form of general exhortations and personal guidance. Spiritual direction is that which is aimed at 'a higher perfection in the Christian life'. So the spiritual director is 'the one to whom a person manifests his state of soul, and to whom he offers himself to be habitually directed . . . in the way of perfection'.[139] De Guibert stresses the habitual and continuous

nature of direction, the freedom of choice in the relationship, and the teaching office of the director. He notes, however, that there are some who set the spiritual director merely as 'a kind of counsellor or friend to whose advice one listens, accepting or rejecting it with perfect freedom'. He makes two important points about the relationship which are central to his viewpoint. First, the spiritual director has no authority which requires obedience. He is not a religious superior or an ecclesiastical official. The person freely chooses a director, and may freely leave him. Indeed, he says, 'there is no theological basis on which to define the nature of the relationship between the soul and the director.'[140] He cites in support of this view the letters of St Francis de Sales who specifically says that the director's role consists of 'counsels, not commands'. However, St Francis certainly stressed that 'it is advisable to have only one spiritual father whose authority ought to be preferred to one's own will on every occasion and in every matter'.[141] Secondly, de Guibert says that the director/disciple relationship is not that of equal to equal, or friend to friend. Rather the director is an educator and teacher, and this involves submission, though it is submission which derives from humility and not from canonical obedience. Yet without such submission, the soul cannot benefit from direction. On the other hand, the director can be called a friend, and indeed St Francis de Sales does call him 'the faithful friend'.[142]

De Guibert held the view that the office of spiritual director cannot be restricted to priests. The tradition includes lay men and women—St Francis of Assisi, St Ignatius Loyola (before his ordination), St Catherine of Genoa, St Teresa of Avila, and so on. However, he also held the view that lay direction was rare. Much of his discussion was concerned with the question of religious vocation, which is not the concern of this study, but his summary of the method of spiritual direction is simple and of general application. First, the director must know the soul, and assist it to express itself. Secondly, the director must teach. Thirdly, good will must be fostered, and resolutions put into practice. De Guibert lists the qualities of a good director as follows: knowledge, especially of spiritual theology and psychology; prudence and good judgement; experience; and holiness. He also summarizes briefly and well the dangers to which spiritual directors will be prone:

Despotism, treating souls as perennial juveniles, or imposing his own ideas and ways on everyone indiscriminately; incompetence, undertaking the direction of every type of soul without preparing himself; vainglory and self-complacency on the number and kind of his clients; waste of time and talkative curiosity; inefficiency, weakness and human respect in his manner of directing, or perhaps even a too-natural liking for his spiritual child; illuminism, i.e., directing the soul according to the lights which he thinks he has received directly from God and which he follows blindly.[143]

In conclusion, de Guibert discusses direction by letter and spiritual friendship. He is wary of the former, because of the danger that letters may be given to others for whom the advice contained is inapplicable, because of the difficulty of maintaining confidentiality, and so on. Nevertheless, he does not exclude letters of direction as an occasional necessity, though he believes that they can only be of value when there is already an intimate knowledge of the soul. On spiritual friendship, he points out that such a relationship can help or hinder spiritual growth. It can be a powerful aid to sanctity, or a hindrance, but either way, it is a relationship essentially different from that of spiritual direction.

Since de Guibert, there have been important changes both in the pattern of spiritual direction in the Roman Communion, and in the kind of thinking which has gone on about the nature of this ministry. The spread of the movement of Catholic Action in Italy after the Second World War made spiritual direction more popular in that country, and it was defined in a manner which made it part of the ordinary pastoral ministry. Thus Don Carlo Gnocchi spoke of it in the 1940s as 'the delegated action of Christ for the edification of his Mystical Body through the ordinary organ of the priesthood'.[144] Father Gabriel, the Professor of Spiritual Theology in the Discalced Carmelites' College in Rome, wrote in 1950 that 'in this age of ours there is an urgent need for thoroughly capable spiritual directors'.[145] But it is during the last few years that there has been some of the most significant writing and thinking in this area, particularly among American Jesuits.

The first substantial work to appear since de Guibert's study on this area was Jean Laplace, *The Direction of Conscience* (1967). Laplace began by observing that 'spiritual direction does not have a good press'. Like most earlier writers he insisted that direction demands a free relationship, but he also emphasized that personal direction can go deeper than group work. 'Discernment by all means, but achieved in peace: that is the objective of personal direction.' In the foreword to Laplace's book, Leo Trese defined spiritual direction as 'simply pastoral counselling with greater spiritual depth than is usually brought to the immediate situation'.[146]

Some recent writers have suggested that direction is not necessary for all. 'Personal spiritual direction', claimed the Jesuit James Walsh, 'becomes useful and necessary only when the individual who is living the life of the Christian community to its fullest possible extent becomes aware of God's *special* call to perfection'. On this view, spiritual direction is *not* the work of the ordinary parish priest, but requires a specialist with special training, while 'what the average priest goes for, first of all, is to get his people to Mass on Sunday'.[147] Another writer, Friedrich Wulf, suggests that much of the work of the spiritual director can now be accomplished through group activity.

> One hears of a 'crisis' of spiritual direction today. And there is an undoubted need to seek for new ways. One form is discussion in small groups: discussion of meditation during spiritual exercises in common, *la revision de vie*, 'sensitivity training'. Such discussion is possible only in homogeneous groups. It does not replace the spiritual direction sought by the individual from a counsellor in private, but makes it more adequate, especially by the possibilities it holds out of better social adjustment.

The main tasks of the director, according to Wulf, are '(a) to help the individual to self-knowledge; (b) to help him to self-acceptance; (c) to help him to detachment from his own ego; (d) to help him to find the actual will of God'.[148]

In a Jesuit symposium of 1972, John H. Wright defines spiritual direction as 'an interpersonal situation in which one person assists another to develop and come to greater maturity in the life of the spirit'. He insists that direction is not in essence informative, therapeutic, or advisory, though it may at times involve all these functions. Rather 'the primary function of spiritual direction is to provide assistance in two areas, that of clarification and that of discernment'. Through the method of conversation, the person is helped to objectify and discern his or her spiritual life and progress. The relationship is not that of parent/child, but adult/adult.

It may at times, because of the difference of development and maturity, participate to some degree in the parent-child relationship, but fundamentally it is not that.

The conversation, says Wright, must include discussion of the details of prayer life (time, problems, and so on), of the person's sufferings, of his or her relationships to others. In the Jesuits' discussion of Wright's paper, however, it was suggested that 'much of our spiritual direction may well be accomplished in the future in groups'.[149]

Two other contributions of importance have come from Gregory Carlson, a Jesuit working in Berkeley, California, and Gerald Keefe of St Paul's Seminary, Minnesota, both written in 1974. Carlson distinguishes spiritual direction from normal friendly advice, problem solving and psychological counselling. He defines it as 'a conversation in which, with the help of another, a person expresses his or her experience of faith and discerns its character and movement'. Within the process, there is a three-fold pattern of conversation, experience and discernment. The director's role also is three-fold: to ask questions in order to clarify and discern; at times to suggest interpretations; and to encourage. He does *not* direct. Carlson stresses the virtues of trustworthiness, experience, discretion, and compassion in the director. Keefe lays a great deal of stress on the Trinitarian nature of direction.

> Spiritual direction strives to reproduce these divine relationships in the human but Spirit-filled dialogue that occurs. So the spiritual director acts as a son as well as a father; that is, he reflects as well as initiates. In the father/son dialogue there is a drawing together in the Spirit. So the entire relationship is seen as a reflection of God's nature and God's relationship with men.[150]

Since Keefe wrote these words, there has been much activity among Roman Catholics. Many women members of religious orders have been sought out as directors by members of other churches. Institutes of spiritual guidance have mushroomed, and there has been a particular revival of Ignatian spirituality and of the Ignatian retreat.[151]

SPIRITUAL DIRECTION WITHIN ANGLICANISM

In seventeenth-century Anglicanism there is a good deal of attention to the area of personal direction. George Herbert, for example, advises his reader to 'dresse and undresse thy soul: mark the decay and growth of it'.[152] In his *A Priest to the Temple* (1632), he describes the pastor as one who 'hath thoroughly digested all the points of consolation', and he gives advice on spiritual direction of various groups of people.[153] Both Herbert and Nicholas Ferrar, his contemporary, were spiritual guides to many people. A major work of seventeenth-century Anglican guidance was Gilbert Burnet's *Discourse of Pastoral Care* (1662), written 'to raise the sense of the obligation of the clergy', while Thomas Wilson's *Instructions for the Clergy* (1708) is also a valuable source book. William Law (1686–1781) laid a high value on spiritual direction, but warned one of his correspondents that, just as 'to be always tampering with physicians and probing one's condition is the way to lose all true judgement', so we can harm our spiritual health 'by running after spiritual advice on every occasion'. Individuals who are 'burdened with troubles' are to be told that 'the state of absolute resignation, naked faith, and pure love of God is the highest perfection'. Law's words have a very Caussadian ring about them. He advises one eager director to 'have a care of too much eagerness to set other people right',[154] and it is striking that his *Serious Call to a Devout and Holy Life* (1728) makes no reference whatever to spiritual direction.

A work which did attempt to provide guidance for Anglican directors was Jeremy Taylor's *Doctor Dubitantium* (1660). 'Our needs remain', Taylor reminded his readers, 'and we cannot be well-supplied out of the Roman store-house.'[155] Taylor was appalled by the low spiritual standards of his age. In his Episcopal Charge of 1661 he said:

> Let every minister teach his people the use, practice, methods and benefits of meditation or mental prayer . . . Let every minister exhort his people to a frequent confession of their sins, and a declaration of the state of their souls; to a conversation with their minister in spiritual things, to an enquiry concerning all parts of their duty; for by preaching and catechizing and private intercourse, all the needs of souls can best be served; but by preaching alone they cannot.[156]

This is an important statement of Caroline spirituality, for while the Carolines stressed the role of the sermon, they assumed that personal spiritual guidance would accompany it. Taylor also wrote *Rules and Exercises of Holy Living* (1650) because he was concerned that many Anglicans had found it impossible to obtain personal spiritual guidance during the Commonwealth period. He himself was spiritual guide to John Evelyn and others. The influence of Taylor was very considerable on the spirituality of the Church of Ireland, and there is abundant evidence of spiritual direction among Anglicans in the seventeenth century in that country.[157]

A little earlier than Taylor, Joseph Hall (1574–1656), who was Bishop of Norwich from 1641, criticized the neglect of spiritual guidance:

> A mean would do well betwixt two extremes: the careless neglect of our spiritual fathers, on the one side; and too confident reliance upon their power, on the other ... The Romish laity make either oracles or idols of their ghostly fathers; if we make cyphers of ours, I know not whether we be more injurious to them or ourselves. We go not about to rack your consciences to a forced and exquisite confession, under the pain of no-remission; but we persuade you, for your own good, to be more intimate with, and less reserved from, those whom God hath set over you, for your direction, comfort and salvation.[158]

Again, the author of *The Whole Duty of Man* (1684) recommends confession to a godly man, as does Francis White in his reply to Fisher (1622), and John Cosin (1594–1672). The Irish Canon 19 of 1634 orders every minister to a parish to toll a bell on the afternoon before Holy Communion

> to the intent that if they have any scruple of conscience, or desire the special ministry of reconciliation, he may afford it to those that need it. And to this end the people are often to be exhorted to enter into a special examination of the state of their own souls; and that finding themselves either extreme dull or much troubled in mind, they do resort with God's ministers to receive from them as well advice and counsel for the quickening of their dead hearts and the subduing of these corruptions whereunto they have been subject, as the benefit of Absolution likewise for the quieting of their consciences by the power of the keys which Christ hath committed to his ministers for that purpose.[159]

The Carolines saw ascetical and moral theology as a unity. 'Causistical divinity', as they termed it, was not merely concerned with the identification and assessment of sinful acts, but with the attainment of the vision of God. Although the Carolines rarely used the term 'spiritual direction', the notion of personal guidance was central to their thinking. Martin Thornton rightly points out that 'it would be hard to find a writer of this age to whom personal spiritual guidance was not a normal and necessary part of Christian living'.[160]

However, the Tractarians tended, in the general area of the confessional, to rely excessively on contemporary French writings. Pusey adapted and edited the *Manual for Confessors* originally produced by the Abbé Jean Joseph Gaume in 1854. In his preface, Pusey referred to spiritual direction which, he claimed, was 'entirely distinct from that of "confession" ', and went on to make it clear that, although he had given what advice he could, he had never undertaken the office of director.[161] He warns against 'over-direction' and quotes Faber in his support. Gaume's work in fact is a fairly exhaustive series of instructions for confessors, and, although a great deal of it is now very dated, there is much that is still of value. Other Tractarians were wary of spiritual direction. Canon T. T. Carter defined direction as ' "ghostly counsel and advice" become habitual', and said, 'I myself greatly prefer the term spiritual guide to that of director'.[162] J. M. Neale distinguished confession very clearly from direction.

> The one is as old as the Apostles, the other the invention of the last three centuries: the one is, though not in all cases necessary, in all cases highly expedient; the other, if sometimes expedient, certainly in many instances pernicious: the one to persons in earnest, scarcely capable of abuse; the other, the more scrupulous the conscience, the more likely to become a snare: the denial of the one, a virtual negation of the power of the keys; the denial of the other, a simple objection to priestly influence. No two things can, as Direction is generally understood, differ more than that system, and the intercourse which must necessarily exist between the priest and penitent . . . Nothing can be more important than to set prominently before English Churchmen this fact: that with Direction of this kind, Confession has no necessary connexion whatever. Incalculable mischief has arisen from the confusion of the two.

But Neale went on to say: 'And, as there is danger of Direction being engrafted on Confession, so also I cannot deny that, in some cases among ourselves, this system has prevailed, and its fruits have been apparent.'[163] On the other hand, John Keble was a spiritual guide to many individuals, as was Pusey, in spite of his rejection of the director's role. Indeed, William Cunningham in his important work *The Cure of Souls* (1908) argues that 'the importance attached to this aspect of the ministerial office has been and is a special characteristic of the Anglican communion: every age and every school of thought in the English Church has done much to insist on and to illustrate the sense of pastoral responsibility'.[164]

In the 1930s a distinctive school of spiritual theology grew up in the Church of England, associated with the names of F. G. Belton, F. P. Harton, Evelyn Underhill, H. S. Box, and Bede Frost. All of these writers contributed major works either on direction and confession (as in the case of Belton and Box) or on the life of prayer (as did the others). Harton's *The Elements of the Spiritual Life* (1932) has been much criticized but is still of great value, as is Bede Frost's *The Art of Mental Prayer* (1931). Frost's book consisted chiefly of a description of six schools of mental prayer, and it contained one chapter on spiritual direction which drew largely on French sources. Belton's *Manual for Confessors* (1916) is now very dated, while H. S. Box's *Spiritual Direction* (1938) is simply a compilation drawn from the works of Scaramelli, Augustine Baker, Faber and other Roman writers. Thornton noted of this 'school' that 'this period still supplies the current text books in spiritual theology, which, whatever their intrinsic value, are the products of a dying theological outlook'.[165] He criticized the school for its authoritarian flavour, and its lack of the distinctively English 'empirical relationship' in spiritual guidance. Its concept of Catholic spirituality was too narrow and too dominated by the thought forms of the Counter-Reformation. During this period in fact the writing on direction tended to rely heavily on continental, particularly French, sources. Thornton's view is that the 1930s' school represented the end of the Oxford Movement, rather than the beginning of something new.[166]

However, two great directors did emerge in this period who had a very wide and rich view of spirituality. One was Reginald Somerset Ward (1881–1962). Ward received a strong call at the age of thirty-four to move into the area of personal guidance, and for many years he became one of the best-known 'full-time' directors in the Church of England. Thornton called him 'probably the most influential spiritual director of modern Anglicanism'.[167] He wrote many pastoral letters and instructions, some of which subsequently appeared in *The Way* (1922), *Following the Way* (1925), *To Jeru-*

salem (1931), *The Way in Prayer* (1932) and *Prayer in Lent* (1956). He also wrote *A Guide for Spiritual Directors*. All these books were written anonymously. Ward was essentially practical, and emphasized the importance of practical disciplines as ways of freeing the soul for expansion and service. 'In most lives', he claimed, 'a practical basis for the ordered life of effective power can be found in a few simple rules concerning the right use of time.'[168]

The other great director was Gilbert Shaw, who died in 1968 as warden of the Sisters of the Love of God, a community which both publishes his work and perpetuates his spiritual outlook. Indeed, one of Gilbert Shaw's most permanent achievements was his influence on his community, and his guidance of it from a rigid and narrow to a rich and free style of Carmelite contemplative life. Shaw's commitment to the recovery of the solitary life for the Church of England was another fundamental element in his work, and the hermits at Bede House in Staplehurst are a monument to his vision. Shaw's other lasting contribution to the guidance of souls was his use of the method of affective prayer, as in his two major collections *The Face of Love* (1959) and *A Pilgrim's Book of Prayers* (1945).

But with few exceptions there was little Anglican writing on the areas of direction and confession during the 1950s. There were several small books and pamphlets on confession. No attempt was made to fill the gap left by the collapse of the ascetical framework which was assumed by the pre-war writers. Meanwhile, in the United States, attention was moving to the pastoral counselling movement, and Britain too saw the beginnings of interest in counselling and therapy in the context of the cure of souls. Groups such as the Guild of Pastoral Psychology, of which C. G. Jung was president, and the Institute of Religion and Medicine were seeking to build bridges between the church and psychotherapy, and it was in this general area that interest in 'personal ministry' seemed to be moving. The main interest, however, cannot be said to have been in the personal area at all, so much as in such questions as liturgical renewal, parish strategy, and social witness. The mood was intensified in the 1960s which was an era of questioning and of 'activism'.

It was against the uncritical activism, or 'multitudinism' as he called it, that Martin Thornton let forth his trumpet blast in 1956 in *Pastoral Theology: A Reorientation*. Thornton saw the priest's primary work to be the spiritual direction of a 'remnant'. In his

Christian Proficiency (1959) he discussed in greater detail the ascetical disciplines which would characterize this remnant of serious Christians or 'proficients', and he returned to the issue of direction in his *English Spirituality* (1963). In this study he expressed his 'conviction, which seems to be widely shared, that spiritual direction is our greatest pastoral need today.' But, he said, it must be consonant with the English tradition and 'central to this tradition is an interpretation of the phrase "spiritual direction" in a much wider sense than is sometimes implied'.[169] Spirituality is concerned with the whole of life, and private devotion is inseparable from liturgy and theology. Thornton sees the Anglican style of direction as empirical, not authoritarian, a mutual working-out of ways towards perfection between two people knit together in Christ. He emphasizes eight elements in the Anglican tradition of direction:

a an empirical relationship established by a brief conversation;
b adequate knowledge of the person, set against a fundamental ascetical map and framework;
c explanation of eucharistic worship and the Divine Office, and insistence on them;
d recollective techniques according to the person's needs;
e formal private prayer to support recollection;
f spiritual reading according to a planned method;
g the encouragement of regular confession;
h the rejection of 'spiritual tension' in relationship, in favour of Jeremy Taylor's 'amiable captivity of the Spirit'.[170]

It was such an 'amiable captivity', a freedom to expand within the liberty of the Spirit, which was the dominating theme of Gilbert Shaw's method of guidance. In one of his manuscripts he defined the nature and purpose of direction thus:

> Direction is the art of guiding souls so that they shall respond most readily to their graces. Few souls, if any, are capable of guiding themselves unless it be by supernatural revelation, and then there is always the danger of being misled as to the reality of such revelation. The self-guided soul is always a prey to delusion.[171]

There has been renewed interest in the work of Thornton and Shaw in recent years. These years have also seen the growth of networks of training for spiritual directors and guides, with a particular emphasis on the laity. The SPIDIR network in the Diocese of Southwark is one of the most developed of such groupings. The retreat movement, which grew out of the Catholic revival of the last century, has grown way beyond its earlier patterns, and the approach to retreats has become far more diverse. There is, however, a real need for a serious study of the Anglican tradition of spiritual guidance as it has developed in the twentieth century, not least because some of the most experienced and widely used directors—Shaw, Somerset Ward, Evan Pilkington, among others— left very little on paper.

PROTESTANT APPROACHES TO SPIRITUAL DIRECTION

The notion of personal spiritual direction has not received so much attention in the Protestant traditions, partly because of the suspicion of 'sacerdotalism' or of any acts which seemed to undermine the place of Christ as the one Mediator. However, while the term may not have been used, there has been at various points within the Protestant traditions a stress on the personal guide and counsellor. Luther, for example, was certainly accustomed to exercise a ministry of personal direction both by word of mouth and by letter. Thus in an early letter to George Spenlein, a fellow student, he urged him to reveal 'the condition of thy soul'.[172] But a more significant figure in the Lutheran tradition is Bucer, whose work *On the True Cure of Souls* (1538) is of some considerable importance. Bucer uses Ezekiel 34:16 as the basis of his five-fold rule for the Christian pastor. He is 'to draw to Christ those who are alienated; to lead back those who have been drawn away; to seek amendment of life in those who fall into sin; to strengthen weak and sickly Christians; to preserve Christians who are whole and strong; and to urge them forward in all good'.[173] As a result largely of the teaching of Luther and Bucer and of such leaders as Philipp Jakob Spener (died 1705), there grew up a pattern of mutual cure of souls by laymen in Lutheranism.

Zwingli recommended confession in God alone, but advised that if it seemed necessary, the Christian should consult a wise counsellor. 'Auricular confession', he claimed, 'is nothing but a consultation in which we receive from him whom God has appointed ... advice as to how we can secure peace of mind.' So 'a wise scholar who looks not at the pocket book but at the conscience' can be a useful guide'.[174] Again, Calvin is an interesting example of a personal spiritual guide within the Reformed tradition. Jean-Daniel

Benoit refers to him as a 'director of souls'. Benoit goes on to argue that there is abundant evidence of spiritual direction in Reformed spirituality, but that there are crucial differences from the Catholic style.[175] Thus the Protestant director does not claim so much authority, does not seek permanence in the relationship, is often a 'crisis counsellor', and so on. Nevertheless, there is in Calvin a deep concern with the question of guidance of conscience, and there is a considerable correspondence consisting of letters of guidance. Calvin always stresses his own subservience in all things to God. He reminds the Duke of Somerset that 'we hold God to be the sole governor of our souls, that we hold his law to be the only rule and spiritual directory of our consciences, not serving him according to the foolish inventions of men'.[176]

In the British Protestant churches, spiritual letters form an important feature of the Scottish Presbyterian tradition, and John Knox wrote many such letters of direction. David Dickson of Irvine (died 1662) wrote a treatise on spiritual guidance, *Therapeutica Sacra* (1656), in which he stressed the role of the pastor or 'prudent friend' as one who gently persuades and guides the soul. It was said too of William Guthrie of Fenwick (died 1665) that 'he was an eminent surgeon at the jointing of the broken soul and at the stating of a doubtful conscience'.[177] The English Puritan Thomas Cartwright (1535–1603), in a lengthy and remarkable letter, recommends confession and 'the direction, establishment and comforte of a man's owne Conscience towardes God', and he goes on:

> Trueth it is, that thou mayest freelye chuse anye discreete Christian man, that is well learned in the holye Scripture and resorte to him for learning, counsell and comfort: but yet for all that, there is none so meete for thy purpose in that behalfe as thine owne Curate (if he be no Papist, neither of corrupt judgement in ye scriptures, but be honest discreete & well exercised in God's holy woord). For he is appointed of God to be heardman of thy soul . . . [178]

The developments in seventeenth-century Puritanism also make it clear that 'the Reformation had not abolished the need for spiritual directors'.[179] The guiding and enlightening of the conscience was a major concern of such works as William Perkins, *The Whole Treatise of Cases of Conscience* (1602), Immanuel Bourne, *The Godly Man's Guide* (1620), William Ames, *De Conscientia* (1631), and so on. It was said of the Puritan guide Robert

Bolton that at the level of personal guidance he was a 'sonne of consolation', while in the pulpit he was a 'sonne of thunder'. Bolton's 'singular dexterity in comforting afflicted and wounded spirits' was said to have been due to the 'grievous pangs' of his own new birth. For 'he never taught any godly point but he first wrought it on his own heart'.[180] Here is the stress on the spiritual man as a man of experience which is so central to the spirituality of the East.

The best known of the Puritans writing in this area was Richard Baxter, whose main works were *A Christian Directory* (1673) and *The Reformed Pastor* (1656). The pastor, says Baxter, must not 'slightly slubber over' the ministry of personal counsel, but must 'do it vigorously'. He lists four groups of people under the general heading of the 'building up of the converted' who need special attention: the immature, those with 'particular corruption which keeps under their graces', 'declining Christians', and the strong. It is the last group, he claims, who need the greatest care.[181] A different emphasis, however, comes through clearly in Bunyan's *Pilgrim's Progress* (1678). Here it is the solitary character of the spiritual journey which is stressed. Christian must go it alone, rejecting the pseudo-guides whom he meets along the way. This sturdy independence, a 'do-it-yourself' spirituality, was to remain one of the central features not only of the Puritans but of wide sections of evangelical Christianity.

The Quakers laid great stress on the guidance which came from within, the 'inner light', though George Fox himself was a spiritual guide. Penn referred to him as a 'discerner of men's spirits', a man who, through the Spirit of God, was able to 'bring people off from their own ways to Christ'.[182] But the distinctive feature of Quaker guidance was the element of mutual admonition and mutual direction. Cotton Mather (died 1728) was one of those who carried this doctrine of mutual guidance through into the tradition of New England Puritanism, and he wrote his *Maneductio ad Ministerium* (1726) as a guide for ministerial students. It was in the Wesleyan band and class meetings, however, that mutual guidance was manifested most strongly. These were groups of people who 'needed to pour out their hearts' to one another, to 'help each other to work out their own salvation'. In the more rigorous band meeting, there was a desire that 'we should come as close as possible . . . cut to the quick, and search your heart to the bottom'.[183] Davies and Rupp refer to 'the strenuous mutual confessional of the band meeting for those who were "pressing on to perfection", and for the rest the only somewhat less searching discipline of the class meeting'.[184] However, by 1841, Daniel P. Kidder was one of those who was lamenting the decline of the class meeting within the Methodist movement.[185]

Wesley himself was particularly concerned with the beginnings of the Christian life. He seems rarely to have referred to the 'cure of souls' and when he did, the reference was to preaching. Certainly, the band and class meetings while they lasted formed an intensive type of mutual spiritual direction and training in the Christian life. But the need for regular personal direction was to some extent undermined by the form which the doctrine of holiness took within the Wesleyan tradition. 'Sanctification in the proper sense', claimed Wesley, 'is an instantaneous deliverance from all sin and includes an instantaneous power then always to cleave to God.'[186] Wesley did believe in relative perfection and in growth within the state of perfection.[187] Other Wesleyans too stressed 'beginnings, process and final issues', seeing sanctification as leading to the 'full eradication of sin' which was to be 'abolished in the wholly sanctified'.[188] So there was here a doctrine of spiritual progress. The Holiness churches which developed the doctrine of entire sanctification also held that perfection was consistent with mistakes and temptations, and that it could be lost and regained. But the stress on the direct action of God tended to lead to the view that a human guide was unnecessary.

During the nineteenth century, John Watson, a Scottish pastor, in *The Cure of Souls* (1896) stressed private consultation as an essential part of the pastor's work, though it assumes a secondary role in William Garden Blaikie's *For the Work of the Ministry* (1873) and Patrick Fairbairn's *Pastoral Theology* (1875), both of which emphasized preaching. In his second edition of 1878, however, Blaikie did add an appendix on spiritual counsel. This ministry cannot be said to have played a central role in most modern Protestant traditions, though some recent studies have seen it as important. Max Thurian, Dietrich Bonhoeffer and Neville Ward in their influential books have laid a high emphasis on confession and on personal guidance.[189]

THE MARKS OF THE SPIRITUAL DIRECTOR
Historically it was from the movement of desert monasticism that we received the idea of spiritual direction within the framework of

Christian practice. As Thomas Merton says, 'spiritual direction is a monastic concept'.[190] It was with the growth of the solitary life in particular that the need for intensive personal guidance was felt. So the *pneumatikos pater* emerges in the spirituality of the East, and later he becomes the *staretz* of the Russian tradition. In the West, we meet spiritual direction in the modern sense, associated closely with the confessional, in the period of the mendicant friars, and a further growth during the Counter-Reformation of a movement of spiritual guides concerned particularly with the guidance of contemplatives. In the twentieth century we have seen a considerable amount of rethinking about the place of direction in the life of the church.

From the tradition, the spiritual director appears, first, as *a person possessed by the Spirit*. The director's role, says Merton, was not in any sense hierarchical, but 'was purely and simply charismatic. It was sanctioned by the father's own personal holiness.'[191] The first and essential characteristic of the spiritual guide is holiness of life, closeness to God. It is this quality too which, in the thought of the eastern Christians, makes the theologian. So Callistus in the fourteenth century urges the seeker to choose 'a man bearing the Spirit within him'. So the Russian *startsy* help their disciples not so much by what they say as by their radiation of sanctity and inner peace.

Secondly, the spiritual director is *a person of experience*, a person who has struggled with the realities of prayer and life. There is no substitute for this experience. Guides who have not encountered their own passions, their own inner conflicts, who do not truly know their darkness and their light, will be of no value in the spiritual battle. The great helpers of humankind are not 'the ideal bearers of final truths' but rather 'the most extraordinarily human members of the community'.[192]

Thirdly, the spiritual director is *a person of learning*, though, as Augustine Baker points out, learning without spiritual maturity can be dangerous. St Teresa, however, puts learning as a very high priority in spiritual guides. The guide must be one who is steeped in Scripture and in the wisdom of the Fathers.

Fourthly, the spiritual director is *a person of discernment*. *Diakrisis* is the word which recurs with tremendous frequency throughout the literature from the Desert Fathers onwards. The spiritual father, according to Cassian, is one from whom we receive *diakrisis*. So spiritual directors must be people of perception and insight, people of vision, who can read the signs of the times, the writing on the walls of the soul.

The spiritual director is, finally, *a person who gives way to the Holy Spirit*. For the relationship of direction is to be one in which the channels of grace are opened, and the Holy Spirit is able to move freely in the Christian person, drawing her to a closer union and a greater freedom as a child of God. 'A spiritual director is then one who helps another to recognize and to follow the inspirations of grace in his life, in order to arrive at the end to which God is leading him.'[193] The director is 'to assist in helping the person read the breathings of the Spirit'.[194] Jean Grou in the eighteenth century was very insistent that the disciple must look beyond the director to God and be prepared to give him up if God so required. Spiritual direction is therefore a means to an end. The end is God, whose service is perfect freedom.

3
Direction, counselling and therapy

Alas there is a great silence. Darkness has fallen upon
us. The saints look at us through the mist of the past.
We cannot understand their ways. The devils shrug their
shoulders and have no comment. Only the sociologists
and anthropologists talk endlessly in a new
vocabulary ... The psychologists too flatter our sense
of self-importance, and we turn the Church of God into
a consulting room with trained counsellors.

ULRICH SIMON[1]

Amid the clinical trends in contemporary pastoral guidance, [the priest] will keep alive the permanent issues
of sin and forgiveness. To be healthy and to be whole
is no substitute for being penitent, forgiven and holy.

MICHAEL RAMSEY[2]

THE PASTORAL COUNSELLING MOVEMENT: A NEW TYPE OF DIRECTION?

A former principal of an Anglican theological college observed in
1975 that 'counselling is now given more attention in Anglican
theological colleges than hearing confessions. It may be questioned
whether this is all gain.'[3] His statement is certainly true. The spread
of interest in 'pastoral counselling' and 'pastoral clinical training',
however desirable in itself, has certainly tended to lead to the
neglect of confession and direction. These disciplines are felt by
some to be obsolete, and to have been superseded by the newer
disciplines of counselling and therapy. So today's clergy are increasingly learning 'therapeutic skills'. Some would suggest that this
union of priest and therapist is simply the recovery of something
which is very ancient. Certainly the historical links between
theology and therapy, priest and doctor, are very close. The Book
of Leviticus contained injunctions which were both priestly and
medical within its framework of law: salvation and healing were

one. The apostles too were sent to preach the Kingdom of God and to heal. Pastoral care and the healing of the sick have been closely associated throughout Christian history. Indeed, on a much wider front, Talcott Parsons pointed out that the doctor has 'very important associations with the realm of the sacred',[4] while Frazer many years ago claimed that magicians and medicine men constituted the oldest professional classes in the evolution of human society.[5]

The revival of the healing dimension in pastoral care was symbolized by the introduction of the word 'clinical' at the end of the 1940s into close association with the word 'pastoral'. The process, however, had begun a good deal earlier. In 1925 Richard C. Cabot had written an article in *Survey Graphic* in the United States in which he called for a 'clinical year' for all theological students, and he supported the experimental chaplaincy work at Massachusetts General Hospital in the early 1930s.[6] In 1930 the Council for Clinical Training was set up with Cabot as president, and in the early 1940s the Institute for Pastoral Care appeared. Other important contributions in the 1930s were Anton T. Boisen's use of theological students at Worcester State Hospital, and the studies by Charles T. Holman[7] and Karl R. Stolz.[8]

So pastoral theology began to emphasize such themes as the cure of souls and 'pastoral counselling'. Two works which marked a turning point in orientation were Seward Hiltner's *Clinical Pastoral Training* (1945) and *Pastoral Counselling* (1949). With studies such as these, pastoral theology was moving away from the concern with ecclesiological details—how to baptize, how to absolve, and so on—towards the concern with what Hiltner called 'the shepherding perspective'.[9] Hiltner certainly brought the wisdom of dynamic psychology and psychotherapy to the service of the Christian minister.

The growth of the pastoral counselling movement was a significant feature of American church life in the 1950s and 60s. By 1960 it was estimated that over 70,000 professional counsellors (including psychiatrists, psychotherapists, psychologists, counsellors, and social workers) were at work in the United States.[10] Clinical pastoral training programmes were set up in American hospitals, and a wide range of other types and levels of counselling was established throughout the United States.[11] Many clergy trained and practised as counsellors. In Britain too in the mid-1930s, Dr Leslie Weatherhead had set up a centre for pastoral

counselling at the City Temple in London, and there were some
other experiments elsewhere, though it was not for some years that
the American ideas spread to Britain.

The growth of the pastoral counselling movement was in marked
contrast to another significant growth in pastoral practice, that of
the managerial and consultancy models of ministry. There has been
a revival recently of this approach, which stresses the minister's
leadership and organizational role as opposed to her personal ministry.[12] The liberal churches, for the most part, were slow to trans-
late their intellectual acceptance of mental health ideas into actual
practice in terms of personal care. Carl Wennerstrom has attributed
this failure to an excessive rationalism leading to a denial or
playing-down of the unconscious, a somewhat naive optimism and
belief in social reform, a concern with leadership and impact at
the expense of more obscure, hidden forms of ministering, and,
particularly, a model of care which stresses the efficient use of
resources, and avoids intimate personal contact. For such a model
of ministry, the safe distance becomes essential:

> Metaphorically speaking, the first liberal (so far as the distance
> goes at any rate) might well have been the man who helped Jesus
> carry the Cross to the place where he was crucified. With a job
> to be done, he was there. With energy to be spent he had it. And
> in carrying a heavy cross, he was not drawn too close together
> with Jesus. Once the spot had been reached and the outcome
> was certain he dropped from sight; we hear no more of this early
> liberal in the New Testament. Perhaps he was off to the Circuit
> Council, hoping against hope to get a reversal of the conviction
> and having the courage to try. Or he may have been investigating
> the future support of Jesus' family or the burial arrangements,
> or he may even have been getting up a petition to Rome about
> Pilate. What he was about was no doubt of great potential
> significance. But at the place of crucifixion he was absent once
> the cross had been delivered. For a liberal the optimal social
> distance.[13]

On this liberal view, the pastor is primarily concerned with the
overall organization of pastoral resources and strategy, and her
intimate ministry to individuals tends to receive little emphasis.
Indeed, the liberal tradition has remained weak on personal guidance, while among conservative evangelicals the ministry of counselling has always contained a more explicitly evangelistic element,

and has been associated particularly with the post-conversion period. Yet as the pastoral counselling movement developed, and gathered momentum, it drew in members of both liberal and evangelical churches. The Christian minister was seen as a personal guide and friend as well as an organizer or a preacher of the Word. Counselling became an acceptable part of the life of the church.

What then is counselling? The word, though it is now used in areas totally alien to the Christian church, owes its origin to the Judaeo-Christian tradition. As one educational psychologist has written, 'It is an old and biblical word which came to be mainly restricted to the legal profession. It travelled to the New World, presumably on the *Mayflower*, and we owe its recent revival to the Americans.'[14] The word is derived from the same source as consul, conciliate, consult, and suggests an interchange, a two-way process. Often it is used to describe a fairly brief session or series of meetings in which a counsellor seeks to help a client to resolve personal difficulties or to reach some decision. Deeper forms of counselling may focus more on motivation and experiences, and may move close to psychotherapy. But as a general rule, counselling is more restricted to specific crises than is the more long-term work of psychotherapy. So while the concept of pastoral counselling is very close to those of psychotherapy, pastoral care and social casework, there are important areas of demarcation. The psychotherapist, certainly if she stands in the Freudian or Jungian schools of depth psychology, may be involved for years with a patient. She is not concerned with immediate crises and she will not often be involved with the patient's life situation and family background. Her concern is with the inner world. The work of pastoral care is sometimes distinguished from that of counselling by the fact that it involves drawing more on one's spiritual resources.[15] Some writers see spiritual direction as 'simply pastoral counselling with greater spiritual depth than is usually brought to the immediate situation'.[16]

Again, the use of the term *casework*, while it is often used more or less synonymously with counselling, does indicate an important difference in orientation. The counsellor is concerned with the achievement of healthy relationships. The social caseworker may share that concern, but he is also involved with practical decisions and their implementation. Again, the social worker is inevitably seen as an authority figure, although there are strong pressures towards greater involvement with social planning and political action on the one hand, and with moral values on the other. Hiltner suggests that, in terms of basic attitudes, approach, method and so on, pastoral counselling does not differ from other types of counselling. It only differs in terms of the setting, and in its use of religious resources. Pastoral counselling, on Hiltner's definition, is 'the attempt by a pastor to help people help themselves through the process of gaining understanding of their inner conflicts'.[17]

Central to the counselling movement has been the I-Thou relationship, the person-to-person encounter, and the concern with personal change. It is this emphasis which has led to frequent comparisons with the Christian ministry. So Paul Halmos has grouped together the professions of clergy, doctors, nurses, teachers, and social workers as professions 'whose principal function is to bring about changes in the physical and psychological personality of the client'. He calls them 'personal service professions'.[18] Halmos identified three main values of the 'counselling ideology': a non-judgemental and non-condemnatory attitude, humble and accepting; a mutually honest and intimate I-Thou relationship; and an opposition to all forms of self-deception, dishonesty, false righteousness and anger. These values did not, of course, originate with the upsurge of counselling during this century, for they were an essential part of the 'moral treatment' ideology which arose at the end of the eighteenth century. This was an ideology which stressed the value and importance of 'close and friendly association with the patient, intimate discussion of his difficulties, and the daily pursuit of purposeful activity . . . It was a way of life offered to the sick, under the direction of physicians whose philosophy of mental illness was based on a high valuation of the individual and belief in his recuperative powers'.[19] 'Moral treatment' was eclipsed in the nineteenth and early twentieth centuries by the development of pharmacology and of the chemical attack on sickness. But it returned in a new form with the growth of psychoanalysis and later of social work. During the inter-war years the emphasis in social work thinking, especially in the United States, was on the shortcomings of the individual, and it is only recently that the movement away from individualism and casework has got under way.

In Halmos's view the counselling movement is very close indeed to Christian spirituality, and he even suggests that the counsellor has stepped into the breach created by the decline of religion. Counsellors, he claims, 'act in lieu of the spiritual consultants and guides of former times'.[20] In particular, the belief in the therapy of love is emphasized. From the early deviant psychoanalyst Ferenczi, who held that 'the indispensable healing process in the therapeutic gift is love',[21] to Erich Fromm's writings, there has been a stress on the centrality of love in therapy which has been carried over into the counselling tradition. Again, many of those working in the areas of counselling and therapy place a high value on spiritual development. Thus Michael Balint, who ran courses in psychotherapy for general practitioners, adapted theological terms to describe his belief in spiritual commitments.[22]

It was in the work of Carl Rogers that the stress on the 'non-directive approach' became an integral part of the counselling relationship, as did the concept of growth. 'The aim is not to solve one particular problem, but to assist the individual to grow'. Rogers stressed the individual, his drive towards wholeness and adjustment, his feelings, and 'the therapeutic relationship itself as a growth experience'. Therapy does bring about change: 'This type of therapy is not a preparation for change, it *is* change.'[23] Throughout Rogers's work one sees the use of concepts such as love, self-respect and maturity, and there is an optimistic view of human potential in which healing and growth are brought together as central themes. Many writers on pastoral counselling also utilized these concepts, and so it is common to find Christians working in this field emphasizing the virtues of non-direction, personal wholeness, integration, authenticity, and so on. The non-directive approach later spread from the sphere of personal counselling into such areas as community development.

Until recently the counselling movement was dominated by the assumptions of psychoanalysis, with its central concern with neurotic forms of behaviour. 'Most counsellors', claimed Halmos, 'no matter how different their clinical and social background, develop their ideas under the influence of published psychoanalytic reflection.'[24] Certainly the strong emphasis on sickness, disease and therapy within the counselling movement testifies to its Freudian clinical origin. Even the most recent arrival on the 'official' counselling scene, the school counsellor, is seen as working in close relationship to the educational psychologist and the child psychiatric clinic.[25] However, in recent years the view that 'depth psychotherapy is not an adequate model for pastoral counselling'[26] has become widely accepted, and it remains to be seen how far the association of counselling with sickness will remain central. Certainly the sickness model is a bad model for spiritual guidance

since, although Christians would wish to use the concepts of healing and wholeness, the emphasis is not so much on the prevention
and treatment of sickness as on the achievement of salvation.
Spiritual guidance therefore is not crisis intervention but a continuous process, the movement to God and in God. Pond and others
have argued that counselling cannot avoid the question of our
understanding of our relationship to the universe,[27] and in the
United States the 'existential' element in counselling has become
particularly important.

In 1958 in Britain a movement called Clinical Theology was
founded by Frank Lake, a psychiatrist with an evangelical Christian
background. A series of groups and seminars began to spread
throughout the Church of England which aimed to help clergy
become more competent in pastoral care of troubled people. Clinical Theology soon became concerned with the pastoral needs of
the clergy themselves. Indeed it has been claimed that 'the major
achievement of the movement has been the insight it has imparted
to its students about their own personality problems and their
religious interpretation—an insight which is vital before much can
be done in helping others with theirs'.[28] Small seminars were set
up which met for three hours on twelve occasions each year, and
particular attention was given to the understanding of depressive,
hysterical, schizoid and paranoid personalities. The priest or minister would, it was hoped, also be helped to understand his own
behaviour patterns, and be freed from emotional immaturity within
himself. So the Clinical Theology Centre, established at Not-
tingham in 1962, has built up an extensive therapeutic ministry
among the clergy themselves.

Lake draws heavily in his system on the writings of St John
and St Paul, St John of the Cross, Simone Weil, Martin Buber and
Kierkegaard and, within psychiatry, on Freud, Klein, Fairbairn
and Fromm among others. He believes that the counselling movement needs the 'clues to the paradoxical that derive from
theology'.[29] In his enormous study *Clinical Theology* (1966) he
attempts a synthesis between theology and psychiatry, on the
assumption that 'since the origin of the model is Christ, and
the Christian is by definition to be a man in whom Christ dwells,
no awkward transition has to be made in the language of communication when we move from the "psychology" to the "spirituality"
of the man of God'.[30] So the language of dynamic psychology and
that of the Bible and the Christian mystics are intermingled. Clini-

cal depression is related to various experiences described in the Old Testament. But the most important part of the book, according to its author, is the section on the schizoid condition, and indeed it could be argued that this represents the heart of the whole system.

In this section, Lake makes a good deal of use of the notion of dread, as illustrated by the prophet Job, Kierkegaard and Simone Weil. He sees the schizoid condition as playing a central role in the life of the church and of its clergy. With Rollo May, on whose work he also draws, he sees 'our schizoid world' to be a world of people out of touch, avoiding close relationships, unable to feel. He sees this condition as prevalent among many younger clergy, and he relates it to the teaching of St John of the Cross about the Dark Night. 'A dark night must be experienced by those who are to move from a schizoid spirituality towards a warm and sensitive union with God.' He also writes: 'The groaning word of Christ crucified speaks into the depths of alienated schizoid sufferers, and to a depersonalized schizoid society. But a schizoid Church carries all the worst features of the disease its Lord set out to cure.'[31]

Clinical Theology then is concerned with the depths of the spiritual life. But it is not spiritual direction. Its concern is with depressive and schizoid states, with psychological and spiritual affliction, and with interpreting these conditions in theological terms. In order to do this, Lake has drawn on a selective range of spiritual writers within the Christian tradition, especially the existentialists, and he has attempted to create bridges between their work and the disciplines of psychiatry. This is open to serious criticism, but in principle such an operation is an essential element in pastoral care. Nevertheless, it is not possible to equate an approach which is so determined by the healing of affliction with spiritual direction, for the concerns of the latter are much wider.

Since the formation of the Clinical Theology Association, there have been many other growths and developments within the Christian section of the counselling world. In the early 1970s the Association for Pastoral Care and Counselling was established. In its constitution, the following definition was given, based on the work of Clebsch and Jaekle:

> The ministry of the cure of souls, or pastoral care and responsibility, consists of helping acts done by representative religious persons, directed towards the healing, sustaining, guiding and

reconciling of troubled persons whose troubles arise in the context of ultimate meanings and concerns.[32]

In recent writing and discussion, the themes which occur are those of development, enabling, and so on. The counsellor, it is said, attempts to create a facilitating environment for growth and development, to assist individuals to become more effective and more human. Terms such as 'full humanness' and 'self-actualization' may be used.

Again, since the formative work of Rogers and others, there has been a great deal of stress on 'unqualified acceptance' and 'full mutuality' in the therapeutic relationship. Rogers points to the need for acceptance of the individual and his potential, and argues that such acceptance is the strongest factor working for change. In recent years, however, a different emphasis has come to the fore: that on confrontation, conflict and the acceptance of personal responsibility. Martin Buber was one writer who had argued for the place of confirmation and struggle. Against the views of Rogers, Buber rejected the equality between therapist and client. There is certainly an I-Thou relationship, he argued, a relationship of trust and mutual partnership, but not of full mutuality. The therapist is engaged in a struggle with the other person against herself.[33] This emphasis on conflict emerges most clearly in the various movements generally classified as 'radical therapy' and 'radical social work' in which the underlying assumptions of conventional psychiatry and counselling are questioned. Casework is seen as a tool to preserve accepted social structures and values. The stress should rather be on responsibility for one's own actions, and on commitment to radical change.[34] This rejection of non-directive tolerance is an integral part of many self-help movements, drug and alcohol recovery programmes such as Synanon, Delancey Street and Phoenix, and a large number of communities in which struggle and aggression are greatly valued.

In recent years also the emphasis has been more on the group as the *locus* of counselling and of therapy. The expression of aggression and fantasy within a group has been central to the work of Fritz Perls and his school of Gestalt Therapy. Berkowitz has labelled Gestalt and similar movements as 'ventilationist' because of their thesis that rage is unhealthy if bottled up, and therefore needs to be released. Most ventilationists—and indeed most therapists and therapeutic schools of any kind!—are to be found in

California. They are, says Berkowitz, 'part of California's contribution to the American Dream, along with Hollywood and Disneyland'.[35] But what is common to Gestalt and to the schools of Reality Therapy and Integrity Therapy associated with the work of Glasser and Drakeford is the insistence on personal responsibility and the rejection of all forms of psychological determinism. The individual is answerable to herself for her own actions. In between the individual and the group, we have also seen the growth of co-counselling, in which two people counsel each other. There is now an extensive industry of counselling courses and programmes, and large numbers of clergy have looked to these disciplines as ways of finding help and support in their ministries.

Can we then see in the pastoral counselling movement a contemporary form of spiritual direction? Is pastoral counselling the form, or one form, which direction and maybe confession should take in the twentieth-century church? Some Christian writers interpret counselling in so broad a sense that it becomes virtually a synonym for the cure of souls. Thus David Jenkins writes: 'The aim of the Christian counsellor is to be used to help people to be themselves ... It is the practice of openness based on justification by faith.'[36] The counsellor knows that his own ability to be himself depends on God's acceptance of him, and God's forgiveness which frees him from fear. He is then released to be an instrument of God's acceptance, forgiveness and love to others. The Christian counsellor does not seek to dominate or dictate, but to be an enabler, enabling the individual to become open to the activity of the Spirit, and to become more truly human. Clearly there is a very close link between such a view of counselling and the traditional Christian ministry of the cure of souls.

Certainly the values expressed in the often tedious jargon of the movement are very close to those which appear in the literature of spiritual direction. The pastoral counsellor works with such ideas as empathy, non-possessive warmth, respect for the integrity of the other, confrontation, support. The Desert Fathers emphasized silence and example, rejected domineering and leadership. The silent witness to authentic living of the hesychast tradition has close parallels with the discipline of analysis. Theodulf wrote of the need for support and salutary counsel. J. N. Grou emphasized mutual respect, courtesy, and the need to avoid over-dependence. Clearly there are similar themes and ideas. Counsellors tend to utilize concepts such as nurturing, consoling, acceptance, non-

judgemental support, all of them with roots in the Christian tradition. However, there are some crucial differences between the
pastoral counselling movement and the tradition of spiritual direction, and it is important to recognize these.

First, the pastoral counsellor's concern has tended to be with
states of emotional distress. Clinical pastoral experience has been
with people under stress, although its exponents have certainly
stressed the importance of a well-integrated spiritual and emotional
life, and not merely the relief of temporary emotional strain. Yet
throughout the literature on counselling, there is the continuous
emphasis on problems and problem-solving, and the counsellor is
seen as performing a crucial role during this critical period. Of
course, there are parallels with the spiritual director, who is also
involved with the experiences of distress and with periods of crisis.
But pastoral care in the Christian understanding is not restricted
to the troubled or distressed or to crisis points in life.

> Pastoral care is more than therapeutic. The pastor is concerned
> certainly with the more obvious needs of people for various
> kinds of help, but it is also concerned with their well-being.
> The pastoral relationship derives its significance for the special
> ministries to those in distress from the fact that it is a continuing
> ministry to life's normality. Unlike the physician, psychiatrist and
> social worker who have no relationship at all except there be
> some kind of distress for which their services are needed, the
> pastor's relationship is just as important when there are no
> problems crying out for immediate attention.[37]

The ministry of spiritual direction indeed is more important when
there are no particular crises. It is a continuous ministry and
involves the healthy as well as the sick. R. S. Lee, in a valuable
discussion on the difference between counselling and confession,
comments:

> They are not the same thing, and they are not optional alterna-
> tives or ways of dealing with the same trouble. In confession, it
> is the spiritually and psychologically mature penitent who is
> most able to gain from it. The disintegrated and mal-developed
> are more likely to become fixed in their weakness. Yet it is these
> who, judged by their actions, are the greater sinners. They stand
> in greater need of counselling. It would be going too far to say

that saints need confession, and sinners counselling, but there is enough truth in it to give point to the saying.[38]

This in fact applies more widely to the whole field of spiritual direction. The priest is primarily concerned with spirituality as the fundamental requirement of health. The therapist or counsellor is primarily concerned with sickness. They move within the same realm of reality, and so it is not surprising that there is considerable overlap. But the priest is a spiritual director, not a therapist, and spiritual direction is not the same as therapy.

Secondly, the counselling movement has been clinic-based or office-based rather than church-based or community-based. It has therefore lacked the continuous involvement with people in their homes and families which is so essential to pastoral care. In the United States, where pastoral counselling has been more developed, the area in which the development is weakest is that of counselling in a parish or congregational framework. Such counselling tends to be 'situational' or very short-term. The movement has been strongest in chaplaincies and in specialized therapy centres. But this is the danger point in terms of contact with the common people and with ordinary life. A recent writer has warned that 'specialized pastoral counselling and psychotherapy in the United States, in spite of honest efforts to the contrary, is gradually losing contact with the moral and spiritual context of the larger church.'[39] Spiritual direction, on the other hand, is firmly located within the liturgical and sacramental framework, within the common life of the Body of Christ. It was this fact which the late R. A. Lambourne insisted upon in his writings. Pastoralia, and therefore pastoral counselling, in Lambourne's view, are set in the church.

> To state the argument very strongly, pastoral care, of which pastoral counselling is a part, is separated from its very life unless it is substantially concerned with the continual renewal of the holiness-in-service of the church as *koinonia* rather than being preoccupied with the ego-formation, identity-righteous-ness, or salvation of its individual members.[40]

Nevertheless, Lambourne's view has not prevailed, and counselling has been separated from the common life of the local church.

Thirdly, the movement has tended to focus excessively on the problems of individuals, a fault which it has shared with social work and with the church at various stages of its history. In 1959

Barbara Wootton warned of the 'reluctance to examine the imper-
fections of our institutions as thoroughly as we examine the faults
or misfortunes of individuals'.[41] In the United States, the preoccupation with pastoral counselling was criticized by Richard Niebuhr
on the grounds that it had led to a neglect of social ethics,[42] and
by Thomas Merton on the grounds that it tended to become
'the instrument for forming and preserving the mentality of the
organization man'.[43] Social adjustment is frequently seen as an
objective, while issues of social criticism are ignored. Kathleen
Heasman even goes so far as to define counselling as 'a relationship
in which one person endeavours to help another to understand
and to solve his difficulties of adjustment to society'.[44]

But adjustment to society is a highly dubious goal for the Christian. One American liberal writer, Daniel Day Williams, strongly
criticized the tendency in the counselling movement to see freedom
from anguish and the attainment of inner peace as an end. To exist
in such a state within a society so marred by injustice and lack of
true peace as ours was, he argued, an untenable position.

> The Christian ideal of life envisions something higher than free-
> dom from anguish or invulnerability to its ravages. Its goal
> cannot be the perfectly adjusted self. In the world as it is, a
> caring love cannot but regard such a goal as intolerably self-
> centred. What does it mean to be completely adjusted and at
> peace in a world so riddled with injustice and the cries of the
> hungry, with the great unsolved questions of human living as
> this? We see why in the end we cannot identify therapy for
> specific ills with salvation for the human spirit. To live in love
> means to accept the risks of life and its threats to 'peace of
> mind'. Certainly the Christian ministry to persons is concerned
> to relieve physical ills, anxieties, inner conflicts. But the relief of
> private burdens is to set the person free to assume more import-
> ant and universal ones.[45]

In Britain, it was again the late R. A. Lambourne who was most
critical of the excessive individualism and the 'problem-solving'
approach within the counselling movement. Lambourne argued in
the early 1970s that

> the pastoral counselling called for in this country during the next
> twenty years cannot be built around a practice and conceptual
> framework derived from professional problem solving and pre-

vention of breakdown. That practice and conceptual framework is based upon the clinical, medical and psychoanalytical models of the U.S.A. of twenty years ago, and it has proved inadequate . . . I believe that the pastoral counselling movement, most highly developed in the U.S.A., must be seen as part of a too general assumption by society, epitomised by the medical profession, that we come to the good life by delineating problems, and then either avoiding them (prevention) or solving them. Pastoral theology has been over-influenced by the puzzle solving view of human progress—a 'hang up' theology which fits only too closely with the medical clinical professional identity.[46]

It was Lambourne's view that much of the movement reflected 'the unrecognized theological prejudices and social patterns of the 50s'.[47] He was at pains to point out that 'pastoral counselling is a political-personal process and that power and justice as well as mercy and weakness are at its very roots. The new awareness in the pastoral counselling movement of the calls of social justice requires this kind of shift in its theology'.[48]

Lambourne's critique of counselling is merely one aspect of a much wider attack in recent years on the ideology of social work, and it is an attack which has a particular relevance for Christian theology. For basically what is in question is the status of social work as a form of social control, defining 'problems' in relation to an accepted social order, encouraging and promoting conformity, and perpetuating injustice by its lack of awareness of social and political dimensions. The same criticism has been made of the church. If the individual is viewed in isolation from the social structure, or if 'society' is seen simply as a neutral backcloth for individual problems, then the accusation of reinforcing social injustice is a correct one. Counselling then becomes a substitute for social change, a way of encouraging adjustment and so reducing discontent.

So in the last few years the casework emphasis and the orientation towards the individual alone have been under very heavy fire from the radical wing of social work. The influence of psychology on social work, they argue, has led to 'an over-emphasis on pathological and clinical orientations to the detriment of structural and political implications'.[49] The best-known and most forceful statement of the anti-casework perspective is in the Case Con Manifesto.

One important tool of professional social work has been casework—a pseudo science—that blames individual inadequacies
for poverty and so mystifies and diverts attention from the real
causes—slums, homelessness and economic exploitation. The
casework ideology forces clients to be seen as needing to be
changed to fit society.[50]

Casework and counselling are always in danger of degenerating
into tools of reaction. They are not an adequate model for Christian
spiritual direction, which is concerned with wider issues than personal adjustment and social adaptation. To establish a 'casework
theology' is an extremely dangerous exercise which threatens to
imprison theology within the confines of a passing outlook, as well
as to privatize its concerns. At the same time, it would be foolish
to deny that the Christian tradition of spiritual guidance has learnt
much from the movements of counselling and clinical pastoral care.

SPIRITUAL DIRECTION AND THE UNCONSCIOUS

If the discipline of spiritual direction is close to that of the pastoral
counsellor, it has links too with those of the psychotherapist, psychiatrist and analyst. Again, there are areas of overlap and areas
of shared knowledge, as well as important lines of demarcation. It
would be as mistaken to see the spiritual guide as a therapist as
it would be to place the 'spiritual' and the 'psychological' in entirely
separate compartments. Spiritual direction necessarily involves the
psyche: it enters the areas of psychological disturbance and psychological health; it concerns itself with issues of distress, inner conflict
and upheaval, and mental pain. The priest, by virtue of her cure
of souls, is plunged into the area of the psyche. So for some years
many priests have been trying to learn from and utilize the insights
and approaches of psychotherapy.

   In recent years also there has been a great deal of attention given
within therapeutic schools to the issues of spirituality and spiritual
values. Both C. G. Jung and R. D. Laing, while their approaches
and their language are widely divergent, lay great stress on the
importance of the recovery of spiritual life. In the 1930s Jung
claimed that 'about a third of my cases are suffering from no
clinically definable neurosis, but from the senselessness and emptiness of their lives. It seems to me that this can well be described
as the general neurosis of our time.'[51] To Laing, as we saw earlier,
the loss of transcendence in our culture is indicative of its death.

What we term 'sanity' is in fact spiritual deprivation. True sanity involves the dissolution and the transcendence of the normal ego. Viktor Frankl, the Viennese analyst, insists that psychotherapy needs to move beyond the dynamics of the neuroses to look at the distress of the human spirit. 'The spiritual dimension cannot be ignored, for it is what makes us human.'[52] Frankl argues that the aim of psychotherapy is to *heal* the soul, while that of religion is to *save* the soul. Psychological health is therefore a necessary side-effect of religion, for salvation presupposes the health of the soul. So today among analysts there is more concern with the areas of values and meaning.

The relationship of the analyst to her patient, however, is of an essentially different character to that of the priest to her parish or community. Analysts, whether Freudian or Jungian in their tradition, receive their patients by referral from doctors, social workers or other analysts, or by self-referral. They are less likely than counsellors to encounter people initially at a point of crisis, and those who go to an analyst expect to continue in that relationship for a long time, maybe years. The analyst will be less concerned than the counsellor with the patient's life situation, his family background, the social problems which face him. Her role rather is to explore the inner world of the unconscious forces, feelings, expectations and fantasies. She seeks, through this exploration, to give life to these unconscious forces. So the analyst listens to what is not being said. Her concern and her method therefore, in a number of crucial respects, differ from those of the priest.

However, the priest cannot ignore the unconscious, and spiritual direction cannot be totally separate from the search for psychological health. Three examples may show the inter-relationship between spiritual and psychological progress. First, the discovery of the self is necessary for emotional maturity. There can be no maturing without self-awareness. But the Christian mystics tell us that such self-awareness is the necessary prelude to the knowledge of God. Secondly, we know how important the body is for psychological health. We speak of the need to 'keep body and soul together'. But the spiritual tradition lays great stress on asceticism, a discipline in which bodily techniques are used to achieve a spiritual goal. Thirdly, there is the need, which many have experienced, to travel the way of the unconscious in order to recover the awareness of God. The work of Laing and his colleagues at the Philadelphia Association has helped us to see what we term 'madness' as a journey. Mary Barnes claimed that it was through madness that she found both herself and God.[53] The Christian gospel is concerned with the human person, with his loves and his fears. So there can be no easy division of that person into 'spiritual' and 'psychological' any more than we can divide him into 'body' and 'soul'. It is the whole person who breathes, experiences, fears, and worships God.

In this century, the analyst C. G. Jung revealed the close relationship between psychology and spirituality, and we can derive a great deal from Jung's work about the characteristics of the spiritual director. Jung was concerned throughout his life with the achievement of wholeness, and with the place of myth and symbol in this quest. It is through symbolism that the conscious mind is able to communicate with the unconscious and to receive communications from it, and it is the unconscious which is the 'mother of consciousness'. Spiritual and psychological health depend on a healthy relationship with the unconscious forces. The ego (conscious mind) may be overwhelmed by the upsurge of too much unconscious material, and may thus be driven into madness. Surrender to the unconscious is therefore not what is needed, but rather the creation of an attitude of friendship between conscious and unconscious, and through this of a self increasingly at harmony. The person who guides others, says the spiritual tradition, must be a soul at peace. On the other hand, lack of contact with the unconscious can be equally, if not more, disastrous. Fear of the inner world, fear of the 'shadow' or dark side of personality, can lead to a very damaged, broken personality, and an unconscious which is out of control. Jung calls the psychological process by which harmony is achieved *individuation*, and his description of the journey towards this condition of wholeness draws heavily on the spiritual tradition of East and West, including that of spiritual direction. 'The patient needs the doctor, the *directeur de conscience*, while the eruption of the unconscious is going on, or he may fall a prey to panic inspired by the overwhelming strangeness of his vision.'[54] Similarly, ritual and dogma are protections against insanity. 'The dogmatic symbol protects a person from a direct experience of God'.[55] Ritual and dogma are like torches in the darkness. They can be abused, as in religiosity, and prevent the journey being undertaken at all, for they become ends in themselves. But the purpose of symbolism (*sumballo*, to totalize, unify) is the unifying of the psyche, conscious and unconscious, rational and irrational.

Jung had thus moved away from Freud's view of religion as an obsessional neurosis, and he had come to see the 'religious problem' as crucial to the search for health. It was vital, he held, for clergy and psychotherapists to join forces, and he was urging this as long ago as 1933.[56] But psychology, the 'science of the soul', must confine itself to its material, and must not trespass into theological areas.[57] Jung was very clear on the limitations on the psychiatrist's role. Nevertheless, his work has thrown considerable light on the process of spiritual growth and on the work of spiritual guidance.

One of the areas in which Jung's work is valuable in spiritual direction is in his classification of psychological types. C. R. Bryant[58] has shown how guidance in prayer can be made more effective and more real by an understanding of the personalities of individuals as illuminated by Jung's work. Jung's division of people into the two attitude types of introvert and extrovert is now well known. The extrovert is one who turns most readily to the external world, the introvert to the inner world. The extrovert sees people and things outside himself as being of supreme importance, while the introvert is more defensive towards them. Each type has strong and weak points. But Jung also subdivided introverts and extroverts into four ways by which they deal with life: through sensation, intuition, thinking and feeling. Bryant shows how an understanding of these variants in personality can be used in helping people to discover the most useful forms of prayer. Thus the extrovert who uses sensation as his strongest function will value outward details, and in prayer will value books and material aids. Corporate worship and the support of a community will be important to him. The introvert who values sensation will also lay great stress on externals, but for him they will be valued more as symbolic pointers to the inner world. Imagination will be a key element in his prayer. Again, the person who is dominated by the function of thought will need to evaluate doctrines and clarify theological positions. Theological reflection will be a positive prelude to prayer. On the other hand, the person who values feelings highly will be drawn more quickly into affective forms of prayer, and will find little help in more 'cerebral' forms. Intuitive persons will be aware of their co-operation with God in service of humankind (if they are extrovert) or of mystical union with God (if they are introvert). These outlines are, of course, grossly over-simplified, but they underline the importance of some understanding of psychology in the approach to spiritual progress.

For Jung also liturgical worship and prayer were key elements in the process of transformation which reaches to the depths of the human spirit. We express through ritual and symbol our fundamental spiritual needs. Spiritual direction therefore is concerned, at its central point, with guiding individuals to discover the 'symbolic life'. But it was the symbolic life, claimed Jung, which was missing in the West. 'We have no symbolic life, and we are all badly in need of the symbolic life. Only the symbolic life can express the need of the soul—the daily need of the soul.'[59] In his important essay on the transformation symbol in the Mass, Jung sees in the Christian liturgy a symbolic rite of integration in which humanity and God are united. He lays great emphasis on the place of liturgy and symbol in the transformation of consciousness and the achievement of integration of the personality.

It is in the *integration* of the inner and outer worlds that true spirituality is clearly distinguished from false. It has been claimed that this is the real distinction between mysticism and psychosis. While the experiences of both are similar, 'the mystic provides the example of the method whereby the inner and the outer world may be joined, the schizophrenic the tragic results when they are separated'.[60] The aim of spiritual direction is the achievement of wholeness of life, an integrated personality, in which the inner and the outer humanity are united. Yet to become whole and integrated is painful, it is a process which involves conflict and crisis, and all spiritual direction is involved in the crises of the soul. The death and resurrection experience is repeated in the life of the soul, and the context of this experience is the area where psychology and theology overlap. For both theologian and therapist are involved with human wholeness, with the inner world, and with the cure of souls. Some therapists identify a distinctive spiritual dimension in their work. Thus Laing:

> Orientation means to know where the orient is. For inner space, to know the east, the origin or source of our experience ... There is everything to suggest that man experienced God ... It seems likely that far more people in our time neither experience the presence of God, nor the presence of his absence, but the absence of his presence.

Laing then goes on to make direct connections between therapeutic and spiritual work.

I believe that if we can begin to understand sanity and madness in existential social terms, we, as priests and physicians, will be enabled to see more clearly the extent to which we confront common problems ... Among physicians and priests there should be some who are guides, who can educate the person from this world and induct him to the other.[61]

From a different angle Viktor Frankl, the founder of the 'logotherapy' school, speaks of 'existential neurosis' and 'existential frustration', resulting from confusion and despair about the meaning of life and of the universe. Psychotherapy, he argues, cannot be indifferent to the issue of meaning. On the contrary, 'there is no such thing as psychotherapy unconcerned with values ... the goal of psychotherapy is to heal the soul, to make it healthy.' While the aim of religion is different—to save the soul—Frankl insists that the side-effect of religion is psychohygienic, for it provides a spiritual anchor. The spiritual dimension, says Frankl, cannot be ignored, and he is critical of those who 'take refuge in psychology by pretending that the spiritual distress of a human being who is looking for a meaning to his existence is nothing but a pathological symptom'.[62]

Another therapist who lays great emphasis on spirituality is the Persian analyst Reza Arasteh, who brings together analytic and mystical approaches in his view of 'final integration'. Integration, Arasteh rightly stresses, is not the curing of neurosis by adaptation to society, but the maturing of the psyche on a transcultural level.[63] Like Frankl, he sees existential anxiety as a summons to growth and to progress.

However, it is obvious that religion, while it can be an agent of wholeness and integration, can also preserve immaturity and inhibit the process of growth. Religion can be unhealthy and pathological. Freud held that all religion was pathological, but to reject his view does not mean that some religion is not of this type. So one of the contributions of psychology to spiritual guidance is to throw light on the pathological features within religious life, and to enable true spirituality to be distinguished from false and distorted forms. When does religion assume pathological forms? The simple answer is: when it ceases to be a means of integration of the personality, and becomes a form of escape from being human. To be 'religious' may be a means of prolonging immaturity, and of preventing the unifying of the personality. Sebastian Moore, writing of the Roman communion, has referred to a 'Catholic neurosis', one of the features of which is 'a tendency for young Catholics to remain strangely immature'. He speaks of the inhibiting in worship of all the ordinary human responses. 'There seems to be a certain *immobility* about religious people, a failure to be quite aware, which goes to the very root of fallen man.'[64] Religion thus becomes a means of preventing life, of preserving death. It may prevent any real confrontation with evil by protecting people in an artificial world. It is this syndrome which Rollo May calls 'pseudo-innocence', a fixation in childhood which is often mistaken for goodness, but in fact is the enemy of spirituality. So 'innocence as a shield from responsibility is also a shield from growth'.[65] It shields people from new awareness, new understandings, new insights. May cites Herman Melville's novel *Billy Budd* to make the point that spirituality is opposed to innocence, for spirituality is based upon experience. A type of religion which prevents experience and preserves innocence must also preserve immaturity.

Religion may, of course, be a cover for deep inner disturbances. It may not further any healing process, but rather increase sickness. The spiritual guide is concerned with sickness and disturbance, and here her ministry requires some considerable understanding of psychological insights. She will need, however, to exercise caution and a critical mind in assessing psychiatric theories, as indeed she will in assessing the spirituality of her clients. Much of what is taken for spirituality is manifestly diseased and deranged. At the same time it needs to be realized that psychiatry is capable of the most stereotyped assumptions about human beings, and psychiatrists are not always sufficiently aware of their own acceptance of labels and models of sickness. To label someone as 'schizoid' or 'psychotic' is not necessarily to tell us very much about them, though it does tell us about the labelling process and the kind of psychological models which the person who is labelling finds most adequate. The model, however, is not the reality.

One of the most commonly used terms in labelling individuals is 'schizoid', which we encountered briefly in describing the movement of Clinical Theology and the work of Lake. Rollo May has argued that our entire culture is schizoid.[66] By schizoid he means out of touch, avoiding close relationships, unable to feel. The schizoid fears the threats and hostilities of the adult world. Lake in his discussion uses the Standard Psychiatric Nomenclature

adopted by the American Psychiatric Association as his basic definition of the schizoid personality. The definition is four-fold:

1 an enduring and malajustive pattern of behaviour manifesting
   avoidance of close relations with others;
2 inability to express hostility and aggressive feelings directly;
3 autistic thinking (i.e. thinking unduly directed towards oneself
   and the inner personal view of the situation, at the expense
   of the information actually available from the external world);
4 a shut-in, seclusive, withdrawn, introverted personality.

Lake then looks at the way in which some writers—such as Kierkegaard and Simone Weil—were able to go behind the defences and
speak of the experience itself, the experience of a split world of
horror and dread.[67] But in many people the experience is too
terrible, and so a range of protections is constructed. It is the
behaviour pattern which results from such protections and defences
which Lake terms the 'schizoid problem', and he believes that
'clinical pastoral care nowadays has to deal predominantly with
schizoid problems in young people, indeed in many younger
clergy'.[68] Holding this view, it is not surprising that he devotes so
much space in his writings to examining the condition.

Most pastors who have been involved in the ministry of personal
guidance would probably agree that what Lake calls schizoid problems do occur frequently among religious people. They become
detached, and cold, using the intellect as a protection against the
body and emotions. As May wrote in an earlier study,

> the typical kind of psychic problem in our day is not hysteria
> (though much of our culture is hysterical, worshipping and cling-
> ing to consumer goods and people treated like consumer
> goods) . . . but the schizoid type, that is to say, problems of
> persons who are detached, unrelated, lacking in affect, tending
> towards depersonalisation, and covering up their problems by
> means of intellectualization and technical formulations.[69]

It is at this point that religious doctrines and forms may become
instruments of fear, of defence against the experience of reality,
instead of signals of enriched experience. Unless there is a real
crisis within the person, religion remains a defence against life, and
against wholeness. It cripples and crushes the person. It does not,
and cannot, liberate. Any pastor has experienced the syndrome in
himself and in others. The pastoral task is to enable the religious

experience to be one which leads to integration and wholeness of personality. But before there can be this change, there must be an experience of darkness, in which the defences of the mind are broken down. This darkness is a terrible experience of alienation, but it is the breakthrough to an experience of warmth and closeness. Lake claims:

> A dark night of the spirit, in which 'god' appears in all the most terrifying forms, such as could put the Christian off wanting to trust him at all, has to be traversed by those who are called to move out of a detached spirituality with schizoid undertones into a life of union with God as he meets and loves us through the touch and sensitivity which others can extend to us as soon as we stop distancing them.

Religion, when it is a form of protection against life and experience, tends to become an end in itself: that is, God is not the end. So religious forms are valued for their own sake. Associated with this kind of religion is religiosity in which the interest in forms and ceremonies becomes obsessive. Undisciplined religiosity is always a positive obstacle to any spiritual progress. Van Zeller stresses how 'religiosity if delayed in must inevitably prolong the night of sense',[70] that is, the process of development towards contemplative prayer, and indeed the entire progress of the spiritual life. In psychological terms, religiosity breeds and prolongs immaturity. Jung, while he rejected the Freudian critique of all religion as pathology, was nevertheless strong in his condemnation of such false religion.

> Woe to them who use religion as a substitute for another side of the life of the soul. They are in error and will be accursed. Religion is no substitute, but is to be added to the other activity of the soul as a completion. Out of the fulness of life shall you bring forth your religion; only then will you be blessed.[71]

His protest, like that of Rollo May, is against pseudo-innocence. So much of what passes for goodness is of this type, and it is very harmful. For example, when the ascetical techniques which were devised to curb violent passions are used by the immature person whose emotional life has not fully developed, and whose instincts are weak and disordered, they can be destructive and not beneficial. Freud believed that religion itself was the result of a failure to transform the sexual desires of early childhood into mature adult attitudes. To question that this is an adequate explanation of all religion is not to deny that it is manifestly true of much of it. True religion requires the maturing of the instincts and the emotions.

The area of sexuality is crucial to the entire discussion. The spiritual director is concerned with union with God, and this process of union demands a profound degree of self-knowledge and maturity. Because we are sexual beings it involves the acceptance of our sexuality, and the integration of sexuality with the rest of life. This integration is one of the central purposes of religion. Hence the insistence in the spiritual tradition that the guide should be a person experienced in the passions. Yet, as we have seen, religion can be distorted so that it becomes itself a form of sexual pathology. Religion and sex are inextricably linked, and the honest facing of human sexuality is vital to spirituality. When it does not happen, spirituality becomes twisted and unbalanced. In fact, Christian history contains many examples of false spiritualities characterized by false and harmful attitudes to sex. To regard sex as a hindrance to holiness of life can hardly be seen as contributing to human wholeness, yet this has been a widespread belief among Christians. The western Christian tradition contains abundant evidence of disparagement of sexuality and of the body, with all the terrible consequences of human misery and confusion which it has brought.

One of the most vital tasks, therefore, for contemporary spirituality is to learn from and work through the contemporary insights and understandings of sexuality, and much of the time of any spiritual director may be taken up with this. Nor can such a task be separated from the work of discovering one's own identity as a sexual being. The spiritual director must be a person who is facing his own sexuality and sexual needs, a person who is on the way towards sexual integrity and wholeness. Spiritual health and sexual health are closely joined, for, as Julian of Norwich wrote, our substance and our sensuality together are in God, and together constitute our soul.[72]

The Christian tradition has been seriously damaged over many centuries by a negative and warped view of sexuality about which a good deal has been written already.[73] It is outside the scope of this study to examine in detail the damage which has resulted from such a distortion, but one result is that the church is widely believed to regard the area of sexuality with a mixture of fear and hostility.

An essential part of spiritual direction is the healing of wounds caused by this and other distorted views, and helping individuals to see the unity of sexual and spiritual life. This must involve the reversal of the tendency, present in the West since Augustine, which has seen the sexual act as tainted with evil, and only justified for purposes of procreation.

Sexuality therefore has to be redeemed from its detractors, and there is a good deal of repentance and humble re-learning required of Christians in the field. But it is not simply sexuality in the narrow sense which has suffered in this way, but the body and the emotional life. Spirituality has come to be seen by some as the rejection of the body. Ashley Montagu has referred to 'a fear associated with the Christian tradition in its various denominations, the fear of bodily pleasures'.[74] In fact, the spiritual person must be one who understands and has integrated into her whole personality the need for physical contact, for touching, for the body, for 'touch and contact are necessarily the most conclusive factor in determining the structure of our world'.[75]

This integration of sexuality and of the physical aspects of being human is therefore of the utmost spiritual importance, and is one of the essential functions of true religion. St Thomas Aquinas writes of insensitivity (*insensibilitas*), the failure to develop these aspects, as a vice. 'Those are called insensitive who are deficient with regard to the pleasures of touch... Now insensitivity is opposed to the virtue of temperance... Therefore insensitivity is a vice'.[76] The insensitive person is an unfeeling person, however much he may try to pass off his immaturity as piety. He is, in Marcuse's phrase, a 'one-dimensional man'. But it is one of Marcuse's central points that the diminution of sexuality is a disease which has affected us all. We have become a culture marked by sensual deprivation, diminished in feeling.[77] It is the poets who have tried to recall us to affection. Thus Allen Ginsberg in 1969, describing the vision of Walt Whitman, pointed out that in Whitman's view,

> unless there were an infusion of feeling, of tenderness, of fearlessness, of spirituality, of natural sexuality, of natural delight in each other's bodies, into hardened materialistic, cynical, life-denying, clearly competitive, afraid, scared, armored bodies there would be no chance for spiritual democracy to take root in America.[78]

Spirituality and sexuality are inseparable. The sexually immature person cannot bypass the quest for sexual integrity in his search for spirituality. If he does, that spirituality will most likely be deranged, and Christian history contains many examples of sexual confusion which finds pseudo-outlets in religious practices.

It was on these grounds that Freud came to see all religion as pathological. But Freud, in spite of his significant recognition of the central place of sexuality in human life, cannot be regarded as a reliable guide today. His understanding of sexuality is extremely negative, as indeed is his attitude to women. Indeed, the psychiatric concern with pathological forms of behaviour is not a helpful model for the study of human sexuality in all its variations. Still less ought the spiritual guide to succumb to the temptation to dismiss those patterns of behaviour or attitudes which infringe current social norms as 'neurotic', 'abnormal' or 'deviant'. Spiritual discernment must include both the wisdom to learn from psychiatric insights, and also the refusal to accept uncritically any of its categories, or to be imprisoned within them. This is particularly important in the sphere of sexuality, where we need desperately to listen and to learn more of this fundamental and yet mysterious area of human life.

But to question the psychiatric tendency to divide humanity into normal/deviant, sane/insane and so on raises the question of the concepts of sanity and madness. The definition of madness is relative. What is considered insane in one social order may become the convention of another. What we need to learn from the work of Laing and his followers is that the discovery of, and living through of, our own hidden forms of madness is a necessary prelude to spiritual maturing. The opposite of both madness and sanity is normality, a dreary state of arrest, of imprisonment within conventions. To find one's true sanity may involve the experience of 'madness'. So Mary Barnes, through her madness, came to find a sense of wholeness and of the self which she had not known before. Certainly there is little support in the Christian spiritual tradition for the conventional idea of sanity. The words of Jacopone da Todi (1228–1306), the Franciscan, are a typical expression of that mad love of those who 'go mad for the beautiful Messiah'.

Whoever goes mad for Christ seems afflicted and in tribulation: but he is an exalted master of nature and theology.

Whoever goes mad for Christ certainly seems crazy to people:

it seems he is off the road to anyone without experience of the state.

Whoever wishes to enter this school will discover new learning: he who has not experienced madness does not yet know what it is.[79]

The madness of which he writes is, of course, a creative experience, a transcendence of limits, an experience of enriched consciousness. It is a breakthrough from constricted existence towards real personal liberation. Now this is certainly not to say that all forms of madness are creative. Nevertheless the Christian must be extremely careful not to accept without question notions of sanity and normality which are based not on any theological principles, but on the social conventions of the day. We must question the notion of sanity as a value, and perhaps this is our central task in this area. It is expressed with great effect in Thomas Merton's meditation on the death of Adolf Eichmann.

One of the most disturbing facts that came out in the Eichmann trial was that a psychiatrist examined him and pronounced him *perfectly sane.* I do not doubt it at all, and that is precisely why I find it disturbing. If all the Nazis had been psychotics, as some of their leaders probably were, their appalling cruelty would have been in some sense easier to understand. It is much worse to consider this calm, well-balanced, unperturbed official, conscientiously going about his dark work, his administrative job which happened to be the supervision of mass murder. He was thoughtful, orderly, unimaginative. He had a profound respect for system, for law and order. He was obedient, loyal, a faithful officer of a great state. He served his government very well . . .

The sanity of Eichmann is disturbing. We equate sanity with a sense of justice, with humaneness, with prudence, with the capacity to love and understand other people. We rely on the sane people of the world to preserve it from barbarism, madness, destruction. And now it begins to dawn on us that it is precisely the *sane* ones who are the most dangerous.

It is the sane ones, the well-adapted ones, who can without qualms and without nausea, aim the missiles and press the buttons that will initiate the great festival of destruction that they, the *sane ones,* have prepared. What makes us so sure, after all, that the danger comes from a psychotic getting into a position to fire the first shot in a nuclear war? Psychotics will be suspect. The sane ones will keep them far from the button. No one suspects the sane, and the sane ones will have *perfectly good reasons*, logical, well-adjusted reasons, for firing the shot. They will be obeying sane orders that have come sanely down the chains of command. And because of their sanity they will have no qualms at all. When the missiles take off, then, *it will be no mistake.*

We can no longer assume that because a man is 'sane' he is therefore in his 'right mind'. The whole concept of sanity in a society where spiritual values have lost their meaning is itself meaningless. A man can be 'sane' in the limited sense that he is not impeded by his disordered emotions from acting in a cool, orderly manner, according to the needs and dictates of the social situation in which he finds himself. He can be perfectly 'adjusted'. God knows, perhaps such people can be perfectly adjusted even in hell itself . . .

I am beginning to realize that 'sanity' is no longer a value or an end in itself. The 'sanity' of modern man is about as useful to him as the huge bulk and muscles of the dinosaur. If he were a little less sane, a little more doubtful, a little more aware of his absurdities and contradictions, perhaps there might be a possibility of his survival. But if he is sane, too sane . . . perhaps we must say that in a society like ours the worst insanity is to be totally without anxiety, totally 'sane'.[80]

Finally, there are some important areas where spiritual direction and psychotherapy overlap or appear to conflict. The first is the question of sin and guilt. It is widely believed that while the priest must condemn sin and induce or encourage guilt, the counsellor, therapist and social worker have no concern with sin, and regard guilt as unhealthy. But this is in fact a serious distortion. It misrepresents the priest's, and the Christian's, posture as one who renounces sin and accepts the sinner with love and understanding. It obscures the difference between guilt which is healthy and necessary, and guilt which is pathological. It ignores the fact that more therapists are now concerned with values, responsibility, issues of right and wrong. Thus Dr Rosemary Gordon, a Jungian analyst, in an important paper on 'Moral Values and Analytic Insights', questions the neglect of ethics in the therapeutic traditions.

While psychoanalysis was predominantly determinist, the prob-

lems of moral values were irrelevant. But the more recent concepts imply that man has a certain amount of choice and
independence. Though they were developed by clinicians on the
basis of their actual experience with patients, they do bring us
closer to the realm of ethics.

She goes on to argue that the development in recent years of a
more personalistic approach in clinical work has led analysts to
propose that 'there seem to be intrinsic in the human psyche certain
characteristics which the moral philosopher would probably incline
to qualify as "good." ' She specifically lists eight such characteristics: creativeness and imagination; the need to discover a true
and authentically experienced self; concern for loved persons and
objects, and values, and an experience of guilt if one hurts or
betrays them; a search for meaningfulness; integration; relationships beyond the self; experience of wonder and awe; and
humour.[81]

More recently the American psychiatrist Karl Menninger argues
for a return to the concept of sin, and provides a study of the seven
deadly sins, which is one of the better guides to self-examination!
Drawing on the earlier work of Hiltner,[82]Menninger describes sin
as defiant withdrawal, supererogation and self-absorption. Sin, he
says, is 'at heart a refusal of the love of others'.[83] The analyst may
not use the word sin because of its strong reproachful quality, but
that does not mean that he is unconcerned with value and ethics.
Indeed there is evidence that it is analysts and other therapists who
are now laying stress on the positive aspects of guilt, while some
theologians are rejecting it as morbid! The acceptance of guilt in
fact is the beginning of renewal.

So long as a person lives under the shadow of real, unacknowl-
edged and unexpiated guilt, he . . . will continue to hate himself
and to suffer the inevitable consequences of self-hatred. But the
moment he . . . begins to accept his guilt and his sinfulness,
the possibility of radical reformation opens up, and a new freedom of self-respect and peace.[84]

Of course, there will be those who cannot distinguish true guilt
from false, destructive, sick guilt. The spiritual director will be
confronted from time to time by those who will benefit more from
therapy of some kind. It is important to recognize that there are
some people who are not sufficiently mature for the kind of adult

relationship which direction implies, and for them the attempt at such a relationship can be harmful. Nevertheless there will be frequent situations in which therapy and spiritual direction run alongside each other. The therapist's concern is to help the person to become a free and autonomous adult. The spiritual director is helping a sinner aided by grace to come to the knowledge of God. Yet they are both involved with the same person, and neither can ignore the various dimensions of her personality, or divide her into 'psychological' and 'spiritual' needs. Her spiritual needs will appear in psychotherapy, and her psychological needs cannot be ignored by the director. But the spiritual director is not primarily concerned with the person as a sick person. Rather, as a French writer, C. Bouchard, has said: 'It is this area of freedom which allows his progress to work through the illness itself. There is no value and no truth in spiritual direction without this knowledge and this respect for a responsible man.'[85] Spiritual direction takes freedom and responsibility as its starting point. The director is looking for signs of the growing freedom of the spirit. Where there is a lack of freedom and of responsibility so that such a relationship cannot even begin, it is a sign that a different kind of relationship is required.

It is a sad fact that, because of lack of knowledge or fear of psychological illness, many priests withdraw entirely from the scene once its presence is suspected. By doing so, they miss some of the most important opportunities for spiritual guidance. Frank Lake lamented this withdrawal.

> The mishandling of spiritual transitional states has other results than the arrest of spiritual growth and maturation. The alien mental contents which are being ejected in the course of sanctification are, in the minds of untrained clergymen, labelled 'for psychiatrists only'. The whole significance of what is going on in this Christian person is missed. The Holy Spirit is moving in, and the clergyman is frantically engaged in trying to stop the dispossessed 'devils' from being pushed out.[86]

R. D. Laing puts the same point more strongly in speaking of the experience of death and rebirth which many people are seeking.

> If they go to a Christian priest, the priest will probably refer them to a psychiatrist, and the psychiatrist will refer them to a mental hospital, and the mental hospital will refer them to the

electric shock machine. And if this is not our contemporary mode of crucifying Christ, what is?[87]

Rather the priest needs to recognize that all Christian experience involves the experience of disturbance, and to look for the movements of the Holy Spirit in the troubled and shaken individual.

Finally it needs to be stressed that priests, therapists and other members of the 'healing professions' could usefully create supportive teams within an area, in order to fulfil their roles more effectively. Inter-disciplinary discussion and sharing of ideas and problems are always valuable, and many have found a particular value in regular groups of priests and doctors to examine the areas of overlap and of collaboration. The achievement of wholeness involves medical, psychological and spiritual needs. Care obviously needs to be taken over confidentiality if priests and doctors meet to discuss an individual, and, where possible, her permission should be sought. It hardly needs to be said that the priest cannot discuss matters raised under the seal of the confessional with any third person unless specific permission has been given to do so. The establishment of such groups for mutual consultation and support could well lead into the study of wider issues in theology and medicine, and illuminate the understanding and practice of both disciplines.

THE HEALING SACRAMENTS

It has been the contention of this chapter that spiritual direction and the attainment of psychological health are intimately connected and that, while the disciplines of spiritual direction and psychotherapy need to be clearly distinguished, they overlap and influence each other at a variety of critical points. The spiritual director is concerned with wholeness of life, with healing for body and spirit. It is the achievement of such healing which is the purpose of the sacraments, and so the sacramental ministry has a central role in direction. It is essential to stress this, for the individual who tries to exercise a ministry of personal guidance from the perimeters of the corporate Christian life is pursuing a course which is highly dangerous both to himself and to those who are subject to his influence. The great Christian mystics were insistent that those seeking spiritual progress must not forsake the sacraments, for they knew the dangers of spiritual pride and isolationism when the individual cuts himself off from the common life.

At the centre of the Christian tradition are the sacraments, and at the centre of sacramental life is deliverance and healing. Spiritual direction therefore always occurs within a direction of spirit, flowing through the organism of the Body of Christ. In the baptismal liturgy, there is both cleansing and deliverance, and also the sealing of the Spirit, the two actions symbolized by the water and the chrism. In absolution, the baptismal process of cleansing followed by strengthening is renewed, for this too is a sacrament of strength as well as of deliverance. The eucharist is a healing sacrament through which the glorified Body preserves our bodies and souls within the direction of eternal life. Whenever these sacraments are celebrated, there is a ministry of healing. An essential area of spiritual direction therefore is concerned with preparing people to *experience* the sacraments, and to enter into the healing process. In the case of baptism, this must mean an end to 'mechanical' celebrations without preparation. The baptismal liturgy should be a splendid event, rich in symbol and ceremony, central to the church's worship, and therefore placed normally within a eucharistic context. It needs to be preceded by a lengthy period of preparation which includes regular prayer for the candidates and their families. And it needs to be followed by the same intensity of prayer, visiting and support. A great deal of time needs to be spent on these areas, and the priest or lay Christian who is preparing the people should see his or her role as one of surrounding the central act with prayer and spiritual guidance. It is the Lord who will act, and spiritual direction, here as always, is aimed at preparing people to receive and respond to that action of grace.

Baptism only happens once (although there can be, and needs to be, a periodic re-enacting and re-living of the experience liturgically, as on Holy Saturday), and therefore the preparation needs to be intensive, and the rite itself needs to express the drama and the once-for-allness. It is a symbolic drowning, the font becomes tomb and womb, grave and mother, and from it emerges the new child of the resurrection. It is a crisis, a slaying of the dragon, a rebirth from the world of death. All spiritual direction in Christ begins at this point.

By that initiation they put the sea of eternal death behind them, and leave their demonic enemies drowning in the font. They put off madness and oppression. They are clothed with holiness and made vocal in thanksgiving to God.[88]

Confession and the eucharist, however, while they occur more frequently and are 'growth sacraments', also need the underpinning of constant prayer. The spiritual guide needs to remember her penitents and pray particularly for them, if possible daily, for they have a relationship with her of special intimacy in Christ. The confession itself must be celebrated within the atmosphere of healing prayer. Again the eucharist is the climax of contemplation, and it is here supremely that people can be brought to experience the divine life. Spiritual direction must aim to awaken people to this experience, and the concern of pastoral liturgy is to make the celebration really manifest and clearly to express it.

Marriage as a sacrament is grossly neglected. This is partly because in England the liturgical celebration has become an unimaginative rite. The priest acts as registrar and only rarely is the service part of a eucharist. So the close association of marriage and the sacramental life of the Christian community is hardly ever manifested. But even where this is so, the liturgy seems to express only the beginning of the marriage, and not its continuing life. Dr Jack Dominian has argued that 'within marriage is likely to be found one of the fundamental sources of the renewal of Christianity'.[89] In marriage, Dominian claims, are contained the three essential features of sustenance, healing and growth, and these correspond to needs in life as a whole. First, sustenance, the need for shelter and food, for psychological and emotional support. Secondly, healing, the way in which, through the marital union, anxieties, fears, loneliness, personal weaknesses are often healed through mutual acceptance and mutual love. Thirdly, growth, the enlarging of experience and development towards maturity which a good marriage can bring. Dominian suggests that marriage belongs at the centre of the church's liturgical life, and that it is through this sacrament that the Christian life can be most fully understood and actualized. Through the experience of marriage can come healing of body and soul. The priest should be working towards ways of helping couples to enter into and deepen the spiritual experience of marriage, the experience of union which anticipates the divine.

The whole of the church's life of prayer and sacrament is concerned with healing. Francis MacNutt in his study *Healing* describes four basic kinds of sickness: sickness of the spirit caused by one's personal sin; emotional sickness caused by the emotional hurts and damage of the past; physical sickness caused by disease or accident; and demonic oppression which may cause any of the preceding. He goes on to suggest that there are four basic methods of prayer which correspond to these forms of sickness—prayer for repentance, for inner healing, for physical healing, and for deliverance; and sacramental rites which also meet the same needs—repentance and inner healing through penance, physical healing through anointing, and deliverance through exorcism.[90]

It is with the sacrament of holy unction that we generally associate the ministry of healing, but it has been suggested above that the entire Christian scheme is deeply involved with healing. However, both laying on of hands and anointing with oil have an important place. Laying on of hands is an act which can be, and is, used frequently and informally in a wide range of circumstances throughout life. In New Testament times it was closely associated with healing, and many have found this to be true today. But in the Bible, the act had a variety of connotations. It could be a blessing, an imparting of functions within the Body of Christ, or a prayer for sending of the Spirit. In the Charismatic movement, the laying on of hands has come to be used widely as an expression of unity and solidarity, as well as for other purposes. But the most specific and most widely known use within the Charismatic groups is the laying on of hands in order that a person may receive 'baptism in the Holy Spirit'. Most people do in fact only receive this experience after hands have been laid on them.

Within a ministry of spiritual guidance, laying on of hands has an important place. It must not be confused with the same action in the sacramental context of confirmation, ordination and (more recently) penance. It is not claimed that the informal and repeated use of laying on of hands is a sacrament, but rather a gesture of private prayer. It can be seen as 'sacramental' in the same way as the signing with holy water, or other similar gestures and actions. In the Old Testament it is used in connection with sacrifice (Leviticus 1:4; 8:22), execution (Leviticus 24:14; Deuteronomy 13:9), ordination (Numbers 8:10) and blessing (Genesis 48:14–20). In the New Testament, Jesus laid hands in blessing (Mark 10:16) and healing (Mark 5:23), and associated the act with healing by his disciples (Mark 16:18). In the Apostolic church, the laying on of hands is associated with the imparting of the Holy Spirit (Acts 8:17; 9:17), and by the third century its use was widespread. The practice does not seem to have been restricted to priests until the fourth-century Apostolic Constitutions which listed it among the priestly works.[91] In the Roman rite to this day, lay people lay hands as godparents, and sponsors in baptism and confirmation. The act may certainly be used by lay people more generally, both within a group and in situations of private prayer. As St Augustine wrote, 'The laying on of hands is not something that can be performed only once like baptism. For what else is it but prayer over a man?'[92] It is in fact a prayer and a transmission of grace which takes place within the context of a developing relationship in Christ, and within that relationship there is healing.

The sacrament of anointing is a more specific act. Its revised western form lays great stress on the healing of the whole person. In contrast to the old rite which stressed forgiveness of sins and proximity to death, the act of unction is now linked with the strengthening and healing power of the Holy Spirit. That these alterations in emphasis were quite deliberate was made clear by Pope Paul VI in his Apostolic Constitution *Sacram Unctionem* of 1 January 1974. Nevertheless, confession of sin is an important preliminary to the sacrament. After the confession there is a silent laying on of hands, followed by the anointing, with the words:

> Through this holy anointing and his great love for you
> may the Lord fill you with the power of his Holy Spirit.
> In his goodness may he ease your suffering
> and extend his saving grace to you
> freed from all the power of sin.

The sacrament is therefore primarily associated with the outpouring of the Holy Spirit, and secondly with deliverance from suffering. It is an element therefore within the overall ministry of spiritual direction, sometimes in fact the final act of a lengthy relationship. There needs to be much prayerful preparation and follow-up, involving a well-trained praying group, and where possible the rite should be administered within a group context.

The association of anointing almost exclusively with death has had harmful results in the West, and fortunately in recent years a fuller and richer theology of the sacrament has developed. But its place within the ministry to the dying remains of the utmost importance, and the role of the dying Christian in spiritual direction is an area which deserves a study in itself. Frequently it is found that through the tribulation of dying, an individual becomes a source of spiritual guidance and of peace to those with whom he or she comes into contact.

The spiritual guide will, of course, always place a very high priority on her personal intercession for those under her care. Particularly in the case of the sick and troubled, intercessory prayer is vital. It is a disciplined activity, involving serious work, although the real work is Christ's.

> Priests today are discovering the power of intercessory prayer as part of their professional practice of spiritual counselling. This prayer is directed at physical and especially inner healing. Serious problems such as drug addiction, alcoholism and long-seated emotional disturbances in some cases seem to have been helped by priests who recognize the appropriateness of joining prayer to the equally necessary professional counselling. They have seen the power of Christ come through them as channels of his love. As yet not many priests have experienced this power, but for those who have the problem of discovering the relevance of their ministry has disappeared.[93]

As well as actual intercession, it is important to realize how one's own God-centred prayer and recollection help to heal the dis-ease of those who are un-centred and fragmented in spirit. Jim Wilson, that great pioneer of the healing ministry, used to stress the place of meditation in healing and the value of meditating on behalf of the sick. This is particularly important with the mentally confused.[94] Again, Paul Tournier, the physician, came to realize the inadequacy of physical treatment alone, and the need to deepen his prayer life and to understand the psyche. To pray for healing is to enter into a spiritual conflict at a profound level. Sometimes it is repentance and forgiveness which bring healing, for personal sin has brought sickness along with it. Often it is deep emotional disturbance which is preventing physical healing. This can be a major obstacle to spiritual progress, and necessitates what recent writers, since Agnes Sanford, have termed 'inner healing'.[95] Inner healing, or the 'healing of the memories', means that the wounds which still remain from the past, and which still affect the present, are healed, and the poison of past hurts and resentments is drained away and replaced by an inflow of love. It is 'the application of Christ's healing power to what we now know of the emotional nature of man'.[96]

Finally, the sacrament of holy order, the sacrament of ministerial priesthood itself. In all that has been said about healing, the priest plays a crucial role, and historically priesthood and healing are closely linked in Christian thought. Indeed, the Apostolic Tradition of Hippolytus in the early third century directed that those who had received healing need not be ordained, for the gift would manifest itself.[97] In the early ordination rites healing was seen as a central element in priestly ministry. Thus the Apostolic Constitutions (fifth century) include a prayer by the bishop that the person being ordained might be 'filled with powers of healing and words of instruction',[98] while the Canons of Hippolytus pray that he may have power to remit sins, to loose bonds of demons and to heal all diseases.[99] The priest then is called to exercise a ministry of reconciliation, to guide individuals in the way of the Spirit, and it is within this ministry that healing holds an essential place. The priest is a minister of healing because she herself, wounded and broken, has received and continues to receive, the healing of the Spirit. She is a 'wounded healer'.[100]

CASTING OUT THE DEMONS

In the New Testament, deliverance is described as deliverance from evil powers which oppress and distort individuals and society. But this belief is part of a wider view of reality in which the spiritual person is set against a network of destructive spiritual forces. The world of spirituality is not universally benign, and there are false spirits, false spiritual directions. Hence the necessity of some treatment of this area in a study of this kind.

The tradition sees 'discernment of spirits' as a key element in spiritual direction. In the Old Testament, while the term does not appear, the idea is present. Saul is motivated by both good (1 Samuel 11:6) and evil spirits (1 Samuel 16:14–23). Moses is given a spirit to enable him to lead (Numbers 11:17, 25). The Lord gives a spirit of confusion in Egypt (Isaiah 19:14). There is a call to discern true prophecy from false (Jeremiah 23:28). In the New Testament, St John instructs us to 'test the spirits if they be of God', and he gives guidelines for distinguishing 'the spirit of truth and the spirit of error' (1 John 4:1–6). St Paul too places the *diakrisis pneumatōn* among the *charismata* of the Holy Spirit (1 Corinthians 12:10). The Desert Fathers emphasized the ministry of discernment, though they had no systematic theology of spiritual conflict. Origen, however, had worked out such a theology based on Ephesians 6:12, and he argued that there were two phases of the conflict—the beginners who struggled against flesh and blood, and the more advanced who struggled against principalities and powers. Evagrius inherited Origen's scheme, but it does not seem to have influenced earlier desert hermits to any great extent. In Evagrius the demons appear as the enemies of contemplation, producing pseudo-visions and deceptions. The protection against them, he says, is *apatheia* and short, intense prayer. Spiritual warfare assumes a central place in the spirituality of St Anthony, where descriptions of encounters with demons are common. Athanasius noted in his life of Anthony:

> There is need of much prayer and self-discipline to gain through the Holy Spirit the gift of discerning of spirits, to detect their nature, namely which of them are the less abandoned, which the more, what is the aim of each, what each affects, and how each is overthrown and ejected.[101]

The life of prayer then is seen as a life of conflict in which evil forces are encountered and defeated. St Anthony warned, 'We have for enemies the terrible, unscrupulous and wicked demons; against them is our warfare.'[102] Abba Serapion (died 362) saw the monastic life as a campaign for Christ 'to witness the defeat of the demons'.[103] In the Rule of St Benedict in the West, spiritual discernment is crucial. Benedict's word is *discretion*, a word which has been misunderstood to mean avoidance of excess, or tactfulness. In fact, in the monastic tradition discretion is a richer, broader concept altogether, and means spiritual discernment whose end is purity of heart and the vision of God.[104] The vision is impeded by the false spirits who invade consciousness. So the *Book of Privy Counselling* warns:

> Do not be overcome with anxious dread if the evil one comes (as he will) with sudden fierceness, knocking and hammering on the walls of your house; or if he should stir some of his mighty agents to rise suddenly and attack you without warning. Let us be clear about this: the fiend must be taken into account. Anyone beginning this work (I do not care who he is) is liable to feel, smell, taste or hear some surprising effects concocted by the enemy in one or other of his senses. So do not be astonished if it happens. There is nothing he will not try to drag you down from the heights of such valuable work.[105]

Again the *Ancrene Riwle* says, 'The higher the hill of holy exalted life, the more and the stronger will be the devil's blasts and the winds of temptation'.[106] This theme of discernment of spirits has been a recurring one in Christian spirituality from Origen, Cyril of Jerusalem, Augustine, Cassian and Gregory the Great through Bernard of Clairvaux, Richard of St Victor, Ruysbroeck and Thomas à Kempis.

From the earliest times, however, there was a realization that many thoughts and impulses come from within our personalities. Thus Origen says, 'We find that the thoughts which arise in our hearts . . . come sometimes from ourselves, at times they are stirred up by counteracting virtues, and at other times they may be sent by God and the good angels.' Or Cassian, 'In truth we should be aware above all that our thoughts have three possible sources— God, the devil and ourselves.'[107] All three sources are encountered within the psyche. Thus the seventeenth-century writer Alvarez de Paz defines a spirit thus:

> A spirit is an internal impulse by which man feels himself urged to do something. It is nothing other than the understanding or judgment of the intellect concerning, and the inclination of the will towards, a work or the omission of a work, to which one is moved by an intrinsic or extrinsic principle.[108]

The basis of discernment of spirits is the undoubted fact that temptations, errors and illusions are commonly encountered on the spiritual path. Writers such as St Ignatius Loyola, St Francis de Sales and J. B. Scaramelli have produced lists of rules for discerning good spirits from bad. Thus Scaramelli's list may be summarized in the table on the following page.[109]

In the work of Ignatius Loyola, discernment of spirits becomes central to spiritual direction. 'It is no exaggeration to say that the *Exercises* have in the end no other purpose than this,' says one Jesuit.[110] St Ignatius in his introduction to the General Examination of Conscience wrote that 'there are three kinds of thoughts in the mind, namely: one which is strictly my own, and arises wholly from my own free will; two others which come from without, the one from the good spirit, and the other from the evil one'.[111] When offering advice to the spiritual director, he says that, while he should not seek to know the private thoughts and sins of his exercitants, yet 'it will be very helpful if he is kept faithfully informed about the various disturbances and thoughts caused by the action of different spirits'.[112] For Ignatius, discernment is 'the discovery of the origin of non-free movements in a prayer situation'.[113] True consolation comes, he claims, from the good spirit,

INTELLECT		WILL	
Signs of good spirit	*Signs of bad spirit*	*Signs of good spirit*	*Signs of bad spirit*
1. True	1. False	1. Inner peace	1. Disquiet
2. Not concerned with useless affairs	2. Useless, vain pre-occupations	2. True humility	2. False humility
3. Illumines intellect	3. Darkness, or deceptive lights in imagination	3. Trust in God	3. Presumption or despair
4. Docility of intellect	4. Obstinate opinion	4. Flexible will	4. Obstinacy of heart
5. Discretion	5. Excess and exaggeration	5. Right intention	5. Devious intentions
6. Humble thoughts	6. Pride and vanity	6. Patience in pain	6. Impatience in pain
		7. Inner mortification	7. Rebellion of passions
		8. Simplicity and sincerity	8. Duplicity and dissimulation
		9. Liberty of spirit	9. Soul bound by earthly ties
		10. Zeal for imitation of Christ	10. Estrangement from Christ
		11. Charity	11. Bitter zeal

and is the sign of authenticity. But St Ignatius insists that one cannot make the *Exercises* without experiencing the movements of the various spirits. In 'exercising oneself' one is opening up the self to the influences of spirits, both good and evil. The Italian writer Iparraguire distinguishes between the intellectual categories of Ignatius's time, and the reality which he wished to express. What is essential is that Ignatius held that a *spirit* was *distinct* from a man's will, but was experienced within, that it *moved* him to some action, and that the different directions led to different results.[114] For Ignatius then the identification of, and conflict with, the forces of evil is of the essence of spiritual direction, and the director's task is to uncover the deceits of Satan and to safeguard the disciple from false choices. So a director can only fulfil his task if he is 'faithfully informed of the various stirrings and thoughts inspired into him by the divers spirits'.[115] Similarly, there is no true spiritual progress which does not include the ability to see through the wiles of the devil. Today the recovery of the tradition of spiritual discernment is in part the recovery of the unity of spirituality and moral and social action. It has been suggested that 'the tradition of discernment . . . may well be the most central thing happening in Christian spirituality today'.[116] Discernment involves clarity of vision: *diakrinein, diakrisis,* discerning, discriminating, judging between truth and falsehood.

St Ignatius says that the best protection against the onslaught of evil spirits is to open one's heart to a confessor and director.

> The enemy also acts like a false lover who wishes to be hidden and does not want to be known ... When the enemy of our human nature tempts a just soul with his tricks and deceits he wants and desires that they be received and kept secret. When they are revealed to a confessor or some other spiritual person who understands his deceits and evil designs, the enemy is greatly displeased for he knows that he cannot win in his evil plan once his obvious deceits have been laid bare.

So in each confession there is a renewal of the baptismal renunciation, a rejection of Satan and all his works. But to reject them involves recognizing them, and this involves discernment of spirits, testing them to see whether they are of God or not.

Is it possible then to think of external forces of evil which impinge upon and harm men and women? St Ignatius seemed less concerned with the objective origin of the forces affecting individuals than he was with the fact of their presence and its results. Whether they were non-human minds external to humankind or disturbing forces from within the psyche, the result was the same: a reduction of human freedom, and spiritual disturbance. Archbishop Michael Ramsey has commented: 'It is arbitrary to assume that we human beings are the only rational beings, knowing good and evil, in the universe, and it seems to me a reasonable assumption that there are, outside the human sphere, beings who can do good and do evil.'[117] But what is important in the tradition of 'false spirits' is *not* the precise structure of demonology, but rather the existence of false spiritual directions, false paths, idols which can become the focus of attention and divert the soul towards a destructive and death-inducing spirituality. In the New Testament, the powers that be in the world are called *angeloi, daimoniai, archai* and *exousiai,* the world rulers of this present darkness, the rudiments of the world (1 Corinthians 2:6–8; Ephesians 6:12; Galatians 4:3; Colossians 2:8). The symbolism, probably derived from the astral beliefs of the time, is one of cosmic warfare, involving an army of invisible beings who 'stand behind what occurs in the world'.[118]

The coming of God's Kingdom and the achievement of spiritual freedom is seen in terms of the setting free of individuals and of creation from slavery to these powers. Christ has conquered the powers. This is not a peripheral belief in the New Testament, but rather 'an altogether central article of faith'.[119] Jesus's exorcisms stood at the heart of his work. In Galilee, exorcism was 'his main occupation'.[120] On the other hand, the cases in the Synoptic Gospels were cases of disease for which we would today offer a different kind of explanation—mental disturbances, epilepsy, convulsions, dumbness, blindness (Mark 5:1–13; 9:15–27; Matthew 9:32–4; 12:22–4; Luke 21:21–2). What is crucial is that in all the cases, physical and mental healing was accompanied by the setting free of the person from oppression, from those forces which stunted and distorted his humanity. It is this liberation, this achievement of human freedom, which is fundamental to spiritual direction, and it is this which is conveyed by the demonic symbol and the theme of deliverance.

The idea of the 'demonic' is often confused with that of 'possession', which has never represented more than a fraction of those cases dealt with by exorcism. The 'possession syndrome' is well known in psychiatry, though it is explained in a variety of ways. Freud in an essay of 1923 noted the similarity between the demonological theory of possession and the psychoanalytic theory of hysteria. 'The neuroses of these early times emerge in demonological trappings. The states of possession correspond to our neuroses ... In our eyes the demons are bad and reprehensible wishes, derivatives of instinctual impulses that have been repudiated or repressed.'[121] Rollo May claims that demonic possession is simply 'the traditional name throughout history for psychosis'.[122] Since the work of Jung in the field of the unconscious, we cannot claim that the categories of theology and psychopathology are alternatives, or mutually exclusive.[123] R. D. Laing has pointed out that to change 'possession' language for the language of 'hysterical dissociation' may only be to exchange one form of metaphorical description for another. All language is symbolic, and the symbol is not the reality.[124]

However, whatever the value of the possession symbol, the idea of exorcism is not essentially connected with it, but is a much wider concept. Exorcism of evil forces was an integral element in the baptismal liturgy from very early times. Many of the Fathers refer to the drowning of the demons in the waters. As early as

Hippolytus there is a pre-baptismal exorcism. The rejection of
Satan's dominion is a crucial element in the baptismal teaching
of St Cyril of Jerusalem and St Gregory of Nyssa. In the modern
Roman baptismal rite, the prayer of exorcism is a prayer that God,
who sent his only Son into the world to cast out the power of
Satan, the spirit of evil, to rescue us from the kingdom of darkness
and bring us into the splendour of his kingdom of grace, should
set the candidate free from original sin, make her a temple of God's
glory and send her the Holy Spirit. Thus exorcism is one element
in a total liturgy of deliverance and healing, in which the realm of
evil is rejected and we are restored to the divine realm.

There will be occasions in the course of spiritual direction when
exorcism is required, though, in the experience of most spiritual
guides, they will be very rare. When it does occur, it is essential
that exorcism is set within the total framework of a healing church,
and if it is not seen in this framework, it is bound to become
distorted. One of the factors which has encouraged the distortion
of exorcism in some areas is the undervaluing of the 'routine'
methods of dealing with evil—prayer, fasting, confession, laying
on of hands, communion, and so on. In most cases they will be
found to be sufficient. Outside the context of the normal sacramental ministry, exorcism can be seriously misunderstood and misused.
A Roman Catholic journal put the point well in discussing the
liturgy of deliverance.

> It would seem that there is urgent need for new sacramental
> rites, both for alleged possession and for alleged infestation,
> which primarily demonstrate that the power and love of God
> are greater than any adverse power, *whatever it may be*, and
> which reintegrate afflicted souls into the normal life of the Christ-
> ian community assured of God's protecting care. This is not to
> say that there is no place for direct authoritative action dismiss-
> ing the evil, but it is safer and wiser to be reticent about the
> precise nature of the evil there. There is also the Gospel warning
> of the empty dispossessed man whose last state was eight times
> worse than his first. Exorcism can only be a first step to rehabili-
> tation.[125]

Francis MacNutt issues a similar warning.

> Prayer for deliverance should not be entered into without real
> prayer and discernment beforehand. Like major surgery it should

not be lightly suggested. Many people have a need for prayers of deliverance, I believe, but the time cannot be hurried, and there is a great need for follow-up. If follow-up cannot be provided, if there is no Christian community to help the person grow, we should hesitate before embarking on a prayer that cannot be finished: the last state of the person may end up worse than the first.[126]

In this area, as in all others, spiritual direction and the movement towards wholeness and maturity, both physical and psychological, must go together.

THE SPIRITUAL DIRECTOR AS HEALER

The spiritual guide stands in a close relationship to the human psyche. In the tradition, the guide plays a central role in helping individuals to move from one phase of life to another to enable them to understand new experiences, and to adjust to them. Spiritual directors and gurus have always been listeners, but the language to which they listen is the 'forgotten language' of myths and dreams and symbols, the language of fundamental human experience.[127] The American Jungian, Morton T. Kelsey, has suggested that the understanding of the unconscious and the language of dreams can lead to a rediscovery of the vital role of priesthood.[128] Certainly the insights of psychotherapy and those of the spiritual traditions of East and West need to be brought into mutual confrontation and dialogue.

One of the essential insights common to both traditions is that the spiritual guide or helper of the soul cannot be seen simply as a technician. Psychotherapy is not an art which can be taught, nor is the priesthood an occupation for which people can be trained. Indeed, an American psychotherapist, Sheldon Kopp, has argued that the process of training may actually impede the effectiveness of the help given.

> Ironically for each it is the very training designed to equip him that handicaps him most when he tries to be an authentic personal guide for another. Psychiatric training breeds a clinical, managerial attitude towards 'patients'. Clinical Psychology encourages an objective, detailed examination of 'subjects'.
>
> Psychiatric Social Workers too often end up becoming sentimental and patronizing towards the 'cases' whose troubled lives they once sought to ease. Finally, seminaries tend to turn out

too many clergymen who would sacrifice themselves to save the 'lost souls' whom they are to shepherd.

So the very process which enables a person to assume the role within our society of a personal helper or guide is the very process which may limit his capacity to fulfil that role.

> So it is that the most important aspect of the development of a psychotherapist occurs outside the context of his professional school training, having more to do with his own personal sufferings, pleasures, risks and adventures. In solitude, and later in the company of one who is already a guru, he must struggle with his own demons and must dare to free himself of them.[129]

Kopp believes that psychotherapy is merely today's name for the age-old activity of the guru. If this is so, it is certainly to use the term in a wider and more continuous sense than is usually the case. Whether or not it is correct to see psychotherapy in this light, there is no doubt that there is a close association with the spiritual director/guru traditions. Kopp identifies the essential feature of the link to be the process of 'illumination by metaphor', that is, a way of knowing based upon an intuitive grasp of situations, an openness to the myths and symbols of experience. The spiritual guide speaks the language of myth and of metaphor. As Paracelsus said, he should not tell 'the naked truth. He should use images, allegories, figures, wondrous speech, or other hidden roundabout ways'.[130] The point is that spiritual guidance is involved with a kind of knowledge which is inaccessible to the scientific mind. Spiritual things are spiritually discerned.

The research into consciousness which has taken place during this century has shattered earlier limited conceptions of the human mind. The unconscious remains an area of great mystery which can be experienced in metaphor and symbol. The Greek Fathers in their day had a strong sense of the mystery of the human mind and the unfathomable depths of human consciousness. The fact that humanity was made in the image of God, the image of the mysterious and unfathomable One, meant that human beings shared in that mystery. St Gregory the Great saw the sea as a symbol of this mystery of humanity.

> The 'sea' is the mind of man, and God enters its depths . . . God penetrates the depths of the sea, when he changes desperate hearts . . . for what abyss is there except the human mind which,

while unable to comprehend itself, is like an obscure abyss, hidden from itself in everything that is . . . God walks, as it were, in the abyss, when he penetrates the dark heart and tramples the invisible waves of sin.[131]

'The dark heart' and 'the abyss' have been opened up to an unprecedented degree by depth psychology. Yet centuries before the arrival of the psychological schools, the great spiritual guides saw the heart as the centre of both consciousness and the unconscious. This was particularly marked in the teachings of the Russian *startsy*. The Macarian homilies describe the heart as the seat of God himself. 'There are unfathomable depths within the heart. God is there with the angels, light and life are there, the kingdom and the apostles, the heavenly cities, and the treasures of grace, all things are there.'[132] It is from these depths, from the 'spark of the soul', that the Holy Spirit comes to us. It is within these depths that the work of spiritual direction is carried on.

4

Prayer and the Christian spiritual tradition

Thank God our time is now when wrong
Comes up to meet us everywhere
Never to leave us till we take
The longest stride of soul man ever took—
Affairs are now soul size.
The enterprise
Is exploration into God.

CHRISTOPHER FRY[1]

THE BREAKDOWN OF THE TRADITION

To pray is to enter into a relationship with God, but it is a relationship in which we stand within a great human movement. The Christian spiritual tradition is vast, rich and diverse, and it is essential that the spiritual guide should be acquainted with this tradition, so that she can find herself in it, use its resources, and guide others within it. One of the weaknesses of the Catholic revival in the Church of England in the nineteenth century was the narrowness of its approach to the tradition, and its copying of the French school of spirituality, a school marked by individualistic piety and active rationalism. We see now that the French school represented a passing phase, and since then there have been powerful movements towards the recovery of the centrality of the liturgy, and the revival of contemplative prayer. Frequently, however, expressions such as 'traditional theology' and 'traditional spirituality' are used in ways which indicate ignorance of the tradition in its diversity. We are in a situation of breakdown so that what often passes for orthodoxy is simply a current convention, and the most deeply rooted orthodox teachings are seen as some novel theory.

Thus one writer can refer to the search for 'words and ideas outside the traditional field of theology', and give as an example of this the term 'ground of our being'.[2] Or we find in John Robinson's *Honest to God* (1963) statements such as this: 'Traditional theology has been based upon the proofs for the existence of God', that is, the existence of God as 'a separate Being'. 'Traditional orthodoxy', in Robinson's view, sees God as an object, 'out there', so that he becomes 'a part of reality', 'the highest person', 'a particular thing'.[3] While it is true that *conventional* western religion has held such unorthodox and narrow views, to label them as 'traditional theology' betrays an appalling ignorance of the tradition. For example, we find the notion of God as the 'ground of being' to be very common in the mystical writers, although Robinson believes that it represents a 'break with traditional thinking'.[4] It is in fact deeply traditional. St Augustine used depth language about God. Indeed, 'every orthodox Christian writer from St Paul onwards has recognized that God is "depth" as well as "height" though with a less crude interpretation of depth than Dr Robinson's'.[5] In the fourteenth century, Eckhart sees God as the source and ground of the soul. 'When the soul enters into her Ground, into the innermost recesses of her being, divine power suddenly pours into her.'[6] 'To gauge the soul, we must gauge her with God, for the Ground of God and the Ground of the soul are one nature.'[7] Julian of Norwich, also in the fourteenth century, sees God as the ground of the soul.[8]

Again, the view of God which Robinson held to be traditional was in fact debated *ad nauseam* and rejected by the Greek Fathers. Thus St Gregory of Nyssa insisted that 'the concepts which we form in accordance with the understanding and the judgment which are natural to us, basing ourselves on an intelligible representation, create idols of God, instead of revealing to us God himself'. Or St John of Damascus says that 'God does not belong to the class of existing things, not that he has no existence, but that he is above existing things, nay even above existence itself'.[9] In the debate between Eunomius and Gregory of Nyssa, Gregory insisted that *all* names were human, even the name *Theos* (God). As David Jenkins commented after *Honest to God*,

> his attempt to be honest to God is so dishonest to the God of, for example, Athanasius, or the fourth century Cappadocian writers, or of Thomas Aquinas, let alone Augustine, or, again, to the author of *the Cloud of Unknowing*, or, say, to the God who is worshipped in and through the shape of the Orthodox Liturgy.[10]

It is now over thirty years since the publication of *Honest to God*, but in many ways it represented the lowest point of collapse of the spiritual tradition, the climax of a process by which Christian people, including bishops, lost touch with and grew ignorant of their tradition and their spiritual history. The breakdown of the wholeness of spirituality within the West is connected with a number of factors. The movements of Liberal Protestantism and of Barthianism, while opposed to each other, were equally hostile to mysticism, which was seen as a hellenistic distortion of Christianity. Moreover the interest in the *practice* of the Christian religion and its application to the needs of the world had not been taken to involve any great concern with prayer; indeed personal devotion had at times been seen as undermining 'practical Christianity'. The loss of a sense of history is another key factor. 'Starting from where we are now' has often in practice meant 'ignore the past', and so old mistakes have been re-committed unnecessarily, while old well-trodden paths have been pursued once again, even though history has shown them to be dead ends.

The suspicion of mysticism among many Christians has led to the widespread idea that the mystical way, while it may be a valid form of experience, is a minority vocation within the Christian frame. This is only true if one adopts a very narrow definition of mysticism, a definition determined by unusual manifestations of paranormal levels of experience. But the heart of mysticism is union with God, and as such, as Thomas Merton points out, 'the mystical life is essentially the normal way of Christian perfection'.[11] Mystical theology is in fact the theology behind the Nicene Creed, a theology which assumes that the reality of God is beyond the limitations of rational thought, a theology in which God is experienced in love and communion. Mysticism is an opening up of mind and heart to a new way of understanding and relating to God. As such it represents 'religion in its most acute, intense and living stage'.[12] Mysticism is not alien to the Christian spiritual tradition. It has its roots in the New Testament, and it is fundamental to Christian orthodoxy.[13]

EXPLORING THE 'GREAT TRADITION'
However, what is often mistaken for orthodoxy today is quite different, a dreary, narrow, emasculated form of religion, and so it is essential to emphasize the need to look again at the neglected world of Christian spiritual theology. It is obviously not possible

here to do more than introduce some of the central themes in the 'great tradition' of guidance in prayer. It is a tradition which contains within it a wide variety of styles and teachers, approaches and techniques, temperaments and personal types of piety. So any introduction must be oversimplified, and any attempt to divide the tradition will be somewhat arbitrary. But it is possible to isolate a series of spiritualities within the whole, each of which had permanent contributions to make to our practice of spiritual direction. Let us examine six such traditions: the spirituality of the desert; Eastern Orthodox spirituality; monastic spirituality; fourteenth-century mystical spirituality; Counter-Reformation spirituality; and Holiness/Pentecostal spirituality.

i Desert spirituality

From pre-Christian times the desert was the place of encounter with God. Yahweh is the God of the desert who found Israel in a desert land, in the howling wastes of the wilderness (Deuteronomy 32:10). Amos looks to the desert age as one of pure spirituality (Amos 5:25). From the desert age comes the revelation of the Divine Name (Exodus 3:2). The desert too is seen as a place of future renewal (Isaiah 35:1, 6; Hosea 2:14). It was natural then that the early Christian solitaries should seek God in the wastes of the desert, and the desert has been a constant theme of Christian spirituality from the days of the Desert Fathers to Charles de Foucauld and Carlo Carretto in our day. Thomas Merton points out that 'the climate in which monastic prayer flowers is that of the desert, where the comfort of man is absent, where the secure routines of man's city offer no support, and where prayer must be sustained by God in the poverty of faith'. It is here then that 'the monk is bound to explore the inner waste of his own being as a solitary'.[14] The Desert Fathers believed that the wilderness was supremely valuable to God precisely because it was valueless to human beings. There was nothing to exploit in the wasteland. So it was the natural dwelling place of those who sought nothing but themselves. But the desert was also 'the country of madness ... the sterile paradise of emptiness and rage',[15] the place where encounter with evil spiritual forces is most terrible and most profound.

So in the desert the early solitaries lived lives of spiritual warfare in attention and silence. 'It was by silence that the saints grew', said Ammonas, the disciple of St Anthony. It was in the desert's silence that there emerged the contemplative life, and Merton in fact has defined contemplative prayer as 'the preference for the desert'.[16] Here too we encounter the first spiritual directors as people sought wisdom and *diakrisis* from the hermit monks around the Nile valley.

The desert tradition is one of renunciation and practical spirituality. In the desert one is confronted by oneself, and the acquiring of *diakrisis* becomes a matter of life and death, since both slackness and asceticism can lead to spiritual disaster. The desert calls for an intense inner discipline of spirit in order to survive and progress, and St Anthony sees that the formation of such inner discipline can only arise from following the example set by the elders. So the guidance given by the Desert Fathers is in the form not of systematic teaching but of answers to questions of life. 'Speak to me a word, father, that I may live.'[17] As a result, 'One of the striking features of the doctrine of the great desert fathers as of all in every century who have reached their spiritual stature, is how little the substance of that doctrine is tied to any external form of life. They often speak to us with an immediacy that is clinically disturbing.'[18] So St Anthony dismisses the false piety of extreme fasting. 'Some wear down their bodies by fasting. But because they have no discretion, it puts them further from God.'[19] In his description of Anthony when he emerged from his cell, Athanasius sees him as the living example of a disciplined Christian life.

> ... the state of his soul was pure, for it was neither contracted by grief nor dissipated by pleasure. It was not pervaded by jollity or dejection. He was not embarrassed when he saw the crowd, nor was he elated at seeing so many to receive him. No, he had himself completely under control—a man guided by reason and stable in his character.[20]

The desert here is seen as a place of purification, or self-knowledge and self-control, of conflict and victory. Out of the struggle of the desert comes the full-grown spiritual person.

The prayer of the desert is silent, simple and short. Cassian, the most systematic of all the desert teachers, recommends silent prayer and the prayer which is brief and frequent. Short verses of Scripture used constantly is the way to make prayer unceasing. By such prayer we are 'folding the recollection of God into the little space of a meditation upon one verse'.[21] He recommends the constant recollection and use of a short text throughout the day.

This you should write on the threshold and door of your mouth, this you should place on the walls of your house and in the recesses of your heart so that when you fall on your knees in prayer this may be your chant as you kneel, and when you rise up from it to go forth to all the necessary business of life, it may be your constant prayer as you stand.[22]

There is much more in the teaching of the early Desert Fathers which is highly relevant to us today. But essentially they were not teachers so much as Spirit-filled figures in whom God was revealed—in Macarius's words, 'men intoxicated with God'.

Today the desert tradition speaks to us of the need for solitude, for that inner purification which can only come from the experience of being alone and in the wilderness. René Voillaume writes of the desert experience as that of helplessness leading to reliance on God alone.

The desert—the real desert—bears in its physical reality the sign of isolation not only from people and human life, but from any semblance of man's presence and activity. Being something that man cannot put to use, it likewise bears the sign of aridity and consequently of the subduing of all the senses, including both sight and hearing. It also bears the sign of poverty, of austerity, and of the most extreme simplicity. In short it bears the sign of man's complete helplessness as he can do nothing to subsist alone and by himself in the desert, and he thus discovers his weakness and the necessity of seeking help and strength in God.[23]

To Carlo Carretto, the Sahara was the place where he learnt to pray.[24] To many thousands of others, the spiritual desert is the place of *katharsis*, of stripping and nakedness, of our terrible aloneness and God's mysterious revealing.

ii The Eastern Orthodox tradition

The spirituality of Eastern Orthodoxy is inseparable from that of the desert and is continuous with it. It was the tradition of the desert which was later to blossom as *hesychasm*, the distinctive spirituality of the Orthodox, based on the Jesus Prayer. The abiding contributions of the Orthodox to Christian spirituality includes several distinct factors. First, their grasp of the unity of theology and mysticism. In Eastern Christian thought, all theology is mysti-

cal. The description 'theologian' is reserved for St John, St Gregory
Nazianzen and St Simeon, all of them exponents of the life of
union and communion with God. The purpose of all theology is
deification (*theōsis*). There is, in the words of Irenaeus, a 'participation (*metochē*) in God'.[25] 'If the Word is made man, it is that
men might become gods.'[26] Origen too speaks of deification: the
spirit is 'deified by that which it contemplates'.[27] St Athanasius
also speaks of humanity's deifying through the vision of God,[28] and
this tradition is encircled in the Alexandrian school, particularly in
St Cyril of Alexandria (370–444). St John of Damascus says that
humanity was created for deification.[29] St Gregory of Nyssa says
that 'God has made us not simply spectators of the power of God,
but also participants in his very nature'.[30] So, in Lossky's words,
'No one who does not follow the path of union with God can be
a theologian. The way of the knowledge of God is necessarily the
way of deification.'[31] This is not some fringe sectarian belief; it
is absolutely central to Orthodox theology and to all Orthodox
spirituality.

Secondly, their insistence on the *unknowability of God*, and on
the importance of what is termed *apophatic theology. Apophasis*,
or negative theology, is at the heart of the spiritual tradition of
Eastern Christianity, and indeed it is 'the fundamental characteristic
of the whole theological tradition of the Eastern Church'.[32] It is
found in Clement of Alexandria and in Dionysius the Areopagite.
Clement says, 'We fling ourselves upon the majesty of Christ. If
we then advance through holiness towards the Abyss (*bathos*), we
shall have a kind of knowledge of God who contains everything,
knowing not what he is, but what he is not.'[33] Dionysius's *Mystical
Theology* is a treatise on the negative way. When one has 'celebrated the principal affirmations of affirmative theology', he says,
it is then necessary to move beyond them towards a theology of
silence.[34] We must move beyond the understanding to a God who is
unknowable. Knowledge of him is only by a process of *unknowing
(agnōsia)*. It was this essential unknowability of God which the
Cappadocians, St Basil and St Gregory of Nyssa, fought for. For
Gregory of Nyssa all concepts relating to God were idols. 'One
does not know God except in terms of our incapacity to apprehend
him.'[35] So the spiritual path involves the *via negativa*, the way of
ignorance, the tradition which T. S. Eliot summed up so well in
East Coker.

In order to arrive at what you do not know
You must go by a way which is the way of ignorance.
In order to possess what you do not possess
You must go by the way of dispossession.
In order to arrive at what you are not
You must go through the way in which you are not.
And what you do not know is the only thing you know
And what you own is what you do not own
And where you are is where you are not.[36]

Thirdly, the development of the Jesus Prayer as the central element in spiritual guidance in the Eastern churches. The Jesus Prayer is seen as the way both to contemplation and to the unification and integration of the personality. The origins of 'heart prayer' centred on the incarnate Lord through his name can be traced to the *Spiritual Homilies* of Pseudo-Macarius in the late fifth century. Later St John Climacus linked the use of the Prayer with breathing techniques, while later writers such as Nicephorus in *The Method of Hesychastic Prayer* treated the prayer itself as a technique. In the fourteenth century the Jesus Prayer was in use on Mount Athos as part of a great movement of hesychastic prayer. In hesychasm (*hesuchia*, silence), the central concern was the attainment of a state of perpetual prayerfulness, and the use of the Jesus Prayer in this quest remains central to Eastern Orthodox prayer today. When a Russian monk is clothed, the abbot says to him, 'Take, brother, the sword of the Spirit which is the Word of God for continual prayer to Jesus, for you must always have the Name of the Lord Jesus in mind and heart and on your lips, ever saying, Lord Jesus Christ, Son of God, have mercy on me, a sinner.'[37] This is the long form of the Jesus Prayer. In its shortest form it is simply the name of Jesus. Again, the purpose of the prayer is deification. 'The Name of Jesus present in the human heart confers upon it the power of deification.'[38]

Finally, the Eastern tradition sees salvation in terms of transfiguration of the world. The symbol of transfiguration is central to Orthodox mysticism. So in the eucharistic liturgy we are seen as lifted up into the heavens.

The east does not think about salvation in terms of the individual soul returning to its maker; it is visualised rather as a gradual process of transfiguration of the whole cosmos. Man is saved not from the world but into the world.[39]

Spirituality is involved in the transforming and redeeming of matter.

iii   Monastic spirituality

It may seem odd to isolate the monastic element since both the Desert Fathers and the great Eastern Orthodox spiritual guides were monks. There is however a distinct element in the spirituality of the monastic movement as it grew up in the West which has become central in Christian life: the recitation of the Divine Office. The Office of prayer at morning and evening has its roots in the Jewish practice of prayer at daybreak and at the lighting of the lamps, and in apostolic times it is clear that other hours of prayer were also observed (Acts 4:24–30). The Canons of Hippolytus refer to prayers in the middle of the night.[40] There was certainly an established framework of hours of prayer before St Benedict, but it was the Benedictines who developed the primitive Office into a definite shape, with divisions of Psalms, readings and chant. The monks saw the Office as a corporate activity, the essential and central monastic work, the *opus Dei*. From the ninth to the thirteenth century the Psalter was the prayer-book of the devout Christian. St Benedict too saw the primary purpose of the Office to be 'the praise of our Creator',[41] and this remains its essential characteristic.

Today the recovery of an Office which can be a focus of objective praise and contemplation is one of the most urgent needs of the church. The serious Christian needs to be able to grow in prayer within a framework which is scriptural, rich, balanced and God-centred, and which provides her with adequate spiritual nourishment. The monastic contribution was to provide such a framework in the regular liturgical diet of the hours of prayer. The recent revision of the Office in the Roman Communion has produced the three- or four-volumed breviary in English which in many respects fulfils the need, though there is still a great deal of adaptation work to be done so that lay people can play their part in the prayer of the church. To enable individuals to do this is at the heart of spiritual direction.

From monasticism too we have received the three vows of poverty, chastity and obedience which have become the characteristic features of many types of religious community in East and West. Today many are seeking to re-evaluate these vows in relation to the needs of our time. New styles of community are emerging, and many feel the need for a close link with the monastic life while remaining in the world. Again, there is a great deal of work which needs to be done in this area.

iv Fourteenth-century mystical spirituality

In the fourteenth century in Europe there was a great flowering of mysticism, and out of this period came some of the greatest spiritual guides of all time whose writings are highly relevant today. A few may be mentioned here. First, Julian of Norwich, the mystic of tenderness and naturalness in the approach to God. The joy of experience of God by 'a simple intuition of truth' is, she claims, 'an experience common to us all'. It is 'for all and sundry'. Prayer is natural, for humankind is created on the pattern of the Trinity. Not only humanity, but the universe, is contained in God. 'I saw the whole Godhead concentrated as it were in a single point, and thereby I learnt that he is in all things.' Julian holds that prayer and the knowledge of God are not difficult, indeed to know God is easier than to know oneself.

> It came also that I was able to see with absolute certainty that it was easier for us to get to know God than to know our own soul ... God is nearer to us than our soul, for he is the ground in which it stands ... So if we want to know our own soul and enjoy its fellowship, as it were, it is necessary to seek it in our Lord God in which it is enclosed.[42]

Because she held strongly this belief in the closeness of humanity and God, Julian has an optimistic assessment of humanity and the universe, and a belief that sin is relatively unimportant. God permits sin in order that good may be achieved, but she claims that there is a part of the soul which never consents to sin. The image of God is indestructible. Moreover, she claims that 'God showed me that sin need be no shame to man but can even be worthwhile'. She seems to mean by this that sins are disguised virtues for 'in heaven what sin typifies is turned into a thing of honour'.[43] Through contrition, compassion and longing for God, the wounds of sin are healed. Julian's theology here represents a rejection of the inadequate judgement theology associated with Augustine, and a return to the older tradition of Gregory of Nyssa, Isaac the Syrian, and Maximus the Confessor, who, while accepting the reality of sin and judgement, see beyond them to the gathering into one of all things in Christ. Merton has called Julian one of the greatest of

English theologians.[44] Her central emphasis is one of cosmic optimism and of the victory of God's love. 'You would know our Lord's meaning in this thing. Know it well. Love was his meaning.'[45] That love, she says, has never slackened nor ever shall. It is a theology of ultimate reconciliation which is expressed in her famous saying, 'All shall be well', the theme which Eliot takes up at the end of *Little Gidding*.

> And all shall be well
> All manner of thing shall be well
> When the tongues of flame are in-folded
> Into the crowned knot of fire
> And the fire and the rose are one.[46]

In Julian's theology, we find the fullest expression of the concept of the *femininity* of God. 'God is really our Mother as he is Father', she says. 'Our precious Mother Jesus brings us to supernatural birth, nourishes and cherishes us by dying for us, giving us the sacraments, especially the Eucharist, and by the guidance of Holy Church.' When we respond to the mother-love of Christ like children, 'the dear gracious hands of our Mother are ever about us, and eager to help'.[47] In developing this theme, Julian is taking up the spirituality of St Anselm (1033–1109), who addresses Jesus as Mother.[48] But the idea is older. Maternal images are used implicitly in Scripture (Isaiah 46:3; 49:15; 66:9ff; Matthew 23:37), in the apocryphal Acts of Peter and in St John Chrysostom, and in such medieval writers as St Francis of Assisi and St Aelred. Julian however is one of the first female theologians in Christian history, and her writing contains a necessary corrective to the masculinity of God-symbolism. Her mysticism brings tenderness and 'homeliness' to the understanding of God our Mother.[49]

Contemporary with Julian is *The Cloud of Unknowing*, that masterpiece of apophatic mysticism which has been rediscovered in recent years by many who have stumbled for the first time on Christian mystical writings. The 'cloud of unknowing' is the sphere of ignorance, *agnōsia*, which marks the path to God. The author is at pains to stress that the book is for a restricted audience, and that it will mean nothing to those who are not ready for its teachings. The central core of the work is the insistence that the knowledge of God comes not through thinking but through love and the *via negativa*, the way of ignorance, the way of dark faith. 'How shall I think of God?', the author is asked.

For thou hast brought me with thy question into that same darkness, and into that same cloud of unknowing, that I would thou wert in thyself. For of all other creatures and their works, yea, and of the works of God's self, may a man through grace have fullhead of knowing, and well he can think of them; but of God himself can no man think. And therefore I would leave all that thing that I can think, and choose to my love that thing that I cannot think. For why; he may well be loved, but not thought. By love may he be gotten and holden; but by thought never.

The way to God then is through the darkness: 'Pierce that darkness above thee. And smite upon that thick cloud of unknowing with a sharp dart of longing love.'[50]

The world of the fourteenth-century mystics is vast. There is the 'fire mysticism' of Richard Rolle, the stress on 'dark silence' and 'abysmal waylessness' in Ruysbroeck, the personal communion stressed by Thomas à Kempis and Walter Hilton. Those who turn to the fourteenth-century mystics for guidance will often find that they have more to teach of the depths of God than many of our modern teachers do.

v Counter-Reformation spirituality

Like those of the fourteenth century, the spiritual classics of the Counter-Reformation period are considerable, and it will only be possible to refer at length to two of the major spiritual writers, St Ignatius Loyola and St John of the Cross. St Ignatius is often portrayed as a dry intellectual, lacking in warmth and affection. It is true that the fear of being charged with 'illuminism' distorted Jesuit interpretations of Ignatius's teachings and led to some suspicion and wariness of contemplation. Thus a certain narrowness and inflexibility distorted the Ignatian tradition which was not present in its founder. Butler noted that 'the fact that St Ignatius in the Exercises is silent concerning contemplation and contemplative prayer has been, probably, the principal reason why so many of the spiritual writers of the Society have looked on meditation as the normal life-long prayer of devout souls'.[51] In the nineteenth century, the Jesuits were very inflexible and literalist in their interpretation of the *Exercises*. In fact, however, the *Spiritual Exercises* are a treasury of spirituality, and the purpose of them is to enable individuals with good direction, to discover the right form of prayer for them. 'Our Father wanted us, in all our activities, as far as possible, to be free, at ease in ourselves, and obedient to the light given particularly to each one.' 'The Father said to me that there can be no greater mistake in his view in things of the spirit than to want to mould others in one's own image.'[52] Nadal, following Ignatius, stresses the role of the spiritual director in the encouragement of Christian freedom. 'When they judge in the Lord that someone is growing in prayer and led by the good Spirit, they are to avoid interfering. They should rather give him heart and confidence, so that he may grow with ease and strength in the Lord.'[53]

Ignatius is by no means obsolete, and his work is of value today in three specific ways. First, in his concern to create 'a way of avoiding the pitfalls of subjectivism and objectivism' and 'his balanced sense of the relationship between the human and the divine'.[54] Secondly, in his very precise guidance on techniques to aid the growth of prayer. He gives instruction about place of prayer, environment, control of the body and the mind, mental recollection, composition, use of imagination, preparatory prayers and so on. Thirdly, in the high value he places on the imagination. Ignatian contemplation is the climax of a process which includes reading, meditation and prayer. In his instructions on spiritual direction, he says that some of the mysteries may be omitted 'for they serve here to afford an introduction and method for better and more complete contemplation later'.[55] So in reading and meditation there is an increase in longing and in sharpening of the senses which leads to contemplation, a divine gift. In Ignatian thought, consolation is inseparably linked to contemplation. So 'the director is to explain clearly to him what consolation is: spiritual happiness, love, a hope of things eternal, tears, and every interior movement which leaves the soul consoled in the Lord'.[56]

St Ignatius saw the purpose of 'spiritual exercises' to be ridding the soul of all 'inordinate attachments', the necessary preliminary to seeking and finding the will of God.[57] The idea of exercises is not a narrow one, for 'under the name of spiritual exercises is understood every method of examination of conscience, of meditation, of contemplation, of vocal and mental prayer, and of other spiritual operations as shall hereafter be declared'. But can these sixteenth-century methods be of any value today? One recent Jesuit writer has claimed that the *Exercises* ought never to be given as group meditations, and that they are potentially dangerous in the group context.[58] Certainly in St Ignatius there is considerable stress on the need for sensitivity, self-knowledge and personal direction. Particular stress is placed on directing the need for 'spiritual discretion' in the making of an Election, that is, a major decision about one's life. The *Exercises* are in fact all about *choice* and about free decisions before God. 'Ignatian spirituality is about choosing.'

So in using the methods of prayer of Ignatius, one is seeking to achieve the freedom of the Christian person, delivered from inordinate attachments and from the wiles of false spirits. The approach has been compared to the work of analysis. Thus in describing the Second Exercise of the First Week, one commentator notes that 'the aim is to bring home to one a realistic picture of himself as a personality deformed by his past'.[59] The aim is to set the person free from slavery and from all obstacles so that she can attain a state of attention to God.

St John of the Cross and St Teresa together present us with the most detailed account of the spiritual path from the Carmelite tradition. Again, as in St Ignatius, there is the insistence that 'God does not lead us all by the same road' and also that 'contemplation is something given by God'.[60] Like St Ignatius, these writers are conscious of the danger of false mystical paths and of becoming absorbed with the delights of visions and raptures. So St Teresa warns that the highest perfection does not lie in such delights but in the conforming of our will to God's.[61] The uniting of prayer and action is stressed throughout. Love is always the primary test of the mystical life. 'In the evening they will examine thee in love', says St John.[62] St Teresa adds, 'It is not a matter of thinking a great deal but of loving a great deal—so do whatever arouses you most to love'.[63] The test of spirituality is practical: 'The Lord is among the saucepans.'[64] St Teresa explains:

> If contemplation and mental and vocal prayer and the care of the sick and serving about the house and doing menial work even of the lowest sort all serve the guest who comes to be with us and to dine and refresh himself with us, why should we concern ourselves whether we serve him in one way or another?[65]

So St Teresa emphasizes that God leads us to perfection by all kinds of ways. Vocal prayer, for example, must not be despised, because it can be the vehicle of perfect contemplation.[66] Nor should books be neglected. St John too insists on the importance of discursive meditation in the beginnings of the life of prayer, and he values the use of images and devotional objects.[67]

The main concern of St John however is with the transition to contemplative prayer, and with the crisis period which he calls the 'dark night'. These will be examined later in this chapter. Neither St John nor St Teresa associates contemplation with a very advanced state in prayer or sanctification. On the contrary, contemplative prayer is often found in ordinary Christians with some experience of prayer and a sense of purpose. But 'there is no state of prayer so exalted that it will not be necessary to return to the beginnings'.[68] Both saints advise against preoccupation with the intellect in prayer. Indeed St John stands in the direct line of apophatic theology, the tradition of Evagrius, Cassian and Gregory of Nyssa. He speaks of the soul being 'blinded and darkened according to the part which has respect for God and spiritual things' and relying on 'dark faith'.[69] He urges us never to be satisfied with what we can understand of God, but rather with what we cannot understand, for this is the meaning of faith. 'Since God is unapproachable and hidden . . . however much it seems to thee that thou findest and feelest and understandest him, thou must ever hold him as hidden and serve him after a hidden manner as one that is hidden.'[70]

In these great Carmelite saints, particularly in St John, we are given a detailed and comprehensive account of spiritual progress. They are of the utmost importance for spiritual direction in any age. 'In these books, the high value of which the church has proclaimed, directors will find set forth in the most perfect and practical way the indispensable knowledge for guiding souls towards the summits of perfection and for helping them effectually in their difficulties.'[71]

vi   Holiness/Pentecostal spirituality

Finally, a tradition which is more recent in origin, though the experiences which gave it birth lie deep in Christian spiritual history: the Holiness/Pentecostal tradition. Modern neo-Pentecostalism is often looked at in isolation not only from classical Pentecostalism but also from the Holiness movement out of which it grew. The modern movements need to be seen in relationship to the Wesleyan doctrine of entire sanctification which led to the founding of Holiness churches such as the Pentecostal Church of the Nazarene of 1900 which laid great stress on the baptism with the Holy Spirit and with fire, though it did not associate the experience with speaking in tongues. The Holiness churches in general held tongues in low esteem as the least of all the spiritual gifts. They held that the proofs of the 'Second Blessing' were to be found in purity of heart (Acts 15:8–9), the fruits of the Spirit (Galatians 5:22–3), perfect love of God and humanity (Romans 5:8; I Timothy 1:5), and power for effective service to Christ (Acts 1:8). However, out of the Holiness movement grew the early Pentecostal churches.[72] Such large groups as the Assemblies of God and the Elim Church, which date from the early Pentecostal movements, have always stressed both speaking in tongues and healing.

A feature of the recent resurgence of Pentecostalism has been its spread within the Roman Communion, that is, within a tradition whose theological categories are not revivalist but sacramental. To Roman Catholics, indeed to all Catholic Christians, the term 'baptism in the Spirit' cannot be used of an experience subsequent to, and different to, the one baptism. Yet many Catholics would hold, with the statement of the Secretariat for Promoting Christian Unity in Rome, that Pentecostalism is 'a spirituality rather than a systematic theology'.[73] So the experience may be accepted, but its interpretation questioned. An American Presbyterian writer has summarized the main characteristics of Pentecostal spirituality under eight heads: stress on the *experience* of the Holy Spirit; stress on the Pentecostal coming of the Spirit as a continuing event in the life of the church; the view that 'Spirit baptism' is an event distinct from and subsequent to conversion; the view that the Holy Spirit acts differently in baptism/conversion, and in 'Spirit baptism'; various ways of expressing the meaning of 'baptism in the Spirit' in terms of a new sense of reality, power, fullness of life, and so on; stress on the background and preparation for 'Spirit baptism' by way of conversion, purification of heart, prayer, yielding, and expectant faith; a denial of any necessary connection between external rites and 'baptism in the Spirit'; and a close relationship between 'baptism in the Spirit' and speaking in tongues.[74] Within the Pentecostal prayer group, one sees these features manifested. There is the strong sense of experience of the Spirit's presence and closeness, leading to a release and opening out of the personality. There is a sense of joy, leading to praise, and of power, a sense too of expectation that the Lord will act.

Prayer is central to all Pentecostal movements. 'No activity is so

typical of Pentecostals as prayer.'[75] Pentecostals see themselves as
a Spirit-filled people, and there are a number of manifestations of
the Spirit's fullness of which speaking in tongues is the one which
has attracted most attention. It is wrong in a sense to see 'tongues'
as being what the movement is about. It is about the fullness of
the Spirit, the fullness of the gospel, the fullness of experience
of spiritual gifts. It is the manifestation of these gifts, of which
tongues is the most widespread, which is the characteristic feature
of Pentecostal worship. Pentecostals insist that when the Holy
Spirit is received in his fullness, he brings about profound changes
in prayer life. The *Life in the Spirit Seminars Team Manual*, for
example, lists some of these changes. They include a deeper sense
of the reality of God, the Bible coming alive, the impetus to tell
others about Christ, a great sense of sharing in Christian communities and changes in character, as well as the showing forth of the
Spirit's gifts.

However, there is the real danger of self-deception and of false
directions, and many Charismatic groups in history have been led
into heresy and into unbalanced forms of spirituality. Groups soon
find the need to test experiences against the experience of the wider
Christian tradition. One prayer group devised six tests of the Spirit.
The Spirit must be the Spirit of Jesus, so any experience which
detracted from Jesus was put aside. It must be consonant with
Scripture, and if there was clear contradiction of scriptural truth,
it was not acceptable. It must be in harmony with the general
teaching of the church. All members of the prayer group must be
living the sacramental life. All manifestations—tongues, prophecy
or counsel—must be tested by the group. Finally, tranquility of soul
and freedom from strain was sought, and any excess emotionalism,
frenzy or undue excitement was rejected as a contra-indication.[76]
So discernment is necessary.

St Paul warns against lack of balance in the Christian life. In 1
Corinthians 13 he stresses that neither tongues, prophecy, phil-
anthropy nor martyrdom are of value without the supreme spiritual
gift of love. It is love which really brings people into the fullness
of the Holy Spirit. His criterion applies to all the Charismatic gifts.
It is possible to abound in 'gifts of the Spirit' and yet remain carnal
(1 Corinthians 14:37; 3:1). It is possible to speak in tongues and yet
merely build up the self (1 Corinthians 14:4). Direction and
discernment are needed in order to discover the balance of the
Christian life, the *analogia* of faith (Romans 12:6). The decisive

question for all Pentecostal movements in all ages is whether they are able to maintain such a balance within the wholeness of Christian truth. It is indeed the decisive question for all spiritual traditions.

THE WISDOM OF THE TRADITION

From the tradition of these great teachers of prayer, we can learn a great deal that will help and guide us in our Christian discipleship. Three specific contributions are of importance. First, the *spiritual necessity of orthodoxy*. The defence of orthodoxy of faith is often portrayed as an exercise in polemics and intellectual debate, while the devout soul, unconcerned with and unaffected by such controversies, seeks God in the pathways of the Spirit where dogmatic disagreements have no place. In fact, nothing could be further from the truth. The Fathers draw the closest connection between dogma and spirituality. There is a story that some people came to see the desert father Agathon in order to abuse him. 'Are you Agathon the fornicator?' 'Yes', he said humbly. 'Are you Agathon the conceited man?' 'Yes' was the reply. And so they went on to accuse him with all the perjorative terms they could find. At length they said, 'Are you Agathon the heretic?' And he said, 'No', which rather baffled them. He had admitted to being a fornicator, a glutton, arrogant, proud, and so on, but he would not admit to heresy. 'All those other things, they are good for my soul. I should accept those. But to be a heretic—that separates from God.' Heresy is the state of putting oneself outside the sphere of God's revelation.

The supposed contrast, even conflict, between the dogmatic and the mystical would have shocked the early Eastern fathers. Orthodoxy meant right *worship*. For 'worship and ethics, the love of God and the love of man together constitute the only milieu in which there can be a true knowledge of God, and therefore authentic theology'.[77] Worship and theology then constitute a dialectical framework in which God is revealed. As St Basil put it, knowledge is manifold and involves perception, ethics and communion.[78] It involves purification and discipleship.

The knowledge of God is not, and cannot be, a conceptual grasp of a reality perceived through the mind. God is not known in the head. God is the hidden God who is known in the process of inner purification and transformation of consciousness. To believe otherwise is to be an idolater, and idolatry is no mere moral lapse but a heresy, a mistaken view of how things are. The true God is

beyond conception and beyond knowledge. In Gregory of Nyssa's
words:

> True knowledge for the one that is searching is to understand
> that to see consists in not seeing because he transcends all knowl-
> edge by being separated from all parts through his incomprehen-
> sibility as by a darkness. This is why John the Mystic who had
> penetrated into this 'luminous darkness' says that 'no one has
> ever seen God', defining through his negation that the knowledge
> of the divine nature is inaccessible not only to man but to every
> intellectual nature. This is why Moses when he had progressed
> in *gnosis* declares that he sees God in the darkness, that is, he
> knows that God is essentially he who transcends all knowledge
> and is outside the grasp of the mind.[79]

In this vein speaks the entire mystical tradition. The way of knowledge is the way of darkness, for 'God is unapproachable and
hidden.'

Again, the early fathers are most insistent on orthodoxy of incar-
national belief, and at this point the second contribution of the
great tradition becomes clear: its insistence on the *materialistic
basis of spirituality*. The heart of Christian mysticism is the Word
made flesh. 'Regard the flesh, the body, matter, as evil, or even
inferior, and one has already begun the deviation from Christian
truth.'[80] It is because the fullness of the Godhead is bodily present
in Christ that union with God is possible. So Irenaeus says that
God 'became what we are that he might make us in the end what
he is'.[81] Athanasius took up this theme. 'He was humanised that
we might be deified.'[82] He went on in a crucial passage for the
understanding of his doctrine of God and his spirituality: 'Man
could not be deified if joined to a creature, or unless the Son were
true God. Nor could man be brought into the Father's presence
unless it had been his natural and true Word who had put on the
body.'[83] Earlier Tertullian had made the same point. 'If Christ's
being flesh is found to be a lie, then everything that was done by
it was done falsely . . . God's entire work is subverted.'[84]

The debates about the nature of Christ in the early church
were not therefore irrelevant arguments but were of the most vital
significance. The conflict with Arianism raised all the fundamental
issues of God and his relationship with human beings and the
world. For Arius, the essence of God was incommunicable. There
could therefore be no real relationship within the Godhead,

between God and humanity, or between people. The Arian world is a world of separation, the Arian god is remote, despotic, one who cannot, and therefore does not, share his nature. Athanasius saw a close connection between the theology of the Arians and their oppression of the poor. 'Human nature is prone to pity and sympathizes with the poor. But these men have lost even the common sentiments of humanity.'[85] In the nineteenth century, Thomas Hancock pointed out the relevance of the Arian controversy for Christian belief.

> If there is no absolute co-eternal Son, there can be no absolute eternal Father. Unless there be an only begotten Son of God, unless this only begotten Son be the One in whom we all consist, we may have an omnipotent Manufacturer—or rather some omnipotent Manufacturer may have us, as the potter has the vessels, but we men can have no Divine Father.[86]

Right belief about God and right relationship with God are therefore intimately connected. Dogma is not irrelevant to, but essential to, sound spirituality. If Christ is true God, and has raised humanity into God, then there is a true sharing in the common life of the Godhead. 'Man with God is on the throne.' God is not a super-object, a remote being in a lonely universe. That is the Arian god, and it was against this kind of idolatry that the dogma of the Trinity was aimed. For the Trinity speaks of a social God, a God who shares, a God of equality, love, and union.

> The Trinity is ... the unshakeable foundation of all religious thought, of all piety, of all spiritual life, of all experience ... If we reject the Trinity as the sole ground of all reality and of all thought, we are committed to a road that leads nowhere; we end in an *aporia* in folly, in the disintegration of our being, in spiritual death. Between the Trinity and hell there lies no other choice.[87]

The third great contribution of the spiritual guides of the past is their view of the *life of prayer as a way of progress*. This is most important, for it is with progress that spiritual direction is concerned. Progress always involves danger, and in the life of prayer the disciple must know that there are dangers on the road. While the beginnings of the way are often filled with joy, warmth and excitement and are 'the easiest time for the soul',[88] the formation of inner disciplines is most necessary at this stage. If this is not achieved, there will be the danger of too much dependence on feelings and on 'spiritual highs', and these may be followed by a sense of despondency and hopelessness. The way of prayer is marked by change and movement, and it is vital in spiritual guidance that one understands the principles involved.

From the very earliest times, writers have seen spiritual progress as involving three stages: purification, illumination and union with God. Clement of Alexandria writes of the three transitions: from paganism to faith, from faith to knowledge and from knowledge to love.[89] Origen speaks too of purification, learning and love.[90] Pseudo-Dionysius refers to internal harmony, intuitive insight (or contemplation) and union. In Dionysius the 'Three Ways' are clearly described. There is

> the Active Life through the Way of Purification, whereby men may become true servants of God; the Inner Life, the Way of Illumination and of real sonship with God; and the Contemplative Life which is the Unitive Way whereby men may attain to true friendship with God.[91]

In Dionysius and Augustine, the threefold division is seen in relation to mystical prayer. Later St Bernard speaks of 'three kisses'—of the feet (the kiss of the penitent), of the hands (the kiss of the growing Christian), and of the mouth (the kiss of intuitive union). It was St Bonaventure, however, who applied the division to the ordinary spiritual development of the ordinary Christian. The Way of Purgation, he said, leads to peace, the Way of Illumination to truth, and the Way of Union to love.[92] From this time onwards, the threefold pattern recurs in many writers and later becomes a standard part of all Catholic spiritual schools.

The origins of the threefold pattern lie in the biblical teaching about repentance, sanctification and union. The New Testament distinguishes between the principles or beginnings of the Christian life, and the perfection or maturity of that life (Philippians 1:6; 3:12; Colossians 1:28; Hebrews 6:1). Repentance is the foundation, and is associated closely with baptism, enlightenment and the giving of the Spirit (Hebrews 6:2–4). It inaugurates a process of renewal, the putting on of the new humanity (Galatians 4:23f). But there is also continual progress towards the maturity of the full-grown person (Ephesians 4:13), the fullness of God (Ephesians 3:19) and of Christ (4:13). There is growth into Christ (Ephesians 4:15), continuance in faith (Colossians 1:23), spiritual warfare (Ephesians 6:12f), increase in knowledge and discernment (Philippians 1:9), in wisdom and spiritual understanding (Colossians 1:9). Within a developing Christian life, there is purgation (Colossians 3:5) while the new person is being renewed. There is also the illumination (*photismon tes gnoseos tes doxes tou Theou*, 1 Corinthians 4:6), the anointing of the Spirit who brings knowledge (1 John 2:20). And there is union, when 'they shall see his face, and his Name shall be on their foreheads' (Revelation 22:4).

John Robinson and others have suggested that today the process of the Three Ways is being reversed, and people often come to the experience of union first.[93] But this is to misunderstand both the processes of prayer and the contemporary scene. There cannot be the experience of union without a radical transformation of consciousness in which there is a transcendence of the ego, and an entering into God-consciousness. This is the purpose of the Illuminative Way, and it cannot begin until self-knowledge and self-discipline have prepared the way. The precise forms in which these developments occur in the individual will vary enormously, but there cannot be a bypassing of the fundamental processes. What is certainly true, however, is that many today become aware of the experience of union, and this can lead to delusions and bogus forms of contemplation.

It is entirely wrong, on the other hand, to associate contemplative prayer with some very advanced stage of holiness. Part of the difficulty here is one of terminology, and often the word is used loosely. In the Middle Ages the word 'contemplation' had a very wide reference indeed. Thus St Thomas Aquinas:

> Contemplation is sometimes taken *strictly* to mean the act of the intellect meditating on divine things . . . [It is] commonly [taken] in another way to mean every act by which one who has withdrawn from external affairs occupies himself with God alone in one of two ways . . . by reading . . . by prayer. Therefore Hugh enumerates the three parts of contemplation as being first, reading, second, meditation, and third, prayer.[94]

Here contemplation is used as a term to cover the whole life of prayer. It is necessary in reading the various writings therefore to be clear in what sense a word is being used, or there can be great confusion.

The classification by Hugh of Saint-Victor (1096–1142) to which

Aquinas made reference represents one of the important contributions to the study of the principles of contemplative prayer.
Hugh distinguishes meditation from contemplation by saying that

> meditation is ... a certain inquisitive power of the soul that
> shrewdly tries to find out things that are obscure and to disen-
> tangle those that are involved. Contemplation is the alertness of
> the understanding which, finding everything plain, grasps it
> clearly with entire apprehension.

In meditation, he says, there is a sort of wrestling match between
ignorance and knowledge, and it is through this conflict that light
is revealed. There is, in the process of prayer, a pattern of struggle,
followed by insight. Hugh identifies the role of meditation as
roughly equivalent to the former, contemplation to the latter.

> Meditation is the concentrated and judicious reconsideration of
> thought that tries to unravel something complicated or scruti-
> nises something obscure to get at the truth of it. Contemplation
> is the piercing and spontaneous intuition of the soul, which
> embraces every aspect of the objects of the understanding.[95]

Struggle followed by rest is a recurrent theme. A little earlier
than Hugh, St Peter Damian (1007-72) wrote that the end of the
Christian way of life is rest, but that such rest is only reached after
much labour and striving, until finally 'the soul may be lifted up
by the grace of contemplation to search for the very face of truth'.
In our day, Bernard Lonergan has described the same process
towards understanding: a period of tension and rational inquiry,
followed by a sudden and unexpected insight.[96] Similarly, the Russian archbishop Anthony Bloom distinguishes meditation, 'an
ascetical exercise of intellectual sobriety ... a piece of straight
thinking under God's guidance', from contemplation, in which
there is a laying aside of thought and of intellectual activity.[97]

It is however in the work of St John of the Cross, and to a lesser
degree in St Teresa, that we find the most systematic and detailed
account of the stages of spiritual progress. At the centre of St
John's account is his theme of the 'dark night of the soul'. This is
a concept which is so frequently misunderstood that it will be
examined at some length.

There is, says St John, a 'dark night through which the soul
passes in order to attain to the Divine light of the perfect union of
the love of God'. God 'will lead the soul by a most lofty path

of dark contemplation and aridity wherein it seems to be lost'.[98] The dark night of St John of the Cross is not a phase, still less is it a pathological feature of the Christian life: it is a symbol of the entire process of movement towards God. Those who enter the night never leave it, though the night changes. St John says that there are three stages associated with the darkness of privation (of human desires), the darkness of faith, and the darkness of God.

> There are three reasons why we may say that this journey which the soul makes towards union with God is called 'night'. First, as concerns the point from which the soul sets out, its desires must be deprived of the delight of all the worldly things which it possessed by being denied them. This negation and privation is as it were night for all the natural senses of man. Second, as concerns the means or way by which the soul must travel to reach this union which is faith. This also is darkness to the understanding and as night. Thirdly, as concerns the goal to which the soul travels which is God. He too is no more and no less than a dark night for the soul in his life. These three kinds of night must pass through the soul, or rather the soul must pass through them, and reach divine union with God.

He goes on to say:

> These three parts of the night are all one night; but like night itself it has three parts. For the first part, which is that of sense, is comparable to the beginning of night, the point at which things begin to fade from sight. And the second part which is faith is comparable to midnight which is total darkness. And the third part is like the close of night which is God, the which part is now near to the light of day.[99]

The night of sense is connected with the Way of Purgation, for St John says:

> This house of sensuality being now set at rest, that is, mortified, its passions extinguished, and its desires set at rest and put to sleep by means of this most fortunate night of sensible purgation, the soul went forth to set out upon the road and way of the spirit which is that of progressives and proficients, otherwise called the Illuminative Way or the way of infused contemplation.[100]

But why is the entry into darkness called the Illuminative Way? St

John explains: 'The clearer the light the more it blinds and darkens the eye of the soul; and the more directly one looks at the sun, the greater the darkness and privation it causes to the visual faculty.'[101] The darkness is thus the subjective experience of the Divine Light. In *The Living Flame of Love*, St John speaks of God as fire and light, and he emphasizes that the fire which glorifies the soul is the same fire which once purged it in the process of drying and stripping. For he says, 'to sight that is weak and not clear, infinite light is total darkness.'[102]

Darkness is inescapable and essential in the spiritual life, but it is necessary to distinguish darkness in general from the dark night of which St John speaks. In the Christian experience of God, there is an encounter with darkness at various levels. There is the darkness of sin and of the loss of God. There is the darkness which is a normal part of the psychological response to God. But the darkness of which St John speaks is a more continuous and a theological experience. Boros notes that 'the Fathers of the church repeatedly experienced God in darkness. This is perhaps the most distinctive and existentially most significant of the names of God ... God comes towards men from out of the darkness'.[103] In saying this, these writers were testifying to an experience which was well known in pre-Christian spiritual traditions. Thus the Bhagavad Gita teaches that 'what is night for all beings is the time of waking for the disciplined soul'.

The darkness is first the experience of purification, of the light of God which dazzles the soul, and which is experienced most strongly in the beginnings of the prayer of contemplation. 'The light of the illuminative way strikes darkness to the soul. Nevertheless it is by the light of the illuminative way that the inwardness of things is finally understood, and the true meaning of love and life is learned.'[104] Van Zeller speaks of 'positive darkness', a darkness which achieves what years of study cannot achieve.[105] So darkness is a purifier, a deepener of the spirit, a light-bringer. But the darkness is painful, and there is no way of avoiding that pain if progress is to be made. Thomas Merton emphasized the vital nature of the experience of darkness and doubt.

> We too often forget that Christian faith is a principle of questioning and struggle before it becomes a principle of certitude and of peace. One has to doubt and reject everything in order to believe firmly in Christ, and after one has begun to believe, one's

faith itself must be tested and purified. Christianity is not merely a set of foregone conclusions. The Christian mind is a mind that risks intolerable purifications and sometimes, indeed very often, the risk turns out to be too great to be tolerated. Faith tends to be defeated by the burning presence of God in mystery and seeks refuge from him, flying to comfortable social forms and safe conventions in which purification is no longer an inner battle but a matter of outward gesture.[106]

The way from knowledge to innocence, the purification of the heart, is a way marked by struggle and conflict. Yet if we stay within the darkness, stick close to the cross, through death we will come to know the God who reveals himself in the process of dying and renewal.

The darkness then is not a description of a psychological condition. It is an integral part of the revelation. God is known in the darkness of Sinai and of Calvary. So Karl Barth says that 'one must know the God who is *above* us and his hidden nature'.[107] The early Eastern fathers would have heartily agreed. They seem to have had no equivalent of the 'dark night of the soul', but they had a strong sense of the 'Divine darkness'.[108] This darkness is related to *agnōsia*, the way of unknowing. So Moses ascends from the level of understanding into the dark cloud. So Clement of Alexandria refers to God as the abyss.[109] Thus Gregory of Nyssa points out that 'the closer the spirit comes to contemplation the more it sees that the divine nature is invisible. The true knowledge of him whom it seeks lies in understanding that seeing consists in not seeing.'[110] Dionysius sees 'transcendent darkness' and 'inaccessible light' as alternative symbols of the God who is beyond knowledge. 'The divine darkness is the inaccessible light where God dwells.' It is 'the superessential ray of the divine darkness'.[111] This is precisely what St John of the Cross teaches. In the path to God 'the soul has to proceed rather by unknowing than by knowing',[112] but the end is deification, the soul becomes 'after a certain manner God by participation'.[113] The way is both light and darkness.

But in the contemplation of which we are speaking, whereof God, in one act, is communicating to the soul light and love together, which is loving and supernatural knowledge, and may be said to be like heat-giving light which gives out heat, for that light also enkindles the soul in love; and this is confused and obscure to the understanding since it is knowledge of contemplation which, as St Dionysius says, is a ray of darkness to the understanding.[114]

So the dark night represents a theological reality, not simply a transitory human experience of forsakenness. It is an essential element in revelation.

> The dark night is a negative way of experiencing God. It is the counterpart of negative or apophatic (dark) theology. Negative theology proceeds by denying to God all the limitations of created reality; in a true sense it is non-knowledge. The dark night is the experience of void, of emptiness, of no-thing and non-being: it is the condition of *kenosis* and poverty of spirit.[115]

St John's concern is both with the theology of contemplation and with the practical guidance of those entering the night. There are three signs, he explains, by which an individual may know if he is being led from the early stages of prayer towards some kind of contemplation. At what point may he safely leave aside the method of discursive meditation? St John insists that, important as this is, it must happen 'neither sooner nor later than when the Spirit bids him'. The three signs are: first, 'his realization that he can no longer meditate or reason with the imagination, neither can take pleasure therein as he was wont to do aforetime'. Secondly, 'a realization that he has no desire to fix his meditation or his sense upon other particular objects, exterior or interior'. The third and surest sign is 'that the soul takes pleasure in being alone and waits with loving attentiveness upon God, without making any particular meditation . . . without any particular understanding'. He adds: 'These three signs, at least, the spiritual person must observe in himself, all together, before he can venture safely to abandon the state of meditation and sense and to enter that of contemplation and spirit.'[116]

The onset of the dark night represents a spiritual crisis, and it is most important that 'at this time the soul must be led in a way entirely contrary to the way wherein it was led at first'.[117] St John explains more fully how one should now pray.

> The way in which souls should behave in this night of the senses is that they should not concern themselves at all with discourse and meditation, for it is no longer a suitable time for such things. Let them leave the soul in tranquility and quietness even though

it may seem clear to them that they are doing nothing and are wasting time.[118]

Dom John Chapman (1865–1933), one of the greatest exponents of Carmelite spirituality, popularized the term 'ligature', originally used by the Jesuit Auguste Poulain (1836–1919), to describe the transition to contemplation. According to Poulain, the term 'ligature' signifies that the soul is somehow bound and can only move with difficulty.[119] But Chapman says that it is simply that one cannot do two things at once, and if the intellect is occupied with God, it cannot also practice meditation on a subject.[120] It is therefore of the utmost importance that the spiritual guide does not attempt to force intellectual or imaginative activity at this point when they are not possible. St John has very harsh words to say about bad direction at this point, which will be noted later. But the essential point is that the transition to contemplative prayer is not unusual. As Trueman Dicken comments:

> It may be confidently said that many many souls in this country at the present day reach this stage of the ligature. Because few directors are able to recognize the state or have sufficient knowledge of the principles involved at this point, only a very small proportion of such souls is adequately directed. Contemplation is far too commonly believed to pertain almost exclusively to the religious life and to accompany an abnormally saintly character ... St John of the Cross and St Teresa make it clear that the ligature is found in souls which are far from perfect and that the condition of contemplative prayer is not near sanctity, but only serious single-minded purpose and a certain amount of experience in prayer.[121]

The readiness of many Christians to enter on a contemplative way of praying and the unreadiness of many spiritual guides to help them is a particularly sad combination which has been the subject of comments for a long period. As long ago as 1930 Father Longridge was complaining that many individuals were ready to move beyond meditation if only they knew about the further stages of prayer and received help and encouragement.[122] Even earlier, in 1903, the French writer Letourneau observed:

> For want of a wise direction such souls may be kept in unsuitable ways of prayer for long years. They persist, in good faith, in trying to make a meditation every morning, when often medi-

tation is useless to them, and morally impossible; and many, understanding nothing of their condition, will end by acquiring a distaste for prayer altogether.[123]

The strongest criticisms of incompetent direction however come from St John of the Cross himself. He devotes a chapter of *The Ascent of Mount Carmel* to 'the harm that certain spiritual masters may do to souls when they direct them not by a good method'.[124] The basic trouble, he says, is 'lack of discretion'. In *The Living Flame of Love* he develops his views on this theme, and what he says here is so important that it merits quotation at length. He begins by asserting,

> ... it is of great importance for the soul that desires to profit, and not to fall back, to consider in whose hands it is placing itself; for as is the master, so will be the disciple, and as is the father, so will be the son. There is hardly anyone who in all respects will guide the soul perfectly along the highest stretch of the road, or even along the intermediate stretches, for it is needful that such a guide should be wise and discreet and experienced. The fundamental requirement of a guide in spiritual things is knowledge and discretion; yet if a guide have no experience of the higher part of the road, he will be unable to direct the soul therein, when God leads it so far. A guide might even do the soul great harm if, not himself understanding the way of the spirit, he should cause the soul, as often happens, to lose the unction of these delicate ointments, wherewith the Holy Spirit gradually prepares it for himself, and if instead of this he should guide the soul by other and lower paths of which he has read here and there, and which are suitable only for beginners. Such guides know no more than how to deal with beginners.[125]

But when contemplation begins, it is vital that the soul should not be kept in the forms of meditation.

> Wherefore in this state the soul must never have meditation imposed upon it, nor must it make any acts nor strive after sweetness or fervour, for this would be to set an obstacle in the way of the principal agent, who, as I say, is God.[126]

The spiritual director therefore needs to remember that the soul is being led into the wilderness in order to experience freedom, and taste the sweet manna.[127] Often however what happens is quite different.

> For whenever God is anointing the soul with some most delicate unction of loving knowledge—serene, peaceful, lonely, and very far removed from sense and from all that has to do with thought—and when the soul cannot meditate or find pleasure in thought, whether in higher things or in lower, or in any knowledge, since God is keeping it full of that lonely unction and inclined to solitude and rest, there will come some director who has no knowledge save of hammering and pounding like a blacksmith.[128]

These directors with 'no understanding of the degrees of prayer or of the ways of the spirit' fail to see that the acts and methods which they urge on the soul belong to its past. So the director 'spoils the wondrous work that God was painting on it [the soul]. In this way the soul neither does one thing nor makes progress in another: it is just as if the director were merely striking an anvil.'[129]

> Let such as these take heed and remember that the Holy Spirit is the principal agent and mover of souls and never loses his care for them: and that they themselves are not agents but only instruments to lead souls by the rule of faith and the law of God, according to the spirit that God is giving to each one. Let them not, therefore, merely aim at guiding a soul according to their own way and the manner suitable to themselves, but let them see if they know the way by which God is leading the soul, and if they know it not, let them leave the soul in peace and not disturb it.
>
> God, like the sun, is above our souls and ready to enter them. Let spiritual directors then be content with preparing the soul according to evangelical perfection, which consists in the detachment and emptiness of sense and of spirit: and let them not seek to go beyond this in the building up of the soul, for that work belongs only to the Lord, from whom comes down every perfect gift.[130]

The director needs to recognize that 'progress' cannot now be evaluated in terms of activity or understanding, for the soul is being led towards the incomprehensible and the transcendent. Directors who themselves have not advanced beyond the meditation stage can disturb the peace of such souls. 'Such persons have no knowledge of what spirituality is, and they offer a great insult and great irreverence to God, by laying their coarse hands where God is working.'[131] He goes on to compare them to 'little foxes which tear down the flowering vine of the soul'.[132] They are to be condemned because 'the business of God has to be undertaken with great circumspection and with eyes wide open'.[133] Even worse, says St John, some directors cling to souls when they cannot help them. They 'tyrannize over souls and take away their liberty'.[134]

St John's analysis is directly applicable to the present day when many individuals are being led to a more direct and simple form of prayer, but where too often the priest or minister who meets them is not only unable to understand them, but even positively hinders them through his or her own lack of insight. Contemplation is by no means an unusual form of prayer, nor should it be seen as a style which is particularly suitable to enclosed monasteries or religious houses. On the contrary, the experience of the Little Brothers of Jesus suggests that it is the form of prayer which is most suited to the conditions of modern life. Abbé Godin, who founded the Mission de Paris, wrote: 'Let all missionaries who consecrate themselves to christianizing the working world be first of all contemplatives.'[135] Contemplatives are to be found in the back streets of cities as well as in cells. Wherever they are, they are the clear eyes of the church, and they need the most special care.

5
The practice of the life of prayer

> I don't think, amateurs at prayer as most of us
> are, that we pay half enough attention to pre-
> prayer. Like all amateurs we see the romance but
> not the pitfalls, the fears and the costly self-giving.
> We have the audacity to suppose that prayer is
> something we ought to be able to do.
>
> MONICA FURLONG[1]

OBSTACLES TO PRAYER

Prayer is the fundamental relationship of humanity to God, a state
of attention to God, involving the whole personality. 'In prayer',
wrote the nineteenth-century Bishop Theophan, 'the principal thing
is to stand before God with the mind in the heart, and to go on
standing before him unceasingly day and night until the end of
life.'[2] This expression 'the mind in the heart' is a favourite one
of the Eastern fathers, and is their way of insisting that prayer
must involve the unifying of the personality, the integration of
mind and heart into one centre. They also insist that prayer is
primarily the action of God. 'Prayer is God', wrote St Gregory of
Sinai in the fourteenth century, 'who works all things in all men.'
In another place he defines prayer as 'the manifestation of baptism'.[3] Prayer then is not essentially a work but the manifesting
and flowering of God's grace in us. All prayer then is charismatic,
all prayer is a gift. There is an Eastern story of a person who came
to a monk and asked, 'Father, what is prayer?' The monk held out
his hands and flames shot up from his fingers. 'That is prayer', he
said. He was a soul on fire, and when necessary he could manifest
the fact. To pray then is to be aflame with God. The purpose of
human effort, and of spiritual direction, is simply to clear away
obstacles to this manifestation of the divine flame.

The most fundamental of these obstacles is, of course, sin. That

may seem a rather obvious point, but it is easily forgotten that
ethics and spirituality are one. Today when we tend to have moralistic notions of sin, we need to recover the theological understanding of the Scriptures, and to remember that 'sin for Jews was seen
as a quenching of the Spirit'.[4] It was thus the very negation and
opposite of the path of prayer. Thus K. E. Kirk defines sin as 'an
impediment to, or even a reversal of, spiritual progress'.[5] Scripture
is emphatic that it is human sin which separates from God. 'The
Lord's arm is not so short that he cannot save, nor his ear too dull
to hear. It is your iniquities that raise a barrier between you and
your God. Because of your sins, he has hidden his face so that he
does not hear you' (Isaiah 59:1–2). Throughout the Bible, there
are a number of specific aspects of human sinfulness which are
named as definite obstacles to prayer.

First, refusal to forgive. Forgiveness in prayer is not possible if
there is a refusal to forgive others (Matthew 6:15). Secondly, anger
and quarrelsome thoughts. Thus St Paul urges prayers to be said
in the congregation by people who 'shall lift up their hands with
a pure intention, excluding angry or quarrelsome thoughts' (1
Timothy 2:8). The implication is that such thoughts hinder or
prevent prayer. Certainly the experience of Christians is that angry
thoughts are among the commonest forms of distraction, and they
may in fact become a form of 'anti-prayer', the shaping of a
consciousness which is of the flesh, not of God. Thirdly, refusal to
be reconciled. The existence of disharmony, linked with injustice
in social relationships, is seen in the prophets as a barrier to prayer.
'When you lift your hands outspread in prayer, I will hide my face
from you. Though you offer countless prayers I will not listen.
There is blood on your hands' (Isaiah 1:15). The context makes
clear that what is actually preventing the prayer from being heard
is the sickness of the nation (1:5–6), and the refusal to seek justice
and mercy (1:17). Similarly Jesus warns that if one is bringing a
gift and suddenly remembers a grievance, it is necessary to sort
this out. 'First go and make peace with your brother and only then
come back and offer your gift' (Matthew 5:23–4).

A fourth area in which prayer can be hindered is that of distorted
sexuality and lust. There is no hint in the Bible of the Manichean
view that sexuality and physical relationships are the enemy of
spirituality. But there is certainly the sense that disorder in sexuality
is related to disorder in the spiritual life. So St Peter urges couples
to conduct their married lives with understanding, and tells hus-

bands to honour the woman's body, because they share together in the grace of God. 'Then your prayers will not be hindered' (I Peter 3:7). Self-control, self-discipline and sobriety are linked to prayer and are its essential prerequisites. The same epistle speaks of 'an ordered and sober life given to prayer' (4:7). St James blames the fact that prayer requests are not answered on the fact that people pray from wrong motives, in particular the quest for pleasure (James 4:2–3).

Fifthly, involvement in the occult and in magical rites is seen in the Old Testament as an impediment to spirituality. The Mosaic Law calls dabbling with wizards, spirits and soothsayers an 'abomination' (Deuteronomy 18:10–12). Disobedience to God's will is a sixth way in which prayer can be frustrated. God listens to those who obey his will (John 9:31). Seventhly, refusal to confess one's sins in the community seems to be suggested as an obstacle by St James, who urges such confession combined with mutual prayer in order that healing may result (James 5:16). The implication is that it may fail to occur if confession and prayer are absent. Finally, greed and avarice are listed in Luke 6:38 where it is pointed out that it is the person who gives generously who will receive from God.

Sin is therefore the first type of hindrance to the life of prayer that must be recognized, and the examination of one's motives and one's life is essential if prayer is to flourish. There can be no spiritual life if ethical demands are bypassed or sins ignored. So all Christian liturgies begin with recollection, confession and the cry for mercy '*Kyrie Eleison*'. Similarly, at the heart of all spiritual discipline is the search for self-knowledge. 'The first step to sanctity', wrote Thomas Merton, 'is self-knowledge.'[6] Merton even defined prayer as 'an awareness of one's inner self'.[7] To go deep into one's own being is an essential step in learning to pray.

> The fact is . . . that if you descend into the depths of your own spirit . . . and arrive somewhere near the centre of what you *are*, you are confronted with the inescapable truth that, at the very root of your existence, you are in constant and immediate and inescapable contact with the infinite power of God.[8]

This introversion, this turning inwards must not stop. We must go beyond the self to God, the deepest centre of consciousness. Yet without self-discovery there can be no further progress. 'In order to find God whom we can only find in and through the depths of

our own soul, we must first find ourselves.'⁹ Without such self-
knowledge our love remains superficial. But the self which we seek
to know is not the fleeting ego which provides one's normal focus
of awareness. The movement which the tradition calls the Purgative
Way is essentially concerned with stripping away the false self, the
removal of illusions. Jung warned that 'whoever goes into himself
risks a confrontation with himself', but he went on to point out
that 'this confrontation is the first test of courage on the inner
way'.¹⁰ It is a confrontation with one's own inner darkness, and it
can be a frightening experience. But it is nevertheless necessary to
wholeness and therefore to prayer. Michael Tippett's oratorio *A
Child of Our Time* contains the exclamation, 'I would know my
shadow and my light, so shall I at last be whole.'

The acquaintance with one's inner depths is intimately connected
with the encounter with God. For, as St Isaac the Surian put it,
'the ladder which leads to the kingdom is hidden within your own
soul. Flee from sin, dive into yourself, and in your soul you will
discover the stairs by which to ascend.'¹¹ The process of self-
discovery is inseparable from personal relationships. It is through
the encounter with others that we grow in self-knowledge. Growth
cannot occur in a vacuum, and so the establishment of sound
relationships within a family is of the utmost importance to the
future health of the spirit. Out of the experience of *lack of love*
can come a spirituality of self-centredness, the fruit of bitter resent-
ment. One experienced spiritual director, John Dalrymple, has
therefore stressed the fact that the initial training in prayer is
always a training in personal relationships. Christian faith, he
insists, cannot be communicated impersonally. 'The thing that
comes first in training for the life of prayer is a healthy relationship
with other people. People do not develop towards God by growing
away from men. The opposite is true.'¹² The sense of interdepen-
dence of relationship with God and relationship with human beings
is very biblical. 'He judged the cause of the poor and needy: then
it was well. Is not this to know me? says the Lord' (Jeremiah 22:16
– RSV). 'If anyone says, "I love God" and hates his brother, he is
a liar: for he who does not love his brother whom he has seen
cannot love God whom he has not seen' (1 John 4:20). So there is
a horizontal dimension in spiritual growth. How can a person
be a friend of God if she is incapable of friendships with people?
Inability to relate at the human level is an impossible basis for the
building up of spiritual relationships.

So the best preparation for the life of prayer is to become more intensely human. Sin diminishes and distorts one's humanity. Lack of self-knowledge and inability to relate to people are both signs that one is far from mature humanity. Both require a degree of depth, and so one of the factors which will always work against growth in prayer is shallowness and lack of inner discipline. The word which most accurately conveys the condition is the word *promiscuity*. Today we tend to restrict the word to the narrow sexual area, and even there it is used imprecisely. We seem in fact to believe in and accept promiscuity in every sphere except the sexual! For the *Shorter Oxford English Dictionary* defines 'promiscuous' as follows:

1 Consisting of members or elements of different kinds pressed together without order; or mixed and disorderly composition or character.

2 That is without discrimination or method, confusedly mingled, indiscriminate.

3 Casual, careless, irregular.

To apply this definition to the life of prayer and to spirituality is to see how dangerous is promiscuity of the spirit. It does not allow prayer to progress. In Jesus's parable of the sower, the seed which falls into good soil is that which bears fruit, while that which falls along the wayside comes to nothing. St Gregory of Sinai put the same point when he said, 'Trees which are repeatedly transplanted do not grow roots.'[13] So in the life of the spirit, there is a vital place for disciplined rule. Without this inner *askesis*, the life will wither for lack of roots. The deeper the degree of self-knowledge, the greater the need for this *askesis* of spirit. For the encounter with the depths of one's consciousness is an encounter with the shadow, the dark side of oneself. In particular one meets the forces of pride and egocentricity, as well as the temptation to despair. The latter may well intensify as the insight into the dark side of one's nature deepens. Spiritual pride, however, is the hazard of all religious people, and it is a major obstacle to spiritual growth. The disciplines of self-examination and confession, of humble service to others, of learning to receive as well as to give, are valuable correctives. Without constant vigilance, they are always likely to occur. Without purity of heart and continuous *metanoia*, spirituality becomes demonic.

THE PRAYER OF THE BODY

Prayer is not an activity of the mind, for God is not in the head. It is an activity of the whole person, and God is in the wholeness. So the *askesis* of the body is vital, and in the preparation for prayer attention needs to be given to the achievement of physical stillness, the acceptance of the rhythm of eating, sleeping and relaxing which are essential to a balanced spiritual life. Spiritual direction will involve a good deal of time spent in these areas, for lack of discretion in these matters can mean spiritual as well as physical harm. The Eastern teachers, both Christian and non-Christian, are more insistent than most of those in the West that 'physical conditions matter a great deal in making possible contemplative prayer',[14] and this includes not only the condition of one's own body, but also physical surroundings. In the attainment of physical relaxation, many have found the disciplines of Yoga useful, and there are valuable studies of the use of Yoga postures in the growth of Christian prayer by Dechanet, Slade and others.[15] But bodily prayer is not peculiarly Eastern, and is assumed by St Thomas Aquinas and by the Nine Ways of Prayer of St Dominic.

The theological basis of the use of the body in prayer is the Incarnation. 'Even what you do in the flesh is spiritual', St Ignatius of Antioch insists, 'because you do everything in Jesus Christ.' St Athanasius seems to have attached theological significance to the fact that when St Anthony eventually died at a ripe old age, there was still nothing wrong with his teeth! The life of prayer certainly presupposes a reasonably balanced bodily condition, for neglect of the body can prevent prayer. 'If you alternately starve and stuff, your prayer will at best be erratic.'[16] One of the important tasks of the spiritual director is to protect the body from abuse, for example, from exhaustion due to overactivity and lack of sleep, or from undernourishment through abuse of fasting.

But there is a positive as well as a negative role in guidance in this area, for the body has a place in prayer itself. The question of posture may seem a trivial one, but it is of the greatest importance, and a lot of time needs to be given to it. People need to experiment in finding the right position for them – standing, kneeling, sitting – all have much to be said in their favour, and none is sacrosanct. (There seems little to be said in favour of the 'shampoo position' so beloved of Anglicans – the body bent over, the head bowed, and one hand raised to shield the eyes.) Father Jim Wilson used to recommend a simple method of relaxing the body in prayer by sitting in an upright position with both feet flat on the floor, straight back and head up, hands on lap and eyes closed. Once in this position, the feet and legs are relaxed, then arms and hands, especially the hands, followed by the stomach muscles, the neck and face, and lastly the eyes. After several deep breaths, the process of mental stillness is begun by use of short phrases of prayer.[17] St Teresa also used to recommend sitting in a comfortable position for prayer. Others find the half-lotus position best, or simply sitting cross-legged on the floor. The question of position is not unimportant, and time spent on it is not wasted.

Again, people need to be encouraged to use the various parts of the body in prayer. This is particularly important because of the overemphasis in our culture and in churches on mental concentration. Of course, attention is a central part of prayer, but continuous attention of the mind is neither desirable nor possible. St Thomas Aquinas points out that even saints do not *always* concentrate, and he stresses the importance of worshipping with the body.[18] In St Dominic's Nine Ways, gestures are emphasized – bowing, prostration, weeping, genuflecting, kneeling, standing with hands outstretched and so on. In the adaptation of Patanjali's Yoga Sutras used by the Anglican priest Herbert Slade, there is use of a series of postures – the deep obeisance, the shoulder stand, the plough, the folded leaf and so on – as well as a stress on the importance of correct breathing and concentration.[19] In Patanjali he finds an approach to the body which is particularly conducive to the growth of contemplation. Thus Patanjali stresses that the posture one adopts must be firm and pleasant, and that when such a posture is attained, the body is freed from disturbances. Similarly breathing correctly removes the veil over the inner light.[20] Slade also uses the method of physical contemplation in the Tai Chi Ch'uan, a Chinese meditation dance, as a way of bringing the body to stillness.

The voice is an organ of the body which should not be despised. Simon Tugwell comments that it is a pity that we tend now to talk about 'praying' rather than 'saying our prayers'. 'Praying' sounds more portentous and ambitious. 'Saying our prayers' is more modest, perhaps more realistic.[21] When St Thomas was asked whether prayer ought to be vocal, he replied with a whole doctrine of the interaction of soul and body.[22] The danger is that we again insist too much on the place of the mind, and therefore 'we do not pray in a sufficiently human way'.[23] We are afraid of speaking our prayers aloud. The early Christians certainly did not share our embarrassment. The nun Aetheria who visited Jerusalem in the early fifth century said that the reading of the Gospel at Mass was greeted with *rugitus et mugitus* – roaring and bellowing – by all the congregation. One of the contributions of the Charismatic renewal of prayer has been to reclaim the voice for the prayer of praise. Again 'there is a time for keeping silent, and a time for speaking' (Ecclesiastes 3:7) and an aim of spiritual direction should be to discern the times.

At this point it is worth making some brief reference to 'praying in tongues', one of the central features of Pentecostal spirituality. There is nothing particularly mysterious about tongues. They are not language, and they have no syntax: they cannot be translated (interpretation of tongues is *not* translation). There are many tape-recordings of tongue-speaking, and they all manifest the same pattern of strings of syllables, sounds taken from a variety of sources, put together haphazardly in units which have a sentence-like shape with rhythm and melody.[24] There is nothing specifically Christian and probably nothing specifically religious about tongues. Indeed from a purely phenomenological point of view, they represent a regression to a kind of 'baby talk'. What then is their religious significance, and have they a value in the life of prayer?

The New Testament throws considerable light on the place of tongues in spirituality, and presents a very balanced and sane view of the issue. To pray in tongues, St Paul says, is to pray in a way which is not normally intelligible either to others or to oneself (1 Corinthians 14:2, 14). It is not ecstasy, and it is subject to control and to discipline, both external (of the local church) and internal (within the individual). Indeed at the time of the Montanist heresy, it was regarded as a mark of orthodox spirituality that the person possessed of spiritual gifts retained his own consciousness.[25] Today the situation is the same: speaking in tongues is frequently a quiet, matter-of-fact unemotional activity, often pursued and practised in private. Simon Tugwell suggests that those who receive the gift most quietly probably gain the most spiritual benefit from it.

> Of course they experience a certain freeing of their prayer, and a certain uplift in their hearts; but essentially what they discover is a new depth of trust in God, a greater assurance that the peace of Christ is really there in their hearts. And this is a very import-

ant factor in spiritual as well as psychological growth. As a result of receiving and using this gift, the range of their response to God's grace in prayer and in their whole lives is, sometimes dramatically, increased, allowing them a far greater involvement in all the 'moods' of God's Spirit, from the most intense joy and exhuberant praise, to utter silence before God, and sometimes acute agony, in union with the suffering of Christ.[26]

So tongues is a gift to use in the praise of God, not given to all but apparently very widespread. Its association with praise – 'speaking in tongues and magnifying God' (Acts 10:26) – is crucial. For praise involves moving beyond the restrictions of the mind. When one prays in tongues, the mind remains barren (1 Corinthians 14:14). It can therefore be a means of setting free the personality to glorify God, freed from the tyranny of mental concepts, set free in the power of the Spirit.

The mind, however, has a place in prayer, to which we shall turn our attention shortly. One area where mind and body combine is in the 'earthing' activity of producing a timetable for prayer. To use a timetable is not 'unspiritual' nor does it imply a legalistic understanding of prayer. It is simply the application of a business-like mind and of an efficient approach to time to the life of the Spirit.

THE DISCIPLINE OF THE MIND

The distinction between meditation and prayer goes back to the earliest Christian periods. 'When the ancient writers speak of prayer, they are careful to distinguish it from meditation which they consider to be the normal preparation for prayer.'[27] The main distinction which is made is that meditation is seen as an activity of mind and thought, while prayer is an activity of the whole being. Prayer is seen as involving the laying aside of thought. The Desert Fathers made a distinction between the outward work, which they compared to the leaves of a tree, and the inward work, which they compared to the fruit. The outward work included study, spiritual reading and the celebration of the liturgy. The inward work is that which should occur throughout, the act of prayer. So meditation, in most Christian usage, is an activity of thought, while prayer is the rejection and transcendence of thought. In meditation, the intellectual faculties are used, while in prayer they are seen as a hindrance and are avoided.

Again confusion of terms can mislead. Some writers use the word meditation in a wide sense to include a variety of spiritual exercises. William Johnston, for example, suggests that mysticism 'is no more than a very deep form of meditation'.[28] Eastern non-Christian teachers tend to use meditation to mean what western writers mean by contemplation, and vice versa. Similarly the word contemplation is used in very wide and very specific senses. Our word comes from the Latin *contemplari*, the work of the Roman augurs who looked for God's will within the sacred enclosure of the *templum*. Patanjali in the Yoga Sutras also stressed the *looking* aspect. He saw the achievement of contemplation (*samadhi*) as a three-stage activity. First, the mind centres on an image in the heart. Secondly, the mind thinks towards the image. Thirdly, the mind is led to a state of mental balance, stillness and insight. This pattern is very similar to the developments described by western writers as the movement from meditation to contemplation. Basic to the whole movement is *concentration*, which Patanjali defines as 'the holding of the heart in one centre'. This leads to meditation or 'the uninterrupted flow of the heart towards the object of concentration', and finally to contemplation, the union between the self and the object.[29]

So meditation and mental discipline are preludes to prayer. As Anthony Bloom points out, 'Meditation and prayer are often confused, but there is no danger in this confusion if meditation develops into prayer; only when prayer degenerates into meditation.' For meditation is an exercise of disciplined, controlled thought. In meditating, we are pursuing one line, renouncing all others; we are focusing our attention upon a point. Bloom calls it 'a piece of straight thinking under God's guidance'.[30] In all the schools of prayer, there is a stress on mental discipline and on practicality, that is, on making the discipline relevant to life. So in all forms of meditation, there is this twofold action: brooding upon a text of passage, and then applying the insights in a practical way.

It is however an exaggeration to regard meditation as an exclusively mental function. Thomas Merton points out that in the monastic tradition, all meditation, all prayer and all reading are seen as involving the whole person and not simply the mind. Meditation is therefore an activity of reflection, a penetration of one's deepest centre, one's inner being. Through such meditation we begin to discover the centre of our personality. It has been assumed by many spiritual guides that meditation of some kind is the form of prayer which is appropriate to beginners. Thus Father Longridge said that it was 'the prayer proper for beginners especially while they are in the purgative way'.[31] Its purpose is seen as a purgative one: to remove from the mind all thoughts and movements which prevent spiritual growth, to purify mind and memory, and to prepare the ground for affective prayer. On the other hand Longridge, writing over fifty years ago, did not make the mistake which so many have made, of assuming that discursive meditation was the only way of mental prayer, and that all Christians would benefit from it. On the contrary, he wrote in 1930:

> We are awaking now to the fact that this is not so. Many souls after a comparatively short time spent in meditation, cease to profit from it, and are ready to advance to affective prayer and the prayer of simplicity, if only they knew about these further stages, and were helped and encouraged by their confessors or directors to go forward.[32]

Many people in fact find deep, reflective reading of more value than a structured form of meditation. Slow reading of Scripture, 'brooding on the Word,' and perhaps group Bible study can often be of greater use than formal meditation in building up an informed and intelligent person, ready for the work of prayer. The purpose of such reading is quite different from that of reading a novel, and the method is therefore different. One is not reading in order to get to the end, but in order to awaken praise and prayer. Once that purpose is achieved, it is very important to put the book down and to enter into the prayer. For many, the time spent in such mental discipline may be quite short. As Thomas Merton says:

> It is clear that those who have progressed a certain distance in the interior life not only do not need to make systematic meditations but rather profit by abandoning them in favour of a simple and peaceful affective prayer, without fuss, without voice, without much speech, and with no more than one or two favourite ideas or mysteries to which they may return in a more or less general and indistinct manner each time they pray.[33]

THE MOVEMENT INTO SILENCE

Physical silence and stillness are not in themselves creative. Silence can be a destructive and disturbing force. The negative silence of solitary imprisonment can crush the human being. There is a silence of hatred, a silence filled with fear and terror, a silence of the unknown. There is a silence which is so threatening that we make sure that all the gaps are filled with synthetic noise. Silence, as in Paul Simon's song 'The Sounds of Silence', can grow like a cancer or, as in Ingmar Bergman's film *The Silence* (1962), can signify the death of God. Silence in Scripture can mean ruin – Isaiah saw Moab put to silence – or death – 'The dead praise not you, O Lord, nor all they that go down into silence.'

Coming to terms with silence is a necessary element in self-knowledge and in prayer. Pascal claimed that 'most of man's troubles come from his not being able to sit quietly in his chamber'. Throughout the writings of all the great spiritual guides, we find the call to inner silence. In the tradition of the desert, the early term for a monk was *hesvchastes*, one who lived in solitude and silence. *Hesvchia* was seen as the essential condition of prayerfulness. It is more than silence, it is a state of soul characterized by sobriety, inner vigilance, attention to God. One of the Desert Fathers, Arsenius, was told, 'Flee, keep silent, be still, for these are the roots of sinlessness.'[34] St John Climacus uses the same language about hesychia which Evagrius used about prayer itself. 'Hesychia is a laying aside of thought.'[35] Closely linked with the idea of inner silence in the hesychast tradition is the stress on breathing. 'Let the remembrance of Jesus be united to your breathing, and then you will know the value of hesychia.'[36] It is this conception which is the background to the Jesus Prayer. Before true prayer can begin, there must be a discipline of thought through the practice of silence and withdrawal, and a discipline of the body through the practice of some degree of physical solitude and stillness. Then, says St Basil, 'When the mind is no longer dissipated amidst external things, nor dispersed across the world through the senses, it returns to itself; and by means of itself it ascends to the thought of God.'[37] It is in this context that silence can help us to grow by reducing the overcrowding of the mind, and enabling the heart to become centred in gentleness and peace.

The practice of silence is, of course, inseparable from the discovery of one's own inner depths. For when one descends into the depths of one's spirit, there is a realization of the closeness of God, the ground of one's being, the depth in which our own soul stands. The eastern church has seen this process of introversion as a return to the heart (*kardia*), the centre of the personality. Through inner silence, one comes to see the inner face, the focal point of spirituality. In the Bible the heart is the seat of intelligence and of life. But it is also from the heart that the depths of wickedness issue forth. The human heart is desperately wicked according to Jeremiah (17:9), and Jesus tells his disciples that it is from the heart that murder, adultery and other evils proceed (Matthew 15:18–19). The heart therefore is in need of purification, and this is an important part of affective prayer. The purpose of silence is to allow the heart to be still and to listen to God. 'When you pray, you yourself must be silent . . . You yourself must be silent. Let the prayer speak.'[38]

To build up inner resources of silence and stillness is one of the central tasks of training in prayer. In a culture which has almost outlawed silence, it is a matter of urgency that Christians create oases, centres in which inner silence can be cultivated. At times, such a search for silence needs to be particularly concentrated, and this is the purpose of retreats. A retreat is a period of silence, lasting usually between one and five days, in which an individual will sever herself from her environment in order to give herself up more completely to the will of God. An annual retreat of some kind is probably an essential feature of serious Christian living, and the conducting of retreats is an important element within spiritual direction. Not all priests are good retreat conductors, but many are, and there is a need to draw more individuals into this growing sphere of work. A retreat is a time of awakening, of new vision and new zest. Hugh Maycock once described the retreat conductor's role as being to 'astonish the soul'.[39] Another major part of a retreat is to allow an individual to relax and to expand at leisure, to give some creative space in which to grow. Von Hügel's wise words are worth recalling.

> No doubt a retreat depends somewhat on the giver of it; yet it really depends far more upon the simplicity and generosity of the soul that makes the retreat. I am sure you already know well that you must evade all straining, all vehemence, all as it were putting your nerves into it. On the contrary, the attention wanted is leisurely expansion, a gentle dropping of distractions, of obsessions. That is the instrument of progress, the recipient of graces.[40]

DISTURBED PRAYER

Meditation is concerned with the discipline of the mind and heart, and lack of this discipline is the key factor in the disturbances and distractions which often trouble those who try to pray. No amount of inner battling with distractions can make up for the steady and regular work of mental discipline. In a useful section on distractions in prayer, W. H. Longridge listed three 'golden remedies': discipline of the mind by practising attention at all times; purifying the heart by resistance to sin; and the use of ejaculatory prayers. He also listed five 'specific remedies' for use within a particular time of prayer.

1 Prepare oneself for prayer by recollection.
2 Attend carefully to posture, punctuality, and detail.
3 Never leave prayer until it is very late.
4 When distractions occur, recall the mind by an act of faith.
5 Accept wearisome conflicts and don't worry about them.[41]

Many other writers give similar advice. One of the earliest was Cassian in the fourth century, who gave the following guidance on troublesome thoughts.

> Thoughts inevitably besiege the mind. But any earnest person has the power to accept or reject them. Their origin is in some ways outside ourselves, but whether to choose them or not lies within us. But because I said it was impossible for thoughts not to come to the mind, you must not put all the blame upon the spirits who assault our integrity. Otherwise the will of man would not be free, and we would make no effort for our own improvement. To a great extent we have the capacity to better the sort of thoughts we receive, to let holy thoughts and secular thoughts grow into our minds. This is the purpose of reading the Bible often and meditating upon it always, to attain a higher state of recollectedness: this is the purpose of singing psalms often, so that feelings of repentance may be continually elicited: this is the purpose of constancy in watchings or fasts or prayer, so that the mind, with its weakened body, may care nothing for the world, but may contemplate the things of heaven. If we neglect these, the mind will surely creep back towards squalid sin and fall.[42]

The methods of meditation taught by the great teachers were based on a realistic assessment of the state of the human mind, fragmented and divided, overcrowded with thought. There was no attempt suddenly to remove these thoughts, but rather to reduce the range by a process of centring and focusing. 'Bind the mind with one thought – or the thought of One only' was the advice of Theophan the Recluse.[43]

There are two aspects of the classic approach to disturbances of thought: the wide question of control, and the specific one of concentration of the heart in one centre. The control of mental activity requires a great deal of discipline *outside* the time of prayer, for it is impossible to expect a disordered and muddled mind to be able to attain peace in the time of prayer. One of the most frequent problems here is the upsurge of memory, which centres the mind in past events, so that it broods on failures, recalls incidents, muses over resentments, and so on. So Evagrius advises those who try to pray to 'guard your memory with all your might . . . for in the time of prayer the memory often lays waste the mind'.[44] The memory, he warns, conjures up the recollections of the past, the images of people who did us ill. Prayer then becomes impossible because we are so involved with these worries. They must be gently laid aside, for 'prayer is a laying down, a casting off of thoughts'.[45] The best and surest method of helping the mind to be recollected in prayer is to nourish it outside the time of prayer. Music, painting, knitting, long walks, enjoyment of natural beauty, reading novels and poetry, physical exercise, gardening and many other activities can all help to make prayer more possible.

However, the great teachers of prayers are unanimous in insisting that during the time of prayer, distracting thoughts should not be fought. The head-on collision method not only rarely works, but it also exhausts the mind and therefore leaves one ill-fitted for prayer. Prayer times then become a battleground in which one wrestles with an agitated mind. The method which they recommend is rather the concentration on a point, visual or vocal: gazing at a crucifix or an ikon, saying the name of Jesus, and so on. More will be said of this later. So the disciple is told not to waste his time and energy on direct contradiction. The sixth-century teacher Barsanuphius advised that this method was too difficult for most people and could lead to exhaustion and despair.[46] To turn aside and focus the mind elsewhere by use of a single word of prayer is the advice most commonly encountered in East and West. The basic principle here is a simple one and illustrated by a modern writer by the analogy of the monkey looking for bananas.

A wise monkey-catcher realizes that the monkey is leaping from branch to branch for a reason; it is looking for something –

more bananas perhaps. He realizes that to chase the monkey round and round the tree is a waste of time. It is much simpler and much quicker to place a pile of bananas at the foot of the tree and the monkey will soon come down of its own accord. By recognizing the inner needs of the monkey he brings it to a state of stillness without any effort, control or chaining down.[47]

So *The Cloud of Unknowing*, like most of the eastern teachers, stresses the use of the single word or phrase.

If you want to gather all your desire into one simple word that the mind can easily retain, choose a short word rather than a long one. A one-syllable word such as 'God' or 'love' is best. But choose one that is meaningful for you. Use it to beat upon the cloud of darkness above you, and to subdue all distractions, consigning them to the cloud of forgetting beneath you. Should some thoughts go on annoying you, demanding to know what you are doing, answer with this one word alone. If your mind begins to intellectualize over the meaning and connotations of this little word, remind yourself that its value lies in its simplicity. Do this and I assure you that these thoughts will vanish. Why? Because you have refused to develop them with arguing.[48]

It is the experience of the great masters of prayer that the danger of inner confusion and loss of bearings becomes greater as the degree of inner exploration deepens. A study of consciousness changes by a group of scientists noted that 'these inner forces are very powerful. Beware the dangers that exist when work like this is done, especially by large numbers of people, without the high values and lifelong disciplines of the great ancient systems.'[49] Hence the urgent necessity of direction. The intensifying of inner conflict as spiritual progress occurs was certainly the experience of the Desert Fathers. St Anthony wrote that the hesychast, while he has escaped from the conflicts of hearing, speaking and seeing, had a continual struggle in the warfare in his own heart. This is of particular importance, since many Christians believe that the fact that they are frequently disturbed in prayer by violent thoughts and feelings, particularly those connected with sexual desire and with great anger, is an indication of their own sinfulness or unfitness for the work. The truth is quite other. Progress in prayer always and inevitably brings with it a deepening awareness of one's own depths, pleasant and unpleasant, and a deeper sensitivity to others. The purpose of the disciplines of the spiritual life is to protect the disciple from the dangers of either being led astray by over-reliance on ecstatic feelings, or of being crushed and brought to despair by disturbed ones. As *The Cloud* puts it, people should 'look over their shoulders' back to God.

TOWARDS CONTEMPLATIVE PRAYER

It was suggested earlier that to see contemplative prayer as an activity reserved for a small minority of atypical Christians was entirely wrong. Many individuals are brought to this way of prayer beyond the confines of the mind. It is an experience of God within which liberates and leads us beyond our limited modes of consciousness, an experience of both emptiness and transcendence. The experience of emptiness is what Zen calls the 'void', the transcending of the subject/object distinction and the experience of simplicity, waylessness and unity. So the fourteenth-century mystic Ruysbroeck:

> The interior man enters into himself in a simple manner, above all activity and all values, to apply himself to a simple gaze in fruitive love. There he encounters God without intermediary. And from the unity of God there shines into him a simple light. This simple light shows itself to be darkness, nakedness and nothingness. In this darkness, the man is enveloped and he plunges in a state without modes, in which he is lost. In nakedness, all consideration and distraction of things escape him, and he is informed and penetrated by a simple light. In nothingness he sees all his works come to nothing, for he is overwhelmed by the activity of God's immense love and by the fruitive inclination of his Spirit . . . becomes one spirit with God.[50]

This process of transformation is of the very essence of the Christian life. In the void the light of God is able to shine. So the aim of methods of prayer is to allow the conditions to emerge in which the light may shine clearly and without interruption, the conditions in which the soul is led to the clear vision of God.

Spiritual direction will therefore concern itself with the area of affective prayer, the encouragement of simplicity, the use of short acts of praise, love and sorrow. In the transition from disciplined thought to simple contemplation, the litany form of prayer comes into its own. For here there is rhythm and repetition, even monotony. 'In this period the so-called litanical prayer thrives.'[51] William

Johnston has stressed the positive value of monotony for it is 'another way of restricting the reflective consciousness ... If ... monotony predominates at the discursive level, the intuitive is allowed to act.'[52] The rosary is a valuable form of prayer in this stage. Carlo Carretto criticizes the view that this is a form of prayer for beginners.

It was in the desert that I came to realise that those who discuss the rosary – as I discussed it in that way – have not yet understood the soul of this prayer. The rosary belongs to that type of prayer which precedes or accompanies the contemplative prayer of the spirit.

It is, he says, 'a point of arrival, not of departure ... a prayer of spiritual maturity.'[53]

In these ways of prayer leading towards contemplative stillness, the single word dominates. The principle of *mantra* is not in origin a Christian one. There are many mantras in the world's spiritual traditions – Hari Krishna, Om Mani Padme Hum, and so on. The commonest Christian mantra is, of course, the name of Jesus, and from early times the name has been used as a means of victory over evil, and as a prayer. 'The remembrance of the Name of God utterly destroys all that is evil.'[54] St John Climacus advised his pupils to use this form of prayer. 'Flog your enemies with the Name of Jesus, for there is no weapon more powerful in heaven or on earth ... Let the remembrance of Jesus be united to your every breath and then you will know the value of stillness.'[55] The use of such a short, concentrated prayer is seen by the eastern teachers as a means of unifying and focusing the personality. 'Through the remembrance of Jesus Christ, gather together your disintegrated mind that is scattered abroad', advised Philotheos of Sinai in the ninth century.[56] The Jesus Prayer is thus a *remembering*, a drawing of Jesus into the memory or rather, a drawing of the self into the memory of Jesus. So the memory is no longer seen as the enemy of stillness, for it is the memory of God, the *anamnesis* of redemption. That *anamnesis* is literally a re-calling, a bringing of God into the present consciousness, so that there is a condition of ceaseless prayer. Theophan the Recluse stresses this aspect of the prayer.

Hold no intermediate image between the mind and the Lord when practising the Jesus Prayer. The essential part is to dwell in God and this walking before God means that you live with the conviction ever before your consciousness that God is in you, as he is in everything: you live in the firm assurance that he sees all that is within you, knowing you better than you know yourself. This awareness of the eye of God looking at your inner being must not be accompanied by any visual concept but must be confined to a simple conviction or feeling.[57]

Earlier St Gregory of Sinai had also advised those using the prayer to 'keep your mind free from colours, images and forms'.[58]

In the path of contemplative prayer there is both self-discovery and self-surrender. The spiritual director therefore is involved in helping in the discovery of identity, and then in the further process of helping the person to die to that self and live from another centre, the deepest centre of one's being, God. It is this God-consciousness, which is the essence of being a Christian. 'Not I, but Christ in me'.

6

Towards a prophetic understanding of spiritual direction

> We can now recognize that the fate of the soul is the fate of the social order; that if the spirit within us withers, so too will all the world we build about us.
>
> THEODORE ROSZAK[1]

> Now spiritual direction, simply regarded as a fact, is a witness against the world, and we commit ourselves to its testimony.
>
> F. W. FABER[2]

Spiritual direction is concerned with healing and reconciliation, not with adaptation to current values, but with the transformation of consciousness. The director, according to the tradition, must be a person of *diakrisis*, discernment, judgement. Her role cannot therefore be restricted to the realm of the personal. How then does the ministry of personal guidance connect with the crises of the age? On the surface there seems to be no connection. For example, what possible social role can the confessional have? One can see the 'social dimensions' of the Mass, but surely not of the confessional.

> To those who see our world as repressive, and struggle effectively against it, the sacrament of penance will appear to confine reconciliation within an unhealthy and inward-looking return to the past. This type of believer will prefer the eucharistic celebration of reconciliation, where they can ratify in participation the actual brotherhood of the struggle and bear witness to a universal hope of unity.

This French Dominican writer continues:

> The existing form, inherited from Irish missionary monasticism, robs sacramental penance of its social character and implies that

forgiveness and reconciliation belong to an inner conscience. Moreover it encourages the sentiment already too prevalent in our society that religion is a private affair.[3]

The recent revisions will help to correct such over-personalized notions, yet the question remains: Is the personal relationship of disciple and director, penitent and priest, one which has any consequences for society?

In our examination earlier in this study of the movement of pastoral counselling, the critique made by the late R. A. Lambourne was cited as an example of dissatisfaction with the over-personalized attitudes in that discipline. After a visit to the United States at the end of the 1960s, Lambourne noted 'a split, perhaps a growing split, between those who are teaching practical theology through pastoral counselling and clinical pastoral care . . . and those who are teaching it through field work in depressed urban situations'. He was very disturbed at the theology of pastoral care which lay behind the counselling movement, for he argued that 'the present theology of pastoral care . . . operates almost entirely with a psychic-affective type of Christology'.[4] As a result, there was an excessive preoccupation with self-development at the expense of justice and matter.

Theology is at the heart of the question of the social relevance of direction. Is this ministry merely concerned with deepening a personal relationship of intimacy with Christ as Saviour? Or is it concerned to deepen perception of the working of God in the structures of society? Is it concerned to enable individuals to live lives of devotion and piety within the accepted framework of the social order, or does it question the spiritual and moral values of that order? Adjustment to society, or the Kingdom of God – which is its perspective? Whether spiritual direction has any social dimension at all is deeply connected with the theological assumptions on which it is based.

The first great spiritual directors in the Christian tradition were monks, and spiritual direction was in origin a monastic concept. To look at the status of the monk will help to illuminate our understanding of direction, and this can be done effectively by looking at the view of monasticism which emerges in the work of Thomas Merton, a great monk and a great spiritual director. It was in fact through Merton's own work as a director that he was led to a deeper awareness of social and political issues. 'He dates his concern with social and political matters to the years he spent as spiritual guide to the student monks.'[5] At the centre of Merton's view of monasticism is his picture of the monk as a social critic, one who questions the fundamental values of society.

Monasticism in Merton's view is not an escape from the incarnation and from the common life, but a specific way of sharing in the redemption of the world. Monastic prayer is a deep confrontation with the alienation of humanity and is thus essential to the undermining of illusion and falsehood. 'Merton understood that the unmasking of illusion belongs to the essence of the contemplative life.'[6] 'The monk', he said in a paper given at Bangkok on the day he died, 'is essentially someone who takes up a critical attitude towards the contemporary world and its structures.'[7] He saw the future of the contemplative life to be closely linked to this critical, prophetic role. 'The great problem for monasticism today is not survival but prophecy.'

Merton's view of the role of the monk in the modern world comes out most clearly in his *Contemplative Prayer* (1969), and in his Bangkok paper on 'Marxism and Monastic Perspectives'. In the former work he argues that

> ... this is an age that, by its very nature as a time of crisis, of revolution, of struggle, calls for the special searching and questioning which are the work of the monk in his meditation and prayer ... In reality the monk abandons the world only in order to listen more intently to the deepest and most neglected voices that proceed from its inner depth.[8]

Earlier, in a 'Message to Poets' read at a meeting of Latin American poets in Mexico City in 1964, Merton compared the poet's task to that of the monk. Both rejected the political art of setting one person against another and the commercial art of setting a price for anyone. Yet it was not in their opposition to these perspectives that their true role was defined. 'Let us remain outside "their" categories. It is in this sense that we are all monks: for we remain innocent and invisible to publicists and bureaucrats.'[9] The monk in Merton's vision is 'a marginal person ... who withdraws deliberately to the margin of society with a view to deepening fundamental human experience'. Existing as he does on the periphery of society and of the church, he remains an enigma to most people, and he 'cannot clearly explain himself to the rest of the world, and he is very foolish if he attempts to do so.' Yet the periphery is in reality the centre, although unrecognized. 'The monk is a man who, in one way or another, pushes to the very frontiers of human experience and strives to go beyond, to find out what transcends the ordinary level of existence.'[10]

Merton's theme of the monk as a 'marginal person' also appears in an important essay by Adrian Hastings on 'Marginality'. Hastings suggests that one of the essential features of the monastic life should be the sense of social non-status, but that monasticism is rarely faithful to this calling. Yet 'the nun and the monk should be the great protesters . . . They should be God's clearest face in the world'.[11] This is true to Merton's idea, and it fits in well too with the vision of Joachim of Flora at the end of the twelfth century, who prophesied the coming of a New Age which would be the age of the Spirit, of little children, of contemplation and leisure, of the absence of money, and of monks!

The point of this for the ministry of direction is that what Merton says of the monastic life is true over a wider area. For the monk is a sign to the whole church, pointing it to the vision of the Kingdom. He is a Kingdom man, a man of the new age. In the same way, the spiritual director is a marginal figure, existing on the periphery of human society, inexplicably committed to a new order, and pointing onwards beyond the conventional and the accepted values of the day.

Spiritual direction is an activity within the sphere of the Kingdom of God, the liberated zone of God's movement. It accepts that the Kingdom is 'the regulative principle of theology',[12] and that all spirituality must be judged by the vision of the coming age. The Kingdom is the standard by which the Christian disciple lives, and by that standard she discerns the signs of the times. *Diakrisis*, that fundamental characteristic of the spiritual director, is a function of *krisis*, judgement; and the central *krisis* of the gospel is the coming of the Kingdom. It is this which determines true prayer, and this fact needs to disturb us. For, as Alan Ecclestone has so truly said:

> If the praying of Jesus took its character from his conviction and announcement of the breaking in upon the world of God's new age, so that his prayer for daily bread and for the forgiveness of sins is prayer for the bread of the new life begun and the wholly new relationships set up, it may be questioned whether many of us pray after this manner at all. . . . Spirituality today must ask

what has happened to this great vision of the Kingdom, with this Gospel engagement with the world of men.[13]

It is the new age of the Kingdom which is both proclaimed and enacted in the eucharistic liturgy. It is the new age which is one of righteousness and *shalom* and joy in the Spirit, which only the spiritually-born can see, and which is to transform the face of the earth. Spirituality which is centred in this hope cannot then be escapist or individualistic, for it is a hope for human society and for the common life.

Yet the vision may be clouded over, and for lack of that vision the people perish. Vision and clear insight are the fruits of contemplation, and they are vital. At heart, the contemplative is one who sees clearly, sees with the eyes of God, the clear light which shines in the emptiness of the human spirit. It is clear vision which enables the truly spiritual person to see beneath the surface of events, to see through the illusion and the phoney claims of human systems, to see beyond the immediate and the transient to the reality. Consequently the contemplative is more of a threat to injustice than the social activist who merely sees the piecemeal need. For contemplative vision is revolutionary vision, and it is the achievement of this vision which is the fruit of true spiritual direction.

A spirituality of clear vision goes hand in hand with love. To see with the eyes of God is to see truthfully and lovingly. Such a love is not sentimental or naïve: it is a love which undermines oppression and burns away illusion and falsehood, a love which has been through the fire, a love which has been purified through struggle. It is a love which has known solitude and despair. No spiritual direction can be seen as adequate in Christian terms unless it is preparing men and women for the struggle of love against spiritual wickedness in the structures of the fallen world and in the depths of the heart. Contemplation is an entering into this struggle because it is a way of looking at reality which cuts through the façades and the bogus claims. Because of this, contemplation is the vital prerequisite for human liberation. The Jesuit Alfred Delp, imprisoned in Nazi Germany, expressed this well when he said that great issues affecting humanity must always be decided 'in the wilderness, in uninterrupted isolation and unbroken silence'.[14]

The vital link between solitude and protest, contemplation and prophecy, is expressed in Taoist mysticism in the symbolism of Yin and Yang. The Tao is known only in the union of Yin-Yang: in isolation they are meaningless. In early symbolic representation, Yin appears as a cloud, symbolizing both the darkness and the source of nourishing water, while Yang is a pennant or banner. The contemplative and the active are necessary for each other. Contemplation must be involved, a clear seeing into the reality of human life and human suffering, not an evasion of that reality. So Gandhi insisted:

> Recall the face of the poorest and the most helpless man whom you have seen, and ask yourself if the step you contemplate is going to be of any use to him. Will he be able to gain anything by it? Will it restore him to control over his own life and destiny?[15]

In such contemplative spirituality lie the resources for resistance to injustice. For resistance can only grow out of improved knowledge and deepened insight (Philippians 1:9).

If this is true, it ceases to be surprising that Charles Elliott, the economist, should end his study *Inflation and the Compromised Church* (1975) with a call to contemplation. Christians, he says, must face in their concrete situation the inequities and miseries with which they are surrounded. They must face the challenge of justice.

> It is then that they begin to reflect the life of Christ and to foreshadow the life of his Kingdom. But they will reflect it only to the extent that they have seen it. Radical action begins with radical contemplation.[16]

Injustice and social fragmentation, on the other hand, are perpetuated through 'partial perception', an unwillingness or inability to see, and therefore to act. So spiritual direction is involved with clarity of perception, with consciousness and awareness, with reality.

To say this, however, is at once to recognize that frequently spirituality and justice do not walk hand in hand. Increased awareness by itself is no guarantee of its use for good. It may mean that businessmen and women, armed with new insights and heightened consciousness, will be better able to exploit the poor, or that politicians, more wakeful through meditation, will be better able to enslave millions and make better bombs. So Daniel Berrigan, in a famous passage, warned of the danger of pseudo-contemplation.

> . . . in the derangement of our culture we see that people move

towards contemplation in despair – even though unrecognized.
They meditate as a way of becoming neutral, to put a guard
between them and the horror around them. . . . So they become
another resource of the culture instead of a resource against the
culture.[17]

'A resource against the culture', 'a witness against the world': the
work of spiritual direction has brought us to the point of *krisis*,
or conflict with the world organized apart from God and from
spiritual values.

The spiritual director exists to be a friend of the soul, a guide
on the way to the City of God. Her ministry is one of *diakrisis*,
discernment of events, and of *liberation*, enabling individuals and
communities to move towards freedom, the freedom of the children
of God. She is not a leader but a guide, and she points always
beyond herself to the Kingdom and the Glory. Through her love,
her silence, her prayer, she seeks to be a light for people in their
search, but she must always remember the demands of freedom.

> You may give them your love but not your thoughts
> For they have their own thoughts.
> You may house their bodies but not their souls
> For their souls dwell in the house of tomorrow,
> Which you cannot visit, nor even in your dreams.
> You may strive to be like them, but seek not to
>   make them like you.
> For life goes not backward nor tarries with
>   yesterday.
> You are the bows from which your children as
>   living arrows are sent forth.[18]

Appendix
Spiritual direction and the sacrament of reconciliation

THE GROWTH OF PRIVATE CONFESSION

The life of the Spirit is both initiated by, and characterized by, *metanoia*, repentance, transformation, and an integral element in spiritual direction is the maintaining of a continuous repentance and sorrow for sin. Indeed, it has been said that 'penitence is . . . the first quality to look for in a spiritual guide'.[1] Although the idea of spiritual guidance is quite distinct from that of sacramental absolution, in practice the two roles are often found together throughout the tradition and at the present time. Jean Grou wrote in the eighteenth century:

> We ought not to draw a distinction between the director and the confessor any more than we draw a distinction between the physician who cures illness and him who prescribes a rule for preserving health. The confessor hears the acknowledgement of our sins, and absolves us from the guilt of them; he tells us what we are to do, that we may avoid sin for the future, and he gives us wholesome advice, that we may advance in virtue. The tribunal of penance, then, includes confession and direction, and it is as essential for it to preserve us from faults as to absolve us from them. Nevertheless, quite as much by the fault of the penitents as of the confessors, there have always been very few confessors who are directors at the same time.[2]

But it is not simply the deficiency of those who hear confessions, but also the distinctions between the two roles which must be considered. Today, more than in Grou's time, the practice of spiritual guidance is far more widespread, less formalized, and more varied in style than is the practice of confession. At the same time, confession and absolution remain important elements within Christian practice. We need then to examine the background of private sacramental confession, with or without spiritual direction, and its place within the church. This appendix will attempt such an examination, and will then consider the changes in thinking about confession in the Roman communion and the revised Order of Penance which embodies some of these changes. It will finally consider the actual practice of hearing confessions and try to supply some basic guidelines for those engaged in this ministry. This section is therefore more limited than is the rest of the book to those living and working within the organized church, though it is hoped that it will not be useful only to them.

In the New Testament, we read of public confession before baptism, at the River Jordan and in the Acts of the Apostles. We read too of sins which cannot be forgiven (1 John 5:16–17; Hebrews 10:26), of excommunication for grave sinners (1 Corinthians 5:4), of prayer for sinners (1 John 5:16; James 5:16). We read too in the early Fathers of confession, apparently public (Didache 14.1; 4.14) and of repentance and restoration (Ignatius, *Ad Philad.* 3.2; 8.1). The earliest reference to private confession seems to occur in Origen (185–253), but this was not the norm. There is a considerable amount of source material for the penitential discipline of the church from the time of Tertullian to that of Gregory the Great, and private confession is not apparent. There was an order of penitents into which candidates were received. They were clothed in penitential robes and joined other penitents in a special area of the church. Here, during the liturgy, they received the laying on of hands. However, the forms of penance were so severe that the system ceased to play any practical part in life, and was seen mainly as a preparation for death! So although sin did not diminish, 'there was no sacramental remedy at their disposal'.[3] Periods of penance during this period would vary from several years in the time of Tertullian and Cyprian to the forty days of Lent which seems to have become the norm by the time of Pope Innocent I. During this period of penance, there was to be strict continence, prayer and almsgiving. But one was only admitted to do penance once. If one subsequently fell into grave sin, it was too bad! In effect, the lapsed penitent became a compulsory religious, condemned to chastity, barred from communion, as indeed he was also banned from military, commercial and other forms of activity.

Private confession seems to have become common in the fifth century, and is evident in the Celtic and Anglo-Saxon penitential books. St Leo the Great in 459 complained of some who were breaking the secrecy of confession, and he commended the practice of private confession: 'Let there be no classified confession of individual sins written out on a chart for public recitation, since it is enough that the state of conscience be indicated in secret confession to the priests alone.'[4] However, public penance did not altogether die out, and Aquinas still refers to it.

In the writings of the early Fathers, confession and absolution are seen as the *recovery of the Spirit*, and it is this emphasis which is being rediscovered today, partly as a result of the Charismatic renewal in the Roman Communion. Once this perspective is accepted, it becomes clear how close is the link with spiritual direction. Both confession and direction are set firmly within the framework of the pouring out of the Holy Spirit. Confession is a sacrament not simply for the removal of sins but for the strengthening power of the Spirit. It is therefore an integral element *within* the movement of spiritual direction, an essential part of Christian progress. So St Jerome in the fourth century writes of the action of absolution:

> He imposes his hand on the subject and invokes the return of the Holy Spirit. And so he who was given over to Satan for the chastisement of the flesh so that his spirit might be saved, led by prayer into the midst of the people, is reconciled to the altar.[5]

In the tenth-century Romano-Germanic Pontifical, the bishop prays that the Holy Spirit may be infused into the penitent. St Ambrose insists that it is the Holy Spirit who forgives sins, but that 'men exercise a ministry in the forgiveness of sins. It is not a right which they exercise.'[6] So confessors become known as *pneumatikoi*, spiritual people.

> He who has been *pneumatized* by Jesus as the apostles and in whom it is possible to recognize the fruits that he has received the Holy Spirit, and is become 'spiritual' in such a manner that under the action of the Spirit he conducts himself in the manner of the Spirit of God in all his rational activity—such a one remits sin which God remits, and retains those which cannot be remitted.[7]

However, the spread of the 'tribunal' concept in the Celtic penitential system had unfortunate results in that it encouraged a legalistic and oppressive approach to confession. Inevitably the concentration on legal moral codes tended to focus excessively on sex, a focus which has plagued us and distorted the ethos of the confessional to this day. 'Moral effort tended naturally to concentrate on prescriptions relating to sexual behaviour.'[8] So in some penitential regimes, all sexual intercourse, even within marriage, was banned under pain of grave sin during Lent, in the weeks before Christmas, and on all Saturdays and Ember Days! Gradually the sense of the sacrament as a Spirit-filling process gave way to a legalistic and moralistic view.

In the Celtic Church the custom was one of repeated confession and absolution. The ministry of absolution was a regular one and was not apparently confined to priests. There is considerable evidence in the early centuries of confessions to, and at times absolution by, lay persons. An anonymous fifth-century monk, writing under the name of Johannes Jejuanator, said, 'God has appointed bishops, priests *and doctors* for the instruction of the faithful monks to hear their confessions.'[9] Women were used as confessors in the Celtic Church. Penitential compendia were compiled very early and seem to have become widespread by the end of the sixth century. They consisted of lists of sins with suitable punishments. Leclercq notes that 'those which survived helped to form the conscience of the west'.[10]

The spread of the practice of frequent confession did not occur without criticism and some alarm. Thus the Spanish bishops complained at the Council of Toledo in 589:

> It has come to our notice that certain people in certain parts of Spain are doing penance for their sins in unworthy fashion and not in accordance with the directives of the church. Every time they sin, they go to the priest for absolution. For this reason and to put an end to such a detestable and presumptuous way of behaving, this holy council has decreed as follows: Penance will be administered in accordance with the old official form, namely the sinner who repents of his sins must receive the laying on of hands many times as a penitent. He is forbidden to go to communion. Once he has in the estimation of his bishop completed his period of expectation he may be readmitted to the Eucharist.[11]

The new practice nevertheless continued to spread, eventually to Rome itself.

Private confession did not totally die out in the Reformation and the post-Reformation traditions. Luther held it to be necessary. 'Secret confession as practised now, though unprovable from Scripture, is highly commendable, useful, and even necessary. Nor would

I have it to cease: in fact, I rejoice that it is in the Church of Christ, since it is the sole [*unicum*] remedy for troubled consciences.'[12] Melanchthon held that 'private absolution is as necessary as baptism', for in it assurance of forgiveness is spoken to the individual 'personally and specifically'. Later the practice ceased to play any real part in most Protestant spirituality, although Wesley advised confession to 'a spiritual guide'.[13] In recent years there has been some revival of the practice among Protestants. In this century, Baptists such as H. E. Fosdick, and Methodists as different in outlook as the late Leslie Weatherhead and J. Neville Ward have testified to its importance and value, as also have members of Lutheran and other traditions.

At the Council of Trent, the emphasis was very strongly on the judicial nature of penance. The absolution, it was emphasized, was not merely the announcement of the gospel, or the declaration of sins forgiven, but 'the absolution is like a judicial act in which the priest himself passes sentence as a judge'. It is seen as a 'judicial process', the penance is 'satisfaction' and must be related to the sin.[14] The division in post-Tridentine Catholic theory between moral and ascetical theology, and the close association of the former with Canon Law increased this judicial and legalistic approach to the confessional which was to dominate the Latin tradition until very recently. Spiritual direction within the confessional was not discouraged. Pope Pius XII associated both reconciling and directing functions within the sacrament.

> Take your place in that divine tribunal of self-accusation, sorrow and forgiveness, as judges in whose breasts beat the hearts of fathers and friends, of physicians and teachers. And while the primary purpose of the sacrament is to reconcile men to God, do not lose sight of the fact that this exalted purpose is splendidly served by spiritual direction.[15]

In actual practice, however, confessions tended to become shorter and more mechanical.

Anglican tradition on the other hand certainly tended to place the practice of confession within the sphere of pastoral theology. The 1549 Prayer Book's exhortation associated confession with 'comfort and counsel' and emphasized that the confessor should be a 'discreet and learned priest'. In the Elizabethan period, Richard Hooker (1554–1600) included advice on confession in his writings, as did Jeremy Taylor (1613–67) in the Caroline period. Taylor

associated confession closely with spiritual direction. There are
references to the practice throughout the seventeenth century.
Canon 19 of the Church of Ireland (1634) urged ministers to offer
'the special ministry of reconciliation' to those who needed it, and
indeed ordered the bell to be tolled for the hearing of confessions
before the Eucharist. During the seventeenth century in Ireland,
this 'special ministry of reconciliation' was not a matter of party
contention, and was very widespread.[16] However, as has been
shown in Chapter Two, within the Tractarian movement there was
a dual tendency, on the one hand to draw heavily on continental
Roman texts for the guidance of confessors, and on the other to
distinguish sharply between confession and direction. The views of
Carter and Neale were cited earlier on this question. In 1866 a
manual entitled *The Priest in Absolution*, an Anglican adaptation
of the study of Abbé Gaume, caused considerable controversy, and
the issue became one of the major conflicts of the anti-Ritualism
campaign.[17]

Today, many Anglican Evangelicals are involved in the ministry
of personal guidance, though the tendency is still to see private
confession more in terms of consultation than of sacramental rite.
'The minister is exercising a pastoral not a priestly function in
soothing a wounded conscience with the ointment of God's word.'[18]
But the practice has been spreading since the 1960s. In 1960 a
small study by Jack Winslow was directed specifically at Anglican
Evangelicals. He pointed out that 'theological colleges of predominantly evangelical outlook do not hesitate to give it a place in their
teaching'.[19] Today the revival of healing ministries and the care of
deeply troubled people has been a major factor in bringing about
a changed attitude towards private confession among many Evangelicals, and the Charismatic movement has undoubtedly also been
a significant factor.[20]

THE REVISION OF THE RITE OF PENANCE

By the 1960s the sense of 'privatization' of the liturgy of penance
was leading some to call for the restoration of its corporate and
social nature. 'The liturgy of penance', wrote John Gustone in
1966, 'has become a purely pastoral instrument of individual
care.'[21] In the same year, Pope Paul's Apostolic Constitution *Paenitemini* announced that 'the Apostolic See intends to reorganize
penitential discipline with practices more suited to our times'.[22] A
French Dominican complained in 1971 that 'the sacrament of

penance, as it is practised today in the Catholic Church, gives rise to many reservations'.[23] From an Anglican standpoint, Martin Thornton in 1974 agreed. 'If the sacrament of penance retains its intrinsic value—as I am sure it does—then does it not demand a revised rite at least as radical as the eucharistic series 3?'[24]

So the Vatican Council's order that 'the rites and formulas for the sacrament of penance are to be revised so that they give more luminous expression to both the nature and effect of the sacrament'[25] was no surprise. It was part of the Constitution's insistence that 'whatever rites . . . make provision for communal celebration . . . this way of celebrating them is to be preferred, as far as possible, to a celebration that is individual and quasi-private'.[26] In similar vein, the liturgist J. D. Crichton in 1973 drew attention to the basic principles which, in his view, should govern any revision of the rite. He stressed that all liturgy was a corporate and not a private act, that it should involve some proclamation of the Word of God, that it should be a visible act, and that it should be possible for the Christian community to take part in its celebration.[27] The work of revision took some time. The Consilium for Liturgy set up a study group in 1966, and at the end of 1969, the Congregation for Worship set up a new working group. Finally, on 2 December 1973 the new *Ordo Paenitentiae* appeared.

Anglicans and other Christians outside the Roman Communion who study the new rites must bear in mind the context of the Roman practice. In various crucial respects the situation is different from that which prevails, for example, in the Church of England: the voluntary nature of confession, the smaller numbers of persons involved, the greater use of Scripture in Anglican worship, the different attitudes to Canon Law, and so on. In spite of these differences, however, the new rites of penance are of the greatest importance, cannot be ignored, and have much of value to give to Christians outside the Roman fold.[28]

There are three separate forms of the rite: the rite for reconciliation of individual penitents, the rite for reconciliation of several penitents with individual confession and absolution, and the rite for reconciliation of several penitents with general confession and absolution. In the form of individual celebration, there is a welcome by the priest ('the priest welcomes him warmly'), followed by the sign of the cross and an invitation to the penitent to have trust in God. There are five alternative invitations. Then follows an optional reading of Scripture, after which the penitent makes his confession. The priest gives a penance and any counsel, and is urged to 'make sure that he adapts his counsel to the penitent's circumstances'. He then asks the penitent to express his sorrow, and there are a number of suggested prayers which can be said by priest and penitent together. The absolution follows during which the priest extends his hands over the penitent's head. After absolution, the priest and the penitent together give thanks to God, and there is a final dismissal.

In the corporate rite, there is provision for a song or hymn, after which the priest greets the congregation and speaks to them about the service and prays with them. Then follows the 'celebration of the Word of God' in which there are two readings, and a Gospel, followed by a homily and an examination of conscience. There follows a general confession of sins, followed by intercessions in litany form. At this point the penitents may make individual confessions, and the priest, after hearing these confessions and offering counsel, immediately gives absolution. When the confessions are over, there is a corporate penance, a proclamation of praise, and a final blessing.

The opening words of the *Ordo Paenitentiae* – '*Reconciliationem inter Deum et homines*' – are crucial, and indicate the change in emphasis. The rite revolves around the theme of reconciliation in its corporate and personal dimensions. Penance is seen as the renewal of baptismal grace and as 'reconciliation with God and the church'.

> In the sacrament of penance, the faithful receive from God's mercy the forgiveness of their offences against him. At the same time they are reconciled with the church, which they have wounded through their sins and which strives for their conversion through charity, example and prayer . . . Penance always implies reconciliation with one's fellow men, who have suffered the effect of one's sin.[29]

So central to the revision is the restoration of the corporate celebration of penance. The penitent is seen as a concelebrant who 'together with the priest celebrates the liturgy of the church which is being perpetually renewed'.[30] There is provision then for a public liturgy. There is emphasis on reading the Word of God, and this is encouraged even in the individual rite. There is provision for singing and for silence, so that those who take part in the rite may respond to the Word. The *Ordo* says:

A community celebration brings out the ecclesial nature of penance. All the faithful hear the Word of God together, and they are all invited to change their lives by God's mercy, which is proclaimed in the readings. At the same time they have an opportunity to reflect on whether or not their present life is in conformity with what they are told in the Word of God, and they help each other with their prayers. When each one has confessed his sins and received absolution, all praise God together for his wonderful goodness towards the people he has made his own through the blood of his Son.[31]

There is provision too for a homily which will stress 'the social aspect of grace and sin',[32] and this will prepare the people for a self-examination. Appendix III of the *Ordo* gives a form for examination of conscience which also lays stress on the social dimensions of sin, though it has been criticized for being simplistic in its approach to sin.[33] The central section, consisting of the general and individual confessions, absolution, praise and thanksgiving, is called 'the rite of reconciliation'. The prayers use the language of wounding and healing rather than the penal and judicial concepts of Trent. In the new form of absolution, there is again the language of reconciliation and emphasis on the power of the Holy Spirit. There is provision for more community-oriented penances in the final exhortation where the priest 'exhorts them to good works by which the grace of repentance will be manifested in the life of each individual and the whole community'.[34]

In the rite for the 'reconciliation of a group of penitents with general confession and absolution', the formula for absolution is longer and more explicitly Trinitarian and scriptural. The language is very significant. God the Father shows *mercy* and gives *peace*. Jesus Christ *frees* from sin and *fills* with the Holy Spirit. The Holy Spirit *purifies* and *fills* with his radiance. The dominant themes are those of peace, freedom and the fullness of the Spirit. The absolution closes with the formula of absolution from the individual rite or with a shortened version of it. Crichton claims that the long form of absolution is 'a remarkable piece of writing' and has 'a pastoral importance of the highest degree', since it is embodied within the service of the Word.[35]

In the individual rite, warmth and kindness are stressed. 'When the penitent comes to confess his sins, the priest welcomes him with a friendly greeting.' He then 'tells the penitent to put his trust in God'. He is urged to 'be careful to adapt himself in every way to the penitent's condition, in what he says and in the kind of counselling he gives'. The reading of Scripture is encouraged but is not obligatory. The confessor 'helps the penitent to make a full confession'. He offers appropriate counsel and helps the penitent to achieve true contrition, reminding him that the sacrament of penance is a re-enactment of the paschal mystery, in which a Christian dies and rises again in Christ.

The pastoral possibilities in these new rites will have to be explored during the next few years, but there are several directions in which changes are likely to occur. First, *a more informal and relaxed approach* to the sacrament. The emphasis on spiritual direction and discernment of spirits will certainly lead to greater flexibility in pastoral practice. The Dutch priest W. Bekkers in the early 1960s was suggesting the creation of 'confessional rooms', and this was supported by F. J. Heggen, and by J. H. Champlin in the United States.[36] Since then such rooms have become common. Certainly, the recommendations of the new rite cannot be easily followed within the framework of the 'box'. The priest's role as healer and counsellor is emphasized, and he is no longer seen as an examining magistrate, treating his penitents like criminals.[37]

Secondly, greater attention to the *corporate self-examination and repentance* and to the *social dimensions of sin*. The view of sin as merely the breaking of a code must be questioned. As Fr Crichton comments, 'For a new and better practice of the sacrament . . . it will be necessary to re-examine the nature of sin, and to recast the examination of conscience. This will have to be based on a deeper notion of sin.'[38] Over ten years ago, the Dutch bishops in their Pastoral Letter on Public Penance (16 March 1965) stressed 'the social and ecclesial dimensions of human guilt',[39] and this restored emphasis is appearing in many of the forms of examination of conscience which are being published to accompany the new rites. We can therefore expect to see more imaginative use of penitential services and of forms of corporate penitence, an area in which the Dutch and Americans have made considerable progress.

Thirdly, *greater use of Scripture* in both public and private celebration. We can expect to see more publications which provide Bible readings and commentaries for use in the service of penance.[40] The link between Scripture, devotion and the practice of penance will become closer, and the roots of penitence in humanity's confrontation with the Word of God will receive greater emphasis.

Brooding on the Scriptures should lead to a fuller and better approach to self-examination.

Fourthly, the association of the sacrament with the *healing ministry*, with *the laying on of hands*, and with *the action of the Holy Spirit*. There is a recovery of the essential theological and pastoral unity of healing and reconciliation. In Macquarrie's words, 'the ministry of healing merges with the ministry of reconciliation'.[41] The healing power of the sacrament of penance is particularly emphasized in the Charismatic renewal groups of the Roman Communion. Francis MacNutt, in welcoming the new rites, stresses the fact that 'healing is desperately needed in order to renew Penance',[42] and he sees the restoration of this emphasis to be central to the future of the sacrament. It is the rediscovery of a very old emphasis, expressed, for example, in the statement of the Council of Florence in 1439: 'If through sin we succumb to sickness of the soul, through penance we are spiritually healed.'

Fifthly, *the correcting of various distorted views and the growth of a richer, theologically sounder understanding*. 'It needs to be realized that we are celebrating the paschal mystery and not just shovelling out and collecting absolutions.'[43] The judicial approach to the sacrament is now noticeably absent. Again, there is greater stress in the new rites on counsel and direction. So the *Ordo* insists that

> in order to fulfil his task properly, a confessor must learn to recognize the diseases of the soul and so be able to apply the appropriate remedies. He must acquire the requisite knowledge and prudence to be able to act as a wise judge, by means of diligent study under the guidance of the church's teaching authority, and especially through prayer.[44]

There is a stress on the 'discernment of spirits'. One commentator on the rites has observed that 'this view of the confessor is deeply traditional, particularly in the spirituality and sacramental practice of the eastern churches, but it will strike many priests today as novel teaching. It involves the confessor in spiritual direction, and one suspects it will demand of all confessors deeper prayer and study.'[45] There is also a richer understanding of the meaning of *metanoia* as change in life. As the rites become more widely celebrated, it is likely that the corporate dimensions, the reconciling ministry of the Body of Christ, and the personal dimensions, involving self-confrontation and spiritual direction, will be equally emphasized. As Rahner predicted some years before the revisions, 'the theory and practice of this sacrament will in future tend towards a *theologically fuller* and also *more personal* accomplishment of this sacrament.'[46]

CONFESSION AND PASTORAL CARE

Confession and forgiveness lie at the very heart of the Christian experience, for it is an experience of being set free from oppression and of being reconciled to God. God has reconciled us to himself in Christ, and has given to the church the *diakonia tēs katallagēs* (2 Corinthians 5:18), the 'work of handing on this reconciliation' (Jerusalem Bible), 'the service of reconciliation' (NEB). The service of reconciliation pervades and shapes the entire Christian community. In the New Testament, reconciliation is a central symbol of the work of Christ and of the church. We were enemies, but have been reconciled through Christ's death: through his death we have gained our reconciliation (*katallagen*, Romans 5:11). The purpose of the cross was to restore peace and reconcile those who were previously hostile (Ephesians 2:15–16; Colossians 1:20). The people of God are involved in the work of reconciling sinners. If one of the brethren is overtaken in a trespass, the spiritual men (*pneumatikoi*) are to 'restore him in a spirit of gentleness' (Galatians 6:1—RSV). Behind the disciplines both of restoration to and exclusion from the community (1 Corinthians 5:5ff; Matthew 18:15–17) lies the strong sense of solidarity of the members of the body with each other. If one member suffers, all suffer (1 Corinthians 12:26). So reconciliation is a community activity, and is indeed a central concern of the parish.

> A parish is made up of a number of redeemed sinners who live in a society which is in large measure unredeemed ... It is a body of people under a divine directive which is to reach out in love to those whose lives are torn and mangled by personal and social sin ... It is a centre of acceptance and relationships ... The object of the parish in the history of the community which it encompasses is peace, salvation, wholeness, unity, health.[47]

The Second Vatican Council described the church as 'the sacrament of reconciliation'.[48] So all our activities within the Body of Christ are part of this ministry. The sacrament of penance therefore is not an isolated element, a forgiveness machine which is separate from the corporate expressions of the church's life. Absolution is

'one of many legitimate expressions of the Gospel . . . a characteristic feature of the forgiven, reconciled community'.[49] It is one
manifestation, the most intimate and most thorough, of a process
of self-scrutiny, self-knowledge and continual penitence which
needs to be spread throughout the entire life of the church. In the
past, Anglicans have tended to avoid *preaching* the confessional,
although the great mission sermons of the older Mirfield Fathers
were notable exceptions. So the sacrament was placed in a corner,
and became seen as a private activity which was permitted, and
might even be encouraged, but ran parallel to the mainstream
liturgical life of the local church. It is essential to rescue the confessional from this position, and see it in relationship to the other
activities through which the ministry of reconciliation is offered.
The Fathers saw forgiveness as effected through a range of actions.
'Forgiveness of sins', claimed Augustine, 'may be found not only
in the washing of holy baptism, but also in the daily recitation of
the Lord's Prayer . . . in which you will discover as it were a daily
baptism.'[50] Caesarius of Arles advised his hearers to 'occupy your-
selves in alms and fasting and prayer: by these means daily sins
are cleansed.'[51]

One of the main actions of this kind is preaching, and it is
essential to relate preaching closely to sacramental confession. Not
only is it possible through the sermon to explain more about the
sacrament, and to allay anxieties and fears, but also the sermon
itself needs to be seen as a vehicle of God's forgiveness. The power
of preaching has, of course, been stressed most within the Protestant traditions. The Westminster Shorter Catechism insisted that
'the Spirit of God makes the reading, but especially the preaching,
of the Word, an effectual means of convincing and converting
sinners, and of building them up in holiness and comfort, through
faith, unto salvation'.[52] Salvation, according to St Paul, is achieved
through the foolishness of preaching (1 Corinthians 1:21). So in
preaching, the word of reconciliation is proclaimed, and God's
forgiveness is offered. Preaching is an essential part of the cure of
souls. It is a liturgical act and it demands a response. Ironically
the call for more use of the pulpit for preaching has come from a
psychiatrist who accuses the church of neglecting preaching in its
concern for pastoral counselling.[53]

It is important also to realize the need for teaching about the
confessional, and a good deal of teaching can be done through
the sermon. Joseph Champlin, in his homily and teaching guide,

advises that a catechesis on penance needs to be spread over a long period, six months to a year at least. There needs to be time for people to absorb the material and to reflect on it. His advice, while it refers specifically to the pastoral use of the new *Ordo*, is even more applicable to the situation in the Church of England, where the practice of confession has not really 'caught on' in many places.[54]

The ministry of reconciliation is exercised also through the other sacraments. In the celebration of baptism, the fundamental act of confession and absolution takes place. We believe in 'one baptism for the forgiveness of sins'. As St Ambrose noted, the church 'possesses both water and tears: the water of baptism and the tears of repentance'.[55] How can the reality of baptism be best conveyed? Certainly, by celebrating the rite within the framework of the public liturgy, and when there is the largest number of persons present. People need to be able to see and to share in the baptismal experience. The renewal of baptismal vows is an extremely valuable means of bringing home the reality of baptism, and this could in effect take place at every celebration of baptism by encouraging the entire congregation to join in the renunciation of evil and the profession of faith. 'We must rediscover Baptism—its meaning, its power, its true *validity* . . . the real rediscovery must take place each time the church celebrates this great mystery and makes all of us its participants and witnesses.'[56] There can hardly be a renewal of the sacrament of penance unless there is a renewal of baptismal spirituality, for penance is itself the renewal of baptismal grace.

The celebration of the Eucharist itself is central to the ministry of reconciliation. Reconciliation is an essential preliminary demand for eucharistic communion, for only those who are in love and charity with their neighbours are invited (cf. Matthew 5:24; 1 Corinthians 11:18). In the rite itself, the mutual confession, the sharing of the sign of peace, and the repeated expressions of corporate unworthiness underline the importance of reconciliation. Christ is offered as 'the Victim of our reconciliation' so that 'we may be brought together through his Holy Spirit'.[57] The blood of the covenant is shed for the forgiveness of sins (Matthew 26:28), and in the Eucharist the forgiveness of sins is conveyed through the power of that redeeming blood.[58]

The emphasis on reconciliation will need to be brought out also not only in the other sacraments, particularly in laying on of hands and anointing, but also in penitential services. These 'meetings of God's people . . . call on men to be converted and renew their lives and . . . proclaim that we have been set free from the bonds of sin by the death and resurrection of Christ'.[59] Within the framework of these services, it is possible to help people to a deeper and more thorough self-examination. But the ministry of reconciliation has to be carried over into all pastoral work—visiting, ministry to the deeply troubled and distressed, mediating in quarrels, struggling for social justice. It is easy to pay lip-service to the reconciling work of the church, but very painful and difficult to practise it in utter truth. For reconciliation is not an easy attainment of harmony, a unity based on sacrificing principles and bypassing conflict. There can be no peace without justice. The prophetic tradition of the Old Testament frequently attacks those who cry 'Peace, peace' when there is no peace. The Christian's role as reconciler in society must never degenerate into an evasion of the issues of justice. 'Reconciliation means in the Bible not the ignoring or explaining away of the contradiction but its effective removal.'[60] Again, there can be no true sense of the need for confession if the social dimensions of penitence are not understood. (They are strongly emphasized in Pope Paul's decree *Paenitemini* of 1966.) It is the whole church, and the local church, which exercise the ministry of reconciliation in and to society. 'The reconciled community which he called into being is itself to be a reconciling community continuing his ministry of reconciliation and continuing to pay the cost of it.'[61]

The hearing of confessions then cannot be isolated from the total reconciling work of the church, and it only makes sense in that context. The confessional stands at the critical point between liturgy and life, the positions adopted in worship and those which prevail in social life. It stands too at the point between the individual response to Christ and the commitment to society. The word of deliverance which is preached is here ministered directly *ad hominem*. The values of the Kingdom are here wrestled with in the life of one person seeking to live them. There is a continuous need for self-examination and confession to be tested against the realities of personal and social life, for without this interaction, the confessional can be twisted and become a pretence. It must remain the place of struggle, the place where good and evil forces fight within the human being, the place where God's clash with the forces of evil is fought out in terms of personal discipleship.

THE PRIEST AS CONFESSOR

It is impossible to teach people to become 'good confessors', for
the qualities which go to make for effectiveness in the ministry of
absolution are simply those which go to make for holy and competent priests and pastors. The 'good confessor' is a priest who is
steeped in prayer, disciplined in his life, acquainted with human
frailty, and endowed with the gifts of wisdom, and knowledge
of the ways of the Spirit. Without these features, no amount of
training or technique will be of much use. Nevertheless, there are
some basic 'dos and don'ts' which are helpful. Nothing is more
disturbing and potentially damaging to a person who wants to
make a confession than to be confronted by a priest who obviously
has no idea what to do, what is expected of him or her and who
flaps about, slightly embarrassed, communicating to the already
nervous penitent nothing but his or her own anxiety, awkwardness
and general muddle. Alas, there is far too much of such muddling
incompetence in the Church of England, and it is important not to
add to it, particularly at a point which for many people is a
personal crisis of a very profound kind. The following observations
then are simply offered as a small contribution towards increasing
priestly competence in this area.

First, it should be stressed that preparation of body and spirit
are vital. Before hearing confessions, a period of prayer and of rest
is sensible. A 'pre-confessional snooze' can help to keep a priest
alert and awake, and can be highly recommended! The hearing of
confessions is not easy and it does require spiritual and physical
alertness. It is essential therefore to give a high priority to the
question of preparing for the sacrament. An exhausted, weary
priest will not be of much use to a distressed penitent. But even
less will he be useful to the strong, mature person, seeking guidance
in his Christian life. Alongside physical preparation must go the
preparation of the mind. Reading and reflection are vital in preparing for this ministry. Indeed the preparation for the liturgy of
penance is identical in many respects with the preparation for all
liturgical worship and for prayer itself. The confessional is a place
of prayer, and should be treated as such. A good rule is to take a
book along. There will be periods when nobody comes—in fact,
nobody may come at all!—and the time spent sitting there can
be used for prayer and study. Whether one takes a book or not, it
is essential to *pray through* the period, penitents or no penitents.

To say the Jesus Prayer can be helpful in keeping oneself God-centred.

Secondly, the usual layout and the geography. In most Anglican churches, confessional boxes do not exist, but there are some, and it is useful to know what to do when one encounters them! The proper 'box' is a structure with a door, and the priest opens the door, draws the curtain if there is one, and sits, separated from the penitent by a grille or screen of some kind. The advantage of this kind of structure is that there is a high degree of anonymity, and this can help some penitents to express themselves. On the other hand, personal contact is reduced to a minimum. It is possible, though difficult, to see the penitent's face, and sometimes difficult to hear her. The stretching out of the hands over her head, as ordered in the new *Ordo*, is impossible, for the grille separates the priest from the penitent. It is arguable, therefore, that the *Ordo* does represent, through this rubric, an indirect abolition of confessional boxes, and certainly in modern Roman Catholic practice the reconciliation room where the penitent faces the priest across a table has become popular. However, in most Anglican churches, what is found is a chair with a kneeling desk for the penitent beside it. There should be a simple form of confession always on the desk, for, while many people prefer to use their own words, others will value a form of words on a card, and they may feel 'at sea' if it is not there. The following is a simple description of the customary form.

The priest sits, wearing a purple stole, and awaits the penitent. When he arrives, he may immediately say 'Bless me, for I have sinned', and the priest will give him a blessing. If he does not, the priest will begin either with a blessing, or, as in the new *Ordo*, with the words 'In the Name of the Father and of the Son and of the Holy Spirit. Amen', followed by a blessing. The penitent will then make his confession. The priest should be careful not to interrupt (unless she is deaf, and needs to tell the person to speak louder, or some similar reason), and not to mistake an awkward pause for the end of the confession. The penitent will usually finish by using the words on the form provided, but if there is a long silence, the priest can ask 'Have you finished?' or 'Is that everything?' When the confession is complete, the priest can encourage the penitent to say, with her, an act of contrition. She may then question the penitent about matters in the confession, and may give him counsel if he requires it. After this she should prescribe a penance, perhaps say with the penitent a simple act of thanksgiving (for example, the Gloria or a Psalm verse), and then give the absolution. The new *Ordo* instructs the priest to stretch out her hands over the penitent's head as she recites the formula of absolution. When she says the words 'I absolve you . . .' she makes the sign of the Cross. Then follow any final prayers and blessing.

It is essential to remember that the primary purpose of confession is forgiveness, *not* advice. It is wise to put on any card some such instruction as 'If you don't want advice, don't ask for it.' Many penitents feel that they are under some obligation to ask for advice, although they know that they do not need it. Equally, many priests insist on giving advice even when it is not needed, or bound to be of little use, or where it may be quite inappropriate for that penitent and in that setting. It needs to be asserted that it is just as normal and acceptable for people to come to confession and not receive advice, as it is for people to come to communion and not hear a sermon. Advice, counsel, or direction is often best given outside the formal structure of the confessional in any case. Where there is a request for advice in the confessional, it should be short, direct and centred on God. If the priest feels that a longer, more relaxed session is appropriate, he should suggest to the penitent that they fix a date, or talk after the confession if that is convenient. But it is *essential* to obtain the penitent's permission to do this, otherwise there is a breach of the seal. The secrecy of the confessional is carried over into the discussion. When such an extension of the confessional occurs, it is very important to let the penitent open the discussion in the same way as he does in the confessional itself.

The priest will often need to ask questions for the purpose of clarification. Penitents should not be allowed to get away with vagueness. 'I have been impure' may mean anything from occasional thoughts of lust or envy to forty years of continuous adultery. As it stands, it is meaningless. The vague penitent needs to see the importance of being specific about the seriousness and the frequency of sin. If a priest is not sure what part of a confession means, he should ask. On the other hand, masses of intimate detail should be avoided, and the priest should be careful not to be a voyeur and pry needlessly into details of sins. He needs enough detail for the confession to make sense, and no more. On no account must he inquire about other persons involved in the events mentioned, and the individual penitent must not mention other people by name. People should only be identified if it is relevant to the nature of the confession—for example, 'I have been resentful of my wife', 'I have neglected my mother', 'I have cheated my employer', and so on.

The purpose of questioning is clarification and discernment on the part of the priest. So she needs to purify her questioning by directing her thoughts away from the penitent and his sins towards God and his purity. Some older manuals give wise, if amusing advice about the questions to be asked. Thus the thirteenth-century *Summa de penitentia* of Thomas of Chabham, the sub-dean of Salisbury, commented:

> And the priest ought to inquire of the penitent, if he was drunk, how he got drunk, whether perchance because he did not know the power of the wine, or because of guests, or because of an exceeding thirst coming upon him . . . The priest ought to inquire of the penitent if he was accustomed to curse men or other creatures; for to be vehemently angry with God's creatures or with cattle, and to curse them, even with the ill will to harm them, which countrymen often do, cursing men and innocent animals, is a great sin; and also many men sin by this kind of sin, who do not believe they are sinning, and few coming to confession confess concerning wrath; and the priest ought to enjoin on the wrathful man silence for a certain time, or for some hour of the day.

The *Memoriale Presbiterorum* (about 1344) warns priests against inquiring too much into the sins of sailors! 'You must be very cautious and careful in inquiring because you should know that the pen can scarcely suffice to write the sins in which they are involved, for such is their wickedness that it exceeds that of all other men.'[62] Questions asked then need to be relevant, brief and careful. K. N. Ross in some guidelines for confessional practice advises that 'it is best to suggest by one's question that one assumes the sin to have been very grave indeed. It is easy then for the penitent to own up to something less serious.'[63]

One important element in clarification is the correction of superficial and distorted ideas of sin. Often a person will confess to happenings which cannot be seen as sinful. A sick person confesses that she didn't come to church, when in fact she could not and ought not to have done so. An adolescent, influenced perhaps by some pious list of sins, confesses to 'impurity' when in fact what he is confessing is healthy sexual desire. A parent confesses to anger towards his children without examining whether there was a right basis for the anger. A person may confess to temptations, thoughts, or distractions, as if they were themselves sinful. Gently but firmly, the confessor needs to draw attention to the dangers of confusion, and therefore of an unbalanced and harmful view of sin. If such views are not corrected, the progress of the Christian person towards wholeness may in fact be twisted, through the confessional, into a hardening of immaturity and childishness, the authentic and deep probing of the self is retarded by a focusing on the trivial and on stereotyped lists of sins. So the priest does not simply *accept* the confession as presented without question. He must aid the penitent in the formation of his conscience and help to free him from legalistic and superficial notions of sin. Sin is not a matter of violating a set of regulations: sin is that which prevents the flowering of man's glory, and delays his progress to perfection.

Again, there are people who cannot accept that they are forgiven. They reject themselves and assume that God does too. It is essential to help them to self-acceptance, including acceptance of the areas of their personality which they find distasteful and disturbing. It is essential, in other words, to preach the gospel of *acceptance*.

> Just as I am thou wilt receive,
> Wilt welcome, pardon, cleanse, relieve,
> Because thy promise I believe . . .

Acceptance and forgiveness cannot be earned, they are free gifts. Christianity is about acceptance: being accepted by God, and accepting that grace which is freely offered. On the other hand, there are always limits to what a person can bear at any given time. The realization of the depths of one's own sinfulness may be an experience which is too traumatic and reduces a person to despair. The confessor needs to learn gentleness and a sensitive approach to the encounter with truth. One of Charles Wesley's hymns prays that he may be allowed to see his sinfulness in proportion to his ability to endure it:

> Show me, as my soul can bear,
> The depth of inbred sin.

This is a vital principle in spiritual guidance, and it is embodied in the western distinction between material integrity and formal integrity.[64] Material integrity refers to what the penitent is obliged to confess if he can remember and is capable of responsible distinctions, free choices, and so on. As Bernard Haring points out, 'at times material integrity is not possible or even not allowed', and that 'there will be times when acceptance of the minimum in legal matters is in the best spiritual interests of a particular penitent . . . No confessor can impose spiritual growth like a law upon his penitent. But, at the same time, no confessor should shrink from encouraging his penitent gently to a higher life.'[65]

In the confessional, the priest needs to maintain an unembarrassed, unshocked, relaxed manner. Many people are deterred from making their confession at all, or are very frightened during it, by the thought that the priest will be shocked, will have a low opinion of them, or will treat them differently in future. It is essential then to show that this is not so. After a while, if one is hearing confessions regularly, one does in fact cease to be surprised by most things. Even today, sexual sins are those which cause most alarm and embarrassment, and people still believe that their sexual failings are unique and do not appear frequently. In fact, the sexual area is not so varied as is sometimes thought, and after a while, one reaches saturation point and ceases to be surprised, if indeed one ever was. There is a limit to the number of things one can actually do, sinful or not! But, even when there is shock or surprise, the priest ought not to show it. She is there not to represent her own feelings, but to be the minister of God's acceptance and reconciliation. This does not, of course, mean that she needs to remain 'impersonal' all the time. It is often helpful to smile, to put the penitent at ease, and at times to laugh. Laughter plays an important, though limited, role in the confessional. The penitent who exaggerates and distorts the significance of some minor sin so that it becomes worse and dominates him needs to be helped to laugh at what he is doing.

Again, the stress on the stretched out hands over the penitent is an important element in the new rite. Different confessors will vary in their approach to physical contact. Some are naturally physically extrovert and warm, others more restrained and reserved. God uses, and works through, all types of confessors. Some priests may need reminding that it is not unknown for some penitents to interpret too expressive a laying on of hands as a sexual advance. Others may find the opposite danger, of being too aloof and remote, raises more pastoral problems for them.

The kind of penance given needs more thought than is usually devoted to it. We need to avoid notions of 'making the penance fit the sin' in a legalistic way, but to recognize the truth that there is a relationship between them. Most penances consist of standard prayers—a collect, the Hail Mary, and so on. One excellent American handbook for confessors suggests a series of penances related to the type of sin. For example, for uncharitable words about another, one might prescribe a deliberate act of speaking positively to that person. Or for irreverent swearing, the saying of the name of Jesus a specified number of times. Or for marital infidelity, a definite act of love such as a gift for no special reason, or taking the initiative in making love, or making up a quarrel. The point to remember is that a penance ceases to be a penance if it becomes too complicated to perform, and it then becomes something else. The late Canon Colin Stephenson once told the story of how, as a young man, he was given a penance, 'Go and make yourself a living sacrifice.' Having worried for some time about how exactly to do this, he eventually sought advice from another priest who told him, 'Don't worry about it, say three Hail Marys.' On the one hand, it is surely a psychological error to make penances so easy and trivial that they are almost an insult to the penitent. The fact is that to come to confession at all has probably meant a reasonable degree of effort and organization, and there can be a sense of anticlimax if a person feels that, after he has put himself out, the priest seems to treat the operation less than seriously. On the other hand, to turn the penance into a kind of community service order is to misunderstand its function. It is vital that Christian people do develop a strong sense of service to their fellow human beings, and this may well be, and should be, one of the results of the practice of penitence. But such a commitment to service is a *result* of penitence, and not the penance itself. If penance becomes too arduous, then it becomes easy to see it as a means of earning forgiveness and a denial of God's free grace and pardon. The Christian life itself is arduous and demanding, but it is not a means of earning God's forgiveness. So the penance should relate to the sin, and should begin to undo some of the damage caused by the sin, and strengthen the person in the opposite direction, the direction of grace and holiness.

Of course, the confessor, like the counsellor, is a listener, and the listening is a vital part of the ministry in the confessional. But there is more to reconciliation than the understanding ear. There is struggle and conflict. Max Thurian says that 'confession may be considered as a sort of exorcism in which Christ does battle against the powers of evil'.[66] It is important to see and express the participation in that shared conflict. The new rite lays emphasis on the fact that priest and penitent celebrate the sacrament together, and there are a number of simple ways in which this mutuality can be brought out. It is helpful to pray aloud with the penitent, to say an act of sorrow together, to say the thanksgiving or the penance together. It is good to personalize the absolution or blessing by saying one's own prayer for the individual penitent before either or both. Before the penitent leaves, and also at other times she should be asked to pray for her confessor.

The seal of the confessional is, of course, absolute.[67] A priest must never speak about sins confessed, or about any other matter raised during a confession, even to the penitent himself, except during the course of spiritual direction and with his permission. Such a conversation must be treated as also subject to the seal. This is extremely important not only in its own right but also as a protection to the priest's reputation. Nothing can undermine one's pastoral work so quickly and so permanently as a reputation for breaking confidences. It should be added that a reputation for gossip and undisciplined chatter, *even unconnected with the confessional*, can also damage a priest's reputation almost irreparably. If people think you are the kind of person who *might* break the seal of the confessional, they are unlikely to take the risk. Careful discipline of the tongue at all times is therefore a basic requirement in the confessor. It is necessary also to remember that some penitents tend to 'play off' one priest against another, and one should beware of the danger of being asked to criticize the advice given by another. Extreme care and discretion are nourished and increased by prayer and the practice of inner silence. It is also worth remembering that there are ways of indirectly breaking the seal. For example, appearing upset or emotionally worried after some serious matter has been confessed, or sighing with relief or weariness after some particularly difficult penitent. Statements such as 'B—is one of my penitents' should be avoided: the priest has no business to announce who does or does not go to confession, or to whom they go, and this kind of statement certainly borders on a breach of the seal.

Finally, it is difficult, and spiritually dangerous, to hear confessions if one is not oneself a regular penitent. The priest who is continually used by others needs to take exceptional care of her own inner resources and inner nourishment. Karl Rahner suggests that monthly reception of the sacrament of penance could be a good norm for those who are serious about the Christian life. Certainly, for a priest to grow slack about her own penitential practice can be disastrous. Bonhoeffer refers to the dangers to the confessor:

> It is not a good thing for one person to be the confessor for all the others. All too easily this one person will be overburdened; thus confession will become for him an empty routine and this will give rise to the disastrous misuse of the confessional for the exercise of spiritual domination of souls. In order that he may not succumb to this sinister danger of the confessional, every person should refrain from listening to confession who does not himself practise it. Only the person who has so humbled himself can hear a brother's confession without harm.[68]

This is strong language, but it is justified by the facts. An important corollary of it is that clergy need to be particularly sensitive to the penitential needs of their fellow clergy. The mutual care of priest for priest includes the sacrament of penance, and there will certainly be some priests who are called to exercise this ministry to a considerable degree. Without such a discipline of continual repentance and continual healing, no priest can hope to survive in the spiritual conflict.

THE CONFESSIONS OF CHILDREN
The question of children's confessions raises special problems which are outside the scope of this study, but some reference ought to be made to the matter. To what extent is a child capable of true *metanoia*? How much consciousness of sin is there in a child? What should be the connection between confession and communion? In traditional Roman practice, first confession and first communion have until recently been closely associated, but this association is now increasingly under question. Anglican practice has been more varied. Often those churches which have taught and practised sacramental confession have either waived the insistence in the case of young children, or have simply advised a preconfirmation confession, and then have quietly dropped the matter. Yet clearly one cannot ignore the issues of repentance, confession and spiritual guidance in the pastoral care of children. Nevertheless, most pastors would agree that 'the young schoolchild at least is still too

young for personal spiritual guidance to be really possible or justified in his case'.[69]

For the first twelve hundred years of the church, there seems to
be no conclusive evidence that children were ever absolved, though
young children were admitted to communion. In 1215 the Lateran
decree that the faithful were to confess annually once they had
reached 'years of discretion' was taken to include young children,
though there were variations about age. The Council of Trent
certainly cleared up one difficulty in that it ruled that confession
was only necessarily related to communion when mortal sin was
involved, and that the annual confession only applied in cases of
mortal sin. Pope Pius X's decree *Quam Singulari* of 1910 was
intended to put an end to the refusal of sacramental absolution to
children, and this decree specifically defined the age of reason as
'approximately the age of seven years'. From this age, children
should be communicated, and therefore absolved. The custom that
confession preceded the reception of communion prevailed virtually from 1910 to the Second Vatican Council in many places,
although since the Council it has become customary for bishops
to permit delay of confession until several years after first communion. So in nearly half of American and Canadian Roman
Catholic dioceses, the custom arose of preparing children for communion at 7–8 years of age, and for confession at 9–12 years of
age. The new rite of penance is certainly not intended for use
by children. However, the General Catechetical Directory (1971)
insisted that first confessions should still precede first communion,
and that when any new practice in this area had begun, those
responsible must communicate with the Holy See. The Declaration
issued by the Roman Curia on 24 May 1973 stated that the widespread practice of admitting children to communion without confession should be ended.

However, the differences of outlook remain. There are many
within the Roman Communion who would discourage private
confession of children altogether.[70] They suggest that young
children should instead take part in a penitential celebration involving common reflection and examination of conscience, a communal
litany and prayer of sorrow. Then each child would approach the
celebrant and say, 'Father, I ask God's forgiveness for all the times
I did wrong', and he would then give individual absolutions followed by the sign of peace which would then be passed to other
members of the congregation. Children would then be gradually

introduced to private confession, and the parents, where possible, would be involved in helping them to understand it. When the Catholic Conference of Canada sought direction on how the Declaration of 24 May 1973 should be interpreted, the two cardinal prefects insisted that 'there is no question of regimenting children in order to make them all pass through the confessional before first communion', but on the other hand, 'neither should they be placed in a climate that would prevent them from receiving the sacrament of penance before their first communion'.[71] The aim was to create a pastoral atmosphere in which the preparation for both sacraments should be given within the same period of time.

At the International Catechetical Congress held in Rome in September 1971, however, the English language working group had made the following recommendation:

> Each child should celebrate the sacrament of penance for the first time when he personally is ready. This readiness, out of respect for the sacrament, implies and requires his own free choice... Each child should be treated as an individual in the matter of the first reception of the sacraments of Holy Eucharist and Penance, and no law should seek to determine the order in which they are celebrated.[72]

Certainly the traditional Roman practice is open to serious criticism. Can it be seriously maintained, on either theological or psychological grounds, that the criteria for assessing readiness for communion are the same as those for confession? Does not the need for nourishment and sharing in the family meal begin earlier than the capacity for sin? Again, does not the child's experience of being *loved* and *received* by God precede the experience of being *forgiven*? In any case, does not the Eucharist itself remit sins? The grounds for insisting on confession before communion in the case of children, irrespective of age, seem very flimsy. Monsignor P. J. A. Moors, the Bishop of Roermond, in 1964 argued that an early age for confession was especially dangerous because it encouraged a pharisaical and legalistic understanding of sin which might actually impede conversion and change of heart.[73] To insist on confession of sin *before* the personal conscience and freedom of moral decision is really developed can be theologically and psychologically harmful.

If we were to continue the practice of introducing our children to confession at an age when it is still impossible for them to have any real insight into the motives behind the actions, then we run the great risk of promoting a view of sin which is limited and incorrect.[74]

In the 'guiding principles' issued by the Bishop of Roermond, the emphasis was therefore on the introduction to confession in phases, so that the development of the child was taken into account.[75] This is both sensible and necessary. To introduce rigid labels at an early stage is likely to lead to immaturity and lack of responsibility in later life, and there are already many adult Christians who are afflicted in this way. Because of this, they are very ill-prepared to cope with the changes and upheavals in present-day society.

Again, in early adolescence, it is all too easy for confession to be obsessive and dangerously associated with sex, and there is enough evidence from the past that serious harm has been done to future sexual life by unhealthy guilt deriving from this kind of association. This is not, of course, to say that sexual sins should be bypassed, still less that the sensitive and complex area of sexual responsibility should be ignored. But two points need to be made. First, as a result of a faulty doctrine of sin, and of the low view of human sexuality which has afflicted much Christian teaching, many young people have been led to believe that the church is *more* concerned with sexual sin than with any other sort of sin, indeed that the church believes that the sexual act is itself sinful or at least sordid. Secondly, to *introduce* confession of sin at the very point in development when sexual identity is becoming so central is fraught with the danger of encouraging these wrong attitudes. Fr Crichton, perhaps the best known Roman Catholic authority on penance in this country, is very emphatic on these dangers.

As a priest who has been in the pastoral ministry for 41 years . . . it is a matter of conviction to me, born of the experience of preparing children through all these years for their first communion, that they are psychologically incapable of making a confession worthy of the name. You can of course teach them formulas, you can make up lists of 'sins', which they will repeat if told to, but they have no apprehension of *sin*, even if they may have some vague notion of 'right' and 'wrong'.[76]

Certainly the thinking behind the Second Vatican Council would discourage a rigid demand for early confession. In the Council's

Declaration on Religious Education, it was stressed that children should be helped to acquire a mature sense of responsibility in pursuing freedom and embracing moral values by personal choice. The Constitution on the Sacred Liturgy also stressed that 'the faithful should take part fully aware of what they are doing, actively engaged in the rite'. Can this be said of young children and the sacrament of penance?

How then can the question of children's confessions be best approached? One German Roman Catholic writer has suggested that 'the power of forgiveness which the parents receive in sacramental confession becomes effective also in the children, and here too salvation is mediated vicariously'. It is also true that the sacrament of penance is not, and never has been, the only method of forgiveness. The early Christian theologians would certainly have been amazed to be told that small children were urged to go to confession every few weeks. Confession, Betz argues, is 'primarily a sacrament of the adult'.[77] It can, and frequently will, be extended to children, but it should be set within the developing experience of love and forgiveness in the wider community of the church.

First, the right context of spiritual guidance and of the experience of forgiveness is the home and family, and pastoral care should be aimed at helping parents to see their vital role. To ask pardon from mummy and daddy and to know what their forgiveness and acceptance means is the right way for the child to come to an understanding of these ideas. Piaget's stages of moral judgement are well known. The child, he argued, judges evil first by the amount of *material damage* caused, later by the degree of *punishment* or *social blame*, and finally by the inner sense of *wrongness*. The American psychologist Lawrence Kohlberg, working from a similar basis, has produced a more comprehensive analysis of the stages of moral judgement. He classifies six stages, the first two of which are pre-moral, and the second two of which are merely concerned with extrinsic or conventional morality.

Kohlberg's Stages of Moral Judgement
1 Fear of punishment
2 Hope of reward
3 Desire for social approval
4 Respect for law and order
5 Respect for the rights of others
6 Appreciation of principles such as justice, goodness, etc.

Kohlberg believes that less than 33 per cent of adults (in the USA) have attained to the fifth stage. Spiritual direction, however, is concerned with helping individuals to move away from the early stages towards a more interior and God-centred moral sense.[78]

Secondly, there can be services of penitence which are designed for children, as the revised rites are not, and the Dutch and American experiments in this area have much to teach us.

Thirdly, when finally the child is introduced to private confession, some simple guidelines are worth noting. There should not be too much talk about sin at an early stage before the child is able to distinguish various kinds of behaviour. If sin is identified in his mind with anti-social behaviour, he will find confession difficult, and it will eventually become trivial and ridiculous. The child must be allowed to express his consciousness of sin in his own way, and must not be forced to an awareness beyond his powers. If the child cannot recognize sins for himself, he cannot be expected to confess them. Young children are not capable of committing serious sins, and a general confession is not only acceptable but is also theologically and psychologically correct. It makes for informality, reduces anxiety, and shifts the emphasis towards God and love. The sense of joy at deliverance from sin needs emphasis, and a party after a first confession is worth considering.

SPIRITUAL DIRECTION AND CONFESSION

It is clear from what has been said that spiritual direction and the practice of confession are closely associated, but are also quite distinct. There can be confession without direction, direction without confession, and often both confession and direction in different times and places but involving the same people. Today, much thinking in the Roman Communion, both in Europe and in Britain, favours 'a clear division between sacrament and counsel'.[79] 'The confessional can serve psychological health only in a very limited sense.'[80] It is argued by many Roman Catholics that 'the sacrament of penance is tied to spiritual direction in a way detrimental to both'.[81]

Of course, the voluntary nature of confession in the Anglican tradition combined with the fact that only a minority of Anglicans are regular penitents has meant that the situation of the Saturday night 'confessional queue' was never a reality except in some central city churches. But it is no longer a reality today for Roman

Catholics either. A Dutch priest, writing over ten years ago, observed that 'the rows of penitents one used to see sitting near the confessionals in almost any church on a Saturday evening, even during the years after the war, have disappeared'.[82] Today it is said that confessions have dropped by some 50 per cent in Europe and by up to 75 per cent in parts of the United States.[83] Among Anglicans the relative concentration of confession and direction in certain churches, particularly in central London, is a phenomenon which seems likely to continue. In the City of London and in some central parishes with fairly small residential populations, some priests have built up valuable ministries of spiritual direction. Clearly, there is a value in such 'specialists'. But it would be both unfair and unrealistic to limit this ministry to them, and ignore the need for a much more widespread growth throughout the church. It is surely important for every priest to see the ministry of absolution as a vital part of his cure of souls. The new *Ordo* is surely right also to stress the necessity for *all* confessors to acquire knowledge of 'the diseases of the soul', 'the needed knowledge and prudence', and 'the discernment of spirits'.[84]

The problem, however, remains of how much spiritual guidance can be usefully given within the structure of the confessional, and what is suggested here is simply based on one priest's experience. There are, in my view, serious objections to the use of the confessional as a *locus* of spiritual direction on a regular basis. First, the structure is not conducive to openness and equality. The penitent is kneeling in a posture of submission, and the priest, representing the church, is sitting facing the opposite direction. It is a situation ideally suited to the symbolism of repentance and restoration, not to that of mutual exploration and progress. These are complementary but distinct aspects of the Christian life. Secondly, the time factor is important. If others are waiting, it is impossible to do more than speak a few words of basic counsel. But to do this as a substitute for direction can be dangerous. True spiritual direction demands time, patience and a relaxed attitude. Thirdly, it is important for people to realize that they come to confession to confess, and not necessarily to receive advice or guidance. There may, of course, be situations where the formality and secrecy of the confessional makes the expression of certain needs, fears and worries easier, and there are certainly some individuals who find this atmosphere an aid to honesty and truthfulness. But many people do not find this so.

The experience of many priests is that where there is a regular and continuing relationship of personal direction, the best approach is to limit the confession period to the actual confession of sins and absolution, a simple liturgical celebration of penitence and praise in which priest and penitent join, and to reserve more lengthy discussion of spiritual progress and problems for a meeting prior to, or following the confession. The seal may, of course, be extended to this discussion, though all ministry of this type needs to maintain its confidential character, whether the official seal applies or not. There may be some situations in which a confession may be made in an informal way. An individual may have some difficulty in formulating what he has to say, and the actual process of confession may take a long time, the confession being mixed up with the discussion of many issues in life. In such cases it may well be sensible to regard the whole discussion as the confession, and to absolve at the end of it, rather than to go through the formality of confession again. Flexibility is essential.

At the present time when the whole framework of sacramental confession is changing, it may be that 'informal confessions' of this type will become increasingly the norm. If so, there will be a greater need than ever to clarify the place of the seal and the unchanging elements within this ministry. The practice of confession does not necessarily suffer because boxes and grilles disappear. It will suffer severely if it loses its character and degenerates into a vague and friendly chat. We should not be surprised if some new formal structure is found necessary. Human beings do not totally abandon rituals; they replace one ritual by another. It is unlikely that the practice of confession, where it remains, will survive without some framework and liturgical shape, and some of the general outlines which have been examined above.

Notes

Introduction

1 W. F. S. Pickering, 'The British priest and the secular world', *Theology* 77 (1974), p. 572.
2 Joseph McCulloch, *My Affair with the Church* (1976), p. 178.
3 Martin Thornton, *English Spirituality* (1963), pp. xiii, 3.
4 Words quoted on the cover of the first UK edition.
5 *Cornish Churchman*, June 1977.
6 Introduction to American edition, Harper and Row 1980, pp. vi–ix.
7 Much of this section is based on my article 'Is spiritual direction losing its bearings?' in *The Tablet*, 22 May 1993. I am grateful to the Editor for permission to reproduce the material here.
8 Jean Leclercq, *Fairacres Chronicle* 12 (1979), pp. 6f.
9 Margaret Guenther, *Holy Listening: the art of spiritual direction* (1992), p. 95.
10 See Philip Rieff, *The Triumph of the Therapeutic* (1966). Christopher Lasch's *The Culture of Narcissism* (1979) is greatly influenced by Rieff's work.
11 On Myers-Briggs see Malcolm Goldsmith and Martin Wharton, *Knowing Me, Knowing You* (1993) and David Kiersey and Marilyn Bates, *Please Understand Me* (1978).
12 See Ira Progoff, *At a Journal Workshop* (1975).
13 Christopher Lasch, 'Probing gnosticism in its modern derivatives', *New Oxford Review*, December 1990, pp. 4–10.

Chapter 1

1 Timothy Leary, *The Politics of Ecstasy* (1968), p. 231.
2 Jeff Nuttall, *Bomb Culture* (1971 edn), p. 164.
3 *Youthquake* (1973).
4 Laurie Taylor in *New Society*, 4 October 1973.
5 R. E. Terwilliger in *The Charismatic Christ* (1974), p. 57.
6 Andrew Greeley, *The Persistence of Religion* (1973), p. 1.
7 *The Non-Medical Use of Drugs* (1971), p. 223.
8 R. D. Laing in *The Role of Religion in Mental Health* (1967), p. 54.
9 Meher Baba, *God in a Pill?* (San Francisco, Sufism Reoriented, 1968).
10 Cited in Baba Ram Dass, *Doing Your Own Being* (1973), p. 33.
11 Cf. Richard Alpert (Baba Ram Dass) in Symposium on World Spirituality, *Cross Currents* 14: 2–3 (Summer/Fall 1974), p. 346.
12 Theodore Roszak, *The Making of a Counter Culture* (1968), p. 177.
13 Michael Hollingshead, *The Man Who Turned on the World* (1973), pp. 130, 211, 241–2.
14 *Heaven and Hell* (1956), p. 63.

15 Benjamin Blood, *The Anaesthetic Revelation and the Gist of Philosophy* (1874); William James, *The Varieties of Religious Experience* (1902).
16 See Brian Inglis, *The Forbidden Game* (1975), Mircea Eliade, *Shamanism* (1964), and P. T. Furst, *Flesh of the Gods* (1972). In recent years not only has LSD returned as a popular drug within youth cultures, but a range of amphetamine derivatives, such as MDMA and MDA, have become integral elements within the 'rave' scene. Yet the issues for spirituality arising from chemical approaches to consciousness remain the same as they were when I first wrote this section.
17 *Where the Wasteland Ends* (1972), p. 73.
18 1971 edn, p. 188.
19 *The Realist*, October 1968.
20 E. F. Schumacher, *Small is Beautiful* (1974 edn), p. 250.
21 *The Greening of America* (1971), p. 395.
22 *The End of our Exploring* (1973), p. 20. Since then, of course, the 'New Age' movements have created a new kind of spiritual counter-culture, though the similarities to the counter-culture of the 1960s are more striking than the differences. The emphasis on the environment, and the millenarian dimension, are more strongly marked in the newer movements. On the New Age and Christian spirituality see Wesley Carr, *Manifold Wisdom: the Church's ministry in the New Age* (1991) and David Toolan, *Facing West from California's Shores: a Jesuit's journey into New Age consciousness* (1987).
23 *Siddhartha* (tr. Hilda Rosner, New York, 1951), pp. 6, 8, 37.
24 Mark Boulby, *Hermann Hesse: His Mind and Art* (Ithaca, Cornell UP, 1967), p. 136.
25 Cited in Theodore Ziolkowski, *Hermann Hesse* (New York, Columbia UP, 1966), p. 14.
26 *The Sunday Times*, 22 July 1973.
27 *The Observer*, 15 July 1973.
28 Sandy Collier, *Man Alive*, BBC 2, 31 May 1972.
29 Glen Whittaker, letter in *The Times*, 11 October 1973.
30 Pamphlet issued by the Spiritual Regeneration Movement.
31 Fred E. Dexter in International Narcotics Conference, 12th Annual Conference, International Narcotic Enforcement Officers' Association, 29 August–3 September 1971, Report, p. 68.
32 Letter, 29 June 1971 cited *ibid.*
33 *The Guardian*, 20 March 1975.
34 *World in Action*, Granada TV, 10 June 1974.
35 *Ibid.*
36 'The Miracle of Being Awake', *Peace News*, 5 December 1975.
37 *Bhagavad Gita Commentary* (1966), p. 193.
38 Una Kroll, *TM: A Signpost for the World* (1974), p. 62.
39 Maharishi Mahesh Yogi, *The Science of Being and Art of Living* (1966), pp. 58–9.
40 Michael Schofield, *The Strange Case of Pot* (1971), p. 182.
41 John A. T. Robinson, *The Difference in Being a Christian Today* (1972), pp. 51–2.
42 F. C. Happold, *Prayer and Meditation* (1971), p. 21. This idea is, of course, common in 'New Age' movements.

43 *A Personal Message to You from the Sixth Man on the Moon*, MS., Institute of Noetic Sciences, Palo Alto, California.

44 *Silent Music* (1974), p. 21.

45 Cited in Thomas Merton, *Mystics and Zen Masters* (1967), pp. 14ff.

46 Nhat Hanh, *op. cit.*

47 *Children of God, Jesus People or Revolution?*, undated. The Children of God, also known since the 1970s as 'The Family of Love' or simply 'The Family', have continued to be controversial. During 1992 and 1993 there were a number of allegations of child sexual abuse within their communities, and children were removed from their centres in various countries including Australia and Argentina.

48 James T. Richardson, 'Alienation and political orientation', MS. 1975. While the Jesus Movement in its 1960s' form no longer exists, I have kept this section essentially as it was, since the main positions and features of that movement have been absorbed into, and are still manifested within, many forms of fundamentalist Christianity. The language of the movement – 'Marches for Jesus', 'The Jesus Army' and so on – are still common.

49 D. W. Basham, *A Handbook on Holy Spirit Baptism* (1969), p. 10.

50 F. A. Sullivan SJ, ' "Baptism in the Holy Spirit": a Catholic interpretation of the Pentecostal experience', *Gregorianum* 55 (Rome 1974), p. 49.

51 Cited in Peter Hebblethwaite, 'The Politics of the Holy Spirit', *Frontier* 18:3 (1975), p. 145.

52 *Renewal*, October-November 1972, pp. 28–9.

53 Kilian McDonnell, 'Statement of the theological basis of the Catholic charismatic renewal', *One in Christ* 10:2 (1974), pp. 206–15.

54 Alistair Kee (ed.), *Seeds of Liberation* (1973), pp. vii, 3.

55 Gustavo Gutierrez, *A Theology of Liberation* (1974), pp. 204–5.

56 Cited in Alain Gheerbrandt, *The Rebel Church in Latin America* (1974), pp. 63–4.

57 A response to Lausanne: statement by about 200 participants.

58 Cited in J.-M. Bonino, *Revolutionary Theology Comes of Age* (1975), p. 38.

59 *Ibid.*, p. xix. On the quest for spirituality within liberation theology see Segundo Galilea, *The Future of Our Past* (1985) and *The Way of Living Faith: a spirituality of liberation* (1988); Gustavo Gutierrez, *We Drink from our Own Wells* (1985); and Jon Sobrino, *Spirituality of Liberation* (1988). For the wider issues see my book *The Eye of the Storm: spiritual resources for the pursuit of justice* (1992).

60 James Cone, *Black Theology and Black Power* (1969), pp. 38, 151.

61 Mary Daly in Alice L. Hageman (ed.), *Sexist Religion and Women in the Church* (1974), p. 138.

62 Rosemary Ruether, 'Male clericalism and the dread of women', *The Ecumenist* 11:5 (1973), p. 69.

63 Nathan A. Scott, *The Wild Prayer of Longing: Poetry and the Sacred* (1971), p. xiv.

64 John A. T. Robinson, *Honest to God* (1963), p. 100.

65 Douglas Rhymes, *Prayer in the Secular City* (1967), p. 84.

66 *Canterbury Pilgrim* (1974), pp. 59–60.

67 See, J.-M. Déchanet, *Christian Yoga* (1960) and *Yoga and God* (1974); J. Winslow, *Christian Yoga* (Poona, 1923); Aelred Graham, *Zen Catholicism*

(1963); William Johnston, *Christian Zen* (1971); H. E. W. Slade, *Exploration into Contemplative Prayer* (1975); Abhishiktananda, *Prayer* (1967); Una Kroll, *TM: A Signpost for the World* (1974); Anita Woodwell, 'TM: a Christian approach', *Encounter and Exchange* 15 (1976), pp. 22–6; Basil Pennington, 'TM and Christian prayer', *New Fire* 4:26 (1976), pp. 28–34.

68 *The Pentecostal Experience* (1970), p. 22.
69 *Anthology of the Love of God* (1953), pp. 123ff.
70 *Ibid.*
71 'Contemplation and Resistance', *Peace News*, 18 May 1973.

Chapter 2

1 *Teach Us to Pray* (1974), p. 41.
2 Igumen Chariton of Valamo, *The Art of Prayer: An Orthodox Anthology*, tr. E. Kadloubovsky and E. M. Palmer (1966), p. 116.
3 *Confession* (1958), p. 69.
4 *The Purple Headed Mountain* (1962), p. 14.
5 *The Charismatic Christ* (1974), p. 46.
6 *The Rock and the River* (1965), pp. 141–2.
7 *De Oratione* 60.
8 *Ladder of Divine Ascent* 30.
9 Vladimir Lossky, *The Mystical Theology of the Eastern Church* (1968 edn), pp. 9, 39.
10 *The Love of God* 6:1.
11 *Evangelical Theology* (1963), p. 160.
12 *English Spirituality* (1963), p. 25.
13 *Spiritual Espousals*, Book 2.
14 P. Pourrat, *Christian Spirituality* (1922) I, pp. 185, 187.
15 *Ibid.*, I, p. v.
16 Martin Thornton, *English Spirituality* (1963), p. 24.
17 *Ethics* 20.
18 Abhishiktananda, *Guru and Disciple* (1974), p. 28.
19 Swami Venkalesananda in *Cross Currents* 24: 2–3 (1974), p. 273.
20 Cited in J. T. McNeill, *A History of the Cure of Souls* (1952), p. 43.
21 *Ibid.*, p. 44.
22 *Cross Currents*, op. cit., p. 277.
23 Cited in R. Garrigou-Lagrange, *The Three Ages of the Interior Life* (1960 edn) I, p. 256.
24 *Apol.* I.18.
25 *Apophthegmata*, Alpha Antonii, n. 38, in Benedicta Ward, *The Sayings of the Desert Fathers* (1975), p. 7.
26 Cited in *Cistercian Studies* 3:1 (1968), p. 17.
27 *Apophthegmata*, Alpha Poemen 174, Ward, p. 160.
28 Owen Chadwick, *John Cassian* (1968), p. 86.
29 Louis Bouyer, *The Spirituality of the New Testament and the Fathers* I (1963), p. 381.
30 Palladius, Lausiac History, in *Ancient Christian Writers*, Vol. 34 (Washington 1964), 38:10.
31 Cited in *Evagrius Ponticus, The Praktikos; Chapters on Prayer* xlv.

32 E. A. W. Budge, *The Book of Paradise Being the Histories and Sayings of the Monks and Ascetics of the Egyptian Desert* I (1904), p. 1043.
33 In Owen Chadwick (ed.), *Western Asceticism* (1958), p. 195.
34 *Ibid.*, p. 214.
35 *Ibid.*, p. 239.
36 E. Kadloubovsky and G. E. H. Palmer, *Early Fathers from the Philokalia* (1964), pp. 162, 263.
37 *Ladder of Divine Assent* I.4.
38 Cited in McNeill, *op. cit.*, p. 307.
39 Kadloubovsky and Palmer, *Writings from the Philokalia* (1961), pp. 100–3, 93, 174–5.
40 Igumen Chariton, *op. cit.*, pp. 62, 97–8, 116, 268–9, 170.
41 Louis Bouyer, *Orthodox Spirituality and Protestant and Anglican Spirituality* (1969), p. 36.
42 Julia de Beausobre (ed.), *Macarius: Russian Letters of Direction 1834–1860* (1947), pp. 23, 28.
43 A. F. Dobbie-Bateman (tr.), *St Seraphim of Sarov Concerning the Aim of the Christian Life* (1936), p. 53.
44 G. P. Fedotov, *A Treasury of Russian Spirituality* (1948), p. 348.
45 *Spiritual Counsels of Father John of Kronstadt*, ed. W. Jardine Grisbrooke (1967), p. 122.
46 Cited in John B. Dunlop, *Staretz Amvrosy* (1975), p. 60.
47 Zossima in *The Brothers Karamazov*.
48 *Regula Pastoralis* 1.1.
49 *Ibid.* 2.2; *Morals on Job* 22: 31–4.
50 A. Owen, *Ancient Laws and Institutes of Wales* (1841) I, p. 28.
51 Cited in Martin Thornton, *English Spirituality* (1963), p. 154.
52 See Rule, chs. 49, Prologue, chs. 3 and 2.
53 J. Leclercq, F. Vandenbroucke and L. Bouyer, *The Spirituality of the Middle Ages* (1968), p. 84.
54 *Opusculum* 7; *Letter* 188.
55 Cited Leclercq *et al.*, *op. cit.*, p. 121, n. 141.
56 Cited Thornton, *op. cit.*, p. 166.
57 *In obitu domini Humberti* 4, cited in J. Leclercq, *Cistercian Studies* 7:2 (1972), p. 132.
58 *Letter* 112 in *The Letters of St Bernard of Clairvaux*, tr. Bruno Scott James (1953), p. 169.
59 *In circumcisione Domini* 3:11.
60 *The Mirror of Faith*, chs. 7, 13.
61 A. Le Bail, 'La spiritualité cistercienne', in *Cahiers du cercle Thomiste feminin* 7 (1927), cited in Amédée Hallier, *The Monastic Theology of Aelred of Rievaulx*, *Cistercian Studies*, Shannon 1969, p. 121, n. 34.
62 *Pastoral Prayer* 7, 8.
63 *Spiritual Friendship*.
64 Introduction to Hallier, *op. cit.*, p. xxvii.
65 *Spiritual Friendship*.
66 A. I. Doyle, *The Age of Chaucer* (1954), p. 70.
67 Cited Leclercq *et al.*, *op. cit.*, p. 324.
68 *Ibid.*, p. 325.

69 Joy Russell-Smith in J. Walsh (ed.), *Pre-Reformation English Spirituality* (no date), p. 192.

70 Bod. Lat. th. e. 26 fol. 127.

71 *Imitation of Christ*, I.4.

72 *A Treatise on the Spiritual Life* by St Vincent Ferrer OP, with Commentary by Mother Julienne Morrell OP (1957), ch. 4., pp. 92–3.

73 W. A. Pantin, *The English Church in the Fourteenth Century* (1962), p. 192.

74 Cited *ibid.*, p. 192, n. 1.

75 I have not been able to locate the exact source of this reference.

76 *Cistercian Studies* 3:1 (1968), p. 3.

77 *Mens Nostra*, 20 December 1919.

78 Paul Molinari SJ in *Spode House Review* 9:102 (1973), p. 28.

79 *The Spiritual Exercises* (cited hereafter as *Exercises*) 15.

80 *Ibid.*, 6, 7, 17.

81 *Directory*, ch. 5.

82 *Ibid.*, ch. 8.

83 *Christian Spirituality* (1924), III, pp. 23–48.

84 Joseph de Guibert, *The Jesuits: Their Spiritual Doctrine and Practice* (1964), p. 167.

85 *Ibid.*, p. 310.

86 *Holy Wisdom*, I.2.2, para. 2.

87 *Ibid.* I.2.2., para. 3.

88 *Ibid.* I.2.2., para. 7.

89 *Ibid.* I.2.2., para. 11.

90 *Ibid* .I.2.2., para. 13.

91 Ibid. I.2.2., para. 19.

92 Pourrat, *op. cit.*, III, p. 282.

93 *Sermon on the Feast of Our Lady of Sorrows*.

94 *Introduction to the Devout Life*, I.4.

95 *Ibid.*

96 *Ibid.*, II.19.

97 *Letter 107* in Elizabeth Stopp (tr.), *St Francis de Sales: Selected Letters* (1960), p. 263.

98 *Ibid.*, Letter 114, p. 276; p. 267, n. 1.

99 Francis Vincent, S. *François de Sales, directeur d'âmes* (Paris 1923), p. 398. On his method see pages 397–547.

100 Letter to Sister Jeanne le Peintre, 23 February 1650, cited in *The Way* 2:3 (1962), pp. 222–3.

101 *Living Flame of Love* 3:33 (Second Redaction).

102 *Dark Night of the Soul* I.10.2.

103 *Living Flame of Love* 3:30.

104 St Teresa, *Life* 13.

105 *Ascent of Mount Carmel*, Prologue.

106 *Living Flame of Love* 3:43.

107 *Ibid.* 3:56.

108 St Teresa, *Way of Perfection* 24:2.

109 *Living Flame of Love* 3:59.

110 *Life* 4:8–9.

111 *Ibid.* 4:6.

112 *Ibid.* 14.

113 *Ibid.* 13.

114 *Ibid.*

115 *Ascent of Mount Carmel* 2:22; 2:18.

116 *Self-Abandonment to the Divine Providence* I.1.1.

117 *Ibid.* II.3.1.

118 *Letters*, Book 3:14.

119 *Ibid.* 5:12.

120 *Manual for Interior Souls*, ch. 21.

121 E. W. Trueman Dicken, 'St John of the Cross and modern English spirituality' in *Mount Carmel* 19:1 (1971), p. 6.

122 F. W. Faber, *Growth in Holiness* (1960 edn), pp. 235, 237–8, 239.

123 *Ibid.*, p. 242.

124 *Ibid.*, p. 244.

125 *Ibid.*, p. 150.

126 *Ibid.*, p. 254.

127 Cited in J. T. McNeill, *op. cit.*, p. 294.

128 Cited in A. Saudreau, *The Degrees of the Spiritual Life: A Method of Directing Souls According to their Progress in Virtue* (1926 edn) I, p. 65.

129 Cited *ibid.* II, p. 151.

130 *Ibid.* II, p. 245.

131 Cited in Dom Raymond Thibout, *Abbot Columba Marmion* (1932), p. 233. See the whole of Chapter 11, 'The Spiritual Director', pp. 229–73.

132 *Ibid.*, pp. 234–5.

133 *Ibid.*, p. 235.

134 Adolphe Tanquerey, *The Spiritual Life* (1950 edn), p. 257.

135 R. Garrigou-Lagrange, *The Three Ages of the Interior Life* (1960 edn), p. 256.

136 *The Soul of the Apostolate* (1946), p. 171.

137 *Praxis theologica mysticae*, Paris 1920.

138 Letter to his sister Marie de Blic, 25 April 1908, cited in *The Way*, 2:3 (1962), p. 222.

139 Joseph de Guibert, *The Theology of the Spiritual Life* (1956), p. 155.

140 *Ibid.*, p. 157.

141 Letters of 11 February 1607 and 24 June 1604, cited *ibid.*, p. 157.

142 *Introduction to the Devout Life* I.4.

143 De Guibert, *op. cit.*, p. 173.

144 *I giovani del nostro tempo e la direzione spirituale*, Roma, Ave, 1940, p. 12.

145 *The Spiritual Director according to the Principles of St John of the Cross* (1951), p. 7.

146 Jean Laplace, *The Direction of Conscience* (1967), pp. 13, 15, 38, 10.

147 James Walsh in *The Way* 2:3 (1962), p. 208.

148 *Sacramentum Mundi*, volume VI (1970), article 'Spiritual Direction', p. 165.

149 J. H. Wright, 'A discussion on spiritual direction' in *Studies in the Spirituality of Jesuits* 4:2 (March 1972), American Assistancy Seminar on Jesuit Spirituality, pp. 41, 42, 49.

150 Gregory I. Carlson, 'Spiritual direction and the Paschal mystery', *Review for Religious* 33 (1974), pp. 532–41; and Gerald E. Keefe, 'Letter to a person beginning spiritual direction', *ibid.*, pp. 542–5.

151 For recent Roman Catholic writing, such journals as *The Way, Spirituality Today* and *Review for Religious* are very valuable sources.
152 *The Church Porch* lxxvi, cited McNeill, *op. cit.*, p. 230.
153 *A Priest to the Temple* (1632), xv, xxxiv.
154 Letter vii, 10 January 1754; Letter xi, undated; Letter xvi, 4 August 1753.
155 Preface.
156 Cited in Martin Thornton, *English Spirituality* (1963), p. 237.
157 See F. R. Boulton, *The Caroline Tradition of the Church of Ireland* (1958), pp. 129–38.
158 *Resolutions and Devotions* III.9.
159 All cited in P. E. More and F. L. Cross (eds.), *Anglicanism* (1957), pp. 513–17.
160 *English Spirituality* (1963), p. 237. See also T. Wood, *English Casuistical Divinity* (1952), pp. 41ff.
161 *Advice for Those Who Exercise the Ministry of Reconciliation through Confession and Absolution, being the Abbé Gaume's Manual for Confessors ... Abridged, Condensed and Adapted to the Use of the English Church &c.* (Parker, Oxford, 1878), clvi, clviii.
162 *Doctrine of Confession in the Church of England* (1869); *Freedom of Confession in the Church of England, A Letter to the Archbishop of Canterbury* (1877), pp. 11–12.
163 J. M. Neale, cited in Pusey, *op. cit.*, pp. clxiii-clxiv.
164 Cited McNeill, *op. cit.*, pp. 245–6.
165 *English Spirituality* (1963), p. 11.
166 'The cultural factor in spirituality' in *The Great Christian Centuries to Come*, ed. C. Martin (1974), p. 183.
167 *English Spirituality* (1963), p. xv.
168 E. R. Morgan (ed.), *Reginald Somerset Ward 1881–1962: His Life and Letters* (1963), p. 56.
169 *English Spirituality* (1963), p. xiii.
170 *Ibid.*, pp. 298–302.
171 On Shaw see R. D. Hacking, *Such A Long Journey* (1988). Recently the Community of Servants of the Will of God, Crawley Down, have produced a series of booklets on the theme of 'One Tradition' which are very much influenced by Shaw, and continue his teaching.
172 Cited in McNeill, *op. cit.*, p. 171. See also. A. Nebe, *Luther as Spiritual Adviser* (1894).
173 Martin Bucer, *On the True Cure of Souls and the Right Kind of Shepherd*, cited in F. Greeves, *Theology and the Cure of Souls* (1960), p. 11.
174 Cited in McNeill, *op. cit.*, p. 196.
175 Jean-Daniel Benoit, *Calvin, directeur d'âmes. Contribution a l'histoire de la piété Reformée* (Strasbourg, 1947); and *Direction spirituelle et Protestantisme. Etude sur la legitmité d'une direction protestante* (Paris, 1940).
176 22 October 1548, cited in McNeill, *op. cit.*, p. 209.
177 *Ibid.*, p. 257.
178 *Cartwrightiana*, Elizabethan Nonconformist Texts, Vol I., ed. Albert Peel and L. H. Carlson (1951), p. 98. For the full text of the letter see pp. 88–105.
179 Owen C. Watkins, *The Puritan Experience* (1972), p. 8.
180 Cited *ibid.*, pp. 9, 15.
181 *The Reformed Pastor* (1656).

182 See G. F. Nuttall, *The Puritan Spirit* (1967), p. 190.
183 R. Davies and E. G. Rupp, *A History of the Methodist Church in Great Britain*, Vol. I (1965), p. 191.
184 *Ibid.*, p. 189.
185 On the Methodist class meeting and its relevance see William H. Dean. 'The Methodist Class Meeting: the significance of its decline', *Proceedings of the Wesley Historical Society 53* (1981), pp. 41–8; and David Lowes Watson, *The Early Methodist Class Meeting: its origins and significance* (Nashville, Discipleship Resources 1985).
186 *Letters of John Wesley*, ed. J. Telford (1931), IV, p. 188.
187 Davies and Rupp, *op. cit.*, I, pp. 169–70.
188 W. B. Pope, *A Compendium of Christian Theology* (Wesleyan Conference Office, 1877) II, p. 64.
189 Max Thurian, *Confession* (1958); Dietrich Bonhoeffer, *Life Together* (1968 edn), pp. 86–96; Neville Ward, *The Use of Praying* (1967), p. 130.
190 Spiritual Direction and Meditation (1975 edn), p. 13.
191 *Ibid.*, p. 14.
192 Sheldon B. Kopp, *Guru* (1971), p. 3.
193 Thomas Merton, *op. cit.*, p. 17.
194 Edward Carter, *The Spirit is Present* (1973), p. 117.

Chapter 3

1 *The Trial of Man* (1973), pp. 11–12.
2 In *The Charismatic Christ* (1974), p. 45.
3 Alan Wilkinson, *New Fire* 3:25 (1975), p. 456.
4 *The Social System* (1952), p. 445.
5 James Frazer, *The Golden Bough* (1949 edn) pp. 105–6.
6 See Richard C. Cabot and Russell C. Dicks, *The Art of Ministering to the Sick* (New York, 1936).
7 *The Cure of Souls* (1932).
8 *Pastoral Psychology* (1932).
9 Seward Hiltner, *Preface to Pastoral Theology* (1958), p. 20.
10 Paul Halmos, *The Faith of the Counsellors* (1965), p. 44.
11 See Ernest E. Bruder, *Ministering to Deeply Troubled Persons* (New Jersey, 1963).
12 Cf. A. E. Harvey, *Priest or President?* (1975).
13 Carl E. Wennerstrom in J. Luther Adams and Seward Hiltner (eds.), *Pastoral Care in the Liberal Churches* (1970), pp. 37–8.
14 Ethel Venables, *Counselling* (National Marriage Guidance Council, 1971), p. 1.
15 Cf. Kathleen Heasman, *An Introduction to Pastoral Counselling* (1969).
16 Leo J. Trese in Jean Laplace, *The Direction of Conscience* (1967), p. 10.
17 *The Counsellor in Counselling* (1950), p. 11; *Pastoral Counselling* (1949), p. 19.
18 Paul Halmos, *The Personal Service Society* (1970).
19 M. Greenblatt, R. H. York and E. L. Brown, *From Custodial to Therapeutic Patient Care in Mental Hospitals* (New York, Russell Sage Foundation, 1955), pp. 107, 411.

20 *The Faith of the Counsellors* (1965), p. 31.
21 Sandor Ferenczi, *Further Contributions to the Theory and Technique of Psychoanalysis* (1920).
22 Michael Balint, *The Doctor, His Patient and His Illness* (1967), p. 226.
23 Carl Rogers, *Counselling and Psychotherapy* (1942), pp. 28–30.
24 *The Faith of the Counsellors* (1965), pp. 108–9.
25 Cf. H. Lytton and M. Craft (eds.), *Guidance and Counselling in British Schools* (1969).
26 H. J. Clinebell in *Contact* 36 (November 1971), p. 26.
27 Desmond Pond, *Counselling in Religion and Psychiatry* (1973), pp. 74ff.
28 M. A. H. Melinsky in *Religion and Medicine: A Discussion* (1970), p. 118.
29 Frank Lake, 'The place of counselling in the church', *The Times*, 19 August 1967.
30 Frank Lake, *Clinical Theology* (1966), p. 32.
31 Frank Lake, *Clinical Pastoral Care in Schizoid Personality Reactions* (1970), p. 17 and front cover.
32 Association for Pastoral Care and Counselling, Constitutional Papers (1973), p. 3. See W. A. Clebsch and C. R. Jaekle, *Pastoral Care in Historical Perspective* (1964).
33 *The Knowledge of Man* (1965), p. 172.
34 Cf. *The Radical Therapist* (Radical Therapist/Rough Times Collective, 1974).
35 Leonard Berkowitz, 'The case for bottling up rage', *New Society*, 17 September 1973, pp. 761–4.
36 D. E. Jenkins, 'The Christian counsellor' in *Living with Questions* (1969), pp. 110–11.
37 C. D. Kean, *Christian Faith and Pastoral Care* (1961), p. 42.
38 R. S. Lee, *Principles of Pastoral Counselling* (1968), p. 116.
39 Don Browning, 'Pastoral care and models of training in counselling', MS. (Chicago, undated).
40 *Contact* 44 (1974), pp. 31–2.
41 *Social Science and Social Pathology* (1959), p. 330.
42 Cited in James Luther Adams and Seward Hiltner (eds.), *Pastoral Care in the Liberal Churches* (1970), p. 217.
43 *An Introduction to Christian Mysticism*, Lectures given at the Abbey of Gethsemani, MS. (1961), p. 145 (in the possession of Bede House, Staplehurst, Kent).
44 *An Introduction to Pastoral Counselling* (1969), p. 1.
45 *The Minister and the Cure of Souls* (New York 1961), pp. 25–6.
46 'Objections to a proposed national pastoral organisation', *Contact* 35 (June 1971), pp. 25–6, 27.
47 *Ibid.*
48 *Contact* 44 (1974), p. 33.
49 Roy Bailey and Mike Brake, *Radical Social Work* (1975), p. 1.
50 *Ibid.*, pp. 145–6.
51 *Modern Man in Search of a Soul* (1933), p. 70.
52 Victor Frankl, *The Doctor and the Soul* (1973 edn), p. 9.
53 Cf. Mary Barnes and Joseph Berke, *Mary Barnes: Two Accounts of a Journey through Madness* (1971).
54 C. G. Jung, *The Integration of the Personality* (1934), p. 43.
55 *Ibid.*, p. 59.

56 *Modern Man in Search of a Soul* (1933), p. 259.

57 Cf. *Psychology and Alchemy* (1944), p. 14.

58 'Helping people to pray', *New Fire* 1 (1969), pp. 15–23.

59 *The Symbolic Life* (Guild of Pastoral Psychology Lecture No. 80, 1954), p. 13.

60 Kenneth Wapruck, 'Mysticism and schizophrenia', *Journal of Transpersonal Psychology* 1:2 (1969), p. 66.

61 *The Politics of Experience and The Bird of Paradise* (1971 edn), pp. 117, 114, 136.

62 *The Doctor and the Soul* (1973 edn), pp. 9, 10, 14.

63 Reza Arasteh, *Final Integration in the Adult Personality* (Leiden, E. J. Brill, 1965).

64 *God Is a New Language* (1967), pp. 18, 28, 74.

65 *Power and Innocence* (1974 edn), p. 64.

66 *Love and Will* (1972 edn), pp. 13–33, 'Our Schizoid World'.

67 *Clinical Pastoral Care in Schizoid Personality Reactions* (Clinical Theology Association, December 1970), p. 17.

68 *Ibid.*

69 *Existence*, ed. Rollo May (New York, 1958), p. 56.

70 Hubert Van Zeller, *Famine of the Spirit* (1950), p. 28.

71 *The Integration of the Personality* (1934), p. 186.

72 *Revelations of Divine Love*, 55, 56.

73 See, for example, D. Sherwin Bailey, *The Man-Woman Relationship in Christian Thought* (1959); Donald Goergen, *The Sexual Celibate* (1974); etc.

74 *Touching: The Human Significance of the Skin* (1972), p. 273.

75 Ortega y Gasset, *Man and People* (New York, 1957), p. 72.

76 *Summa Theologica* 2.2, q. 142, a. 1.

77 Herbert Marcuse, *One Dimensional Man* (1966), *Eros and Civilisation* (1962), etc.

78 Cited in Dennis Altman, *Homosexual: Oppression and Liberation* (1974 edn), p. 183.

79 For this and other references see John Saward, 'The fool for Christ's sake in monasticism east and west', in A. M. Allchin (ed.), *Theology and Prayer* (Studies Supplementary to Sobornost, Fellowship of St Alban and St Sergius, 1975), pp. 29–55.

80 *Thomas Merton on Peace* (New York, 1971), pp. 160–2.

81 Rosemary Gordon, 'Moral Values and Analytic Insights', *British Journal of Medical Psychology* 46:1 (1973), pp. 6, 10.

82 Cf. Seward Hiltner, 'Christian understanding of sin in the light of medicine and psychiatry', *Medical Arts and Sciences* 20 (1966), pp. 35–49.

83 Karl Menninger, *Whatever Became of Sin?* (1973), p. 19.

84 O. Hobart Mowrer, *The Crisis in Psychiatry and Religion* (Princeton, New Jersey, 1961), pp. 54–5.

85 C. Bouchard, 'Direction spirituelle d'un sujet en psychothérapie', *La Vie Spirituelle*, Supplement 68 (February 1964), p. 37.

86 *Clinical Theology* (1966), p. xxvii.

87 In *The Role of Religion in Mental Health* (1967), p. 57.

88 Austin Farrer, *A Study in St Mark* (1951), p. 80.

89 'The domestic liturgy of marriage', *Christian Celebration* 3:2–3 (Autumn 1974), p. 5.

90 Francis MacNutt, *Healing* (1975 edn), pp. 162–4.
91 *Didascalia et Constitutiones Apostolorum* III.x.1 (ed. F. X. Funk, 1905), I, p. 301.
92 *De baptismo* 3.16.21.
93 *The Spiritual Renewal of the American Priesthood*, ed. Ernest Larkin and Gerald Broccolo (Washington, DC, US Catholic Conference, 1973), p. 18.
94 *Go Preach the Kingdom, Heal the Sick* (1962), pp. 51ff.
95 Agnes Sanford, *The Healing Gifts of the Spirit* (1966).
96 MacNutt, *op. cit.*, p. 190.
97 *Apostolic Tradition*, I.15.
98 *Apostolic Constitutions* 8.17.
99 Canon 17 in W. K. Lowther Clarke, *Liturgy and Worship* (1954), p. 475.
100 Cf. Henri Nouwen, *The Wounded Healer: Ministry in Contemporary Society* (1972).
101 *Vita Antonii* 22.
102 *Ibid.* 21.
103 *Epistola ad Monachos* 11. See Basil Krivoshein, 'Angels and demons in the eastern orthodox spiritual tradition' in *The Angels of Light and the Powers of Darkness*, ed. E. L. Mascall (1954), pp. 22–46.
104 See Sister Augusta M. Raabe, 'Discernment of spirits in the Prologue to the Rule of St Benedict', *American Benedictine Review* 23:4 (1972), pp. 397–423.
105 Ch. 7.
106 Tr. M. B. Salu (1958), p. 78.
107 Cited in de Guibert, *The Theology of the Spiritual Life* (1956), p. 130.
108 *Ibid.*, p. 131.
109 See J. B. Scaramelli, *Discernimento degli Spiriti* (1753), chs. 6–9.
110 Heinrich Bacht, 'Good and evil spirits', *The Way* 2:3 (1962), p. 188.
111 *Exercises* 32.
112 *Annotation* 7.
113 Brian O'Leary, 'Good and evil spirits', *The Way* 15:3 (1975), p. 180.
114 Ignacio Iparraguire, *Vocabulario de Ejercicios Espirituales* (Rome, 1972), p. 103.
115 *Exercises* 17. On the Ignatian tradition see also John Futrell, 'Ignatian discernment', *Studies in the Spirituality of the Jesuits* 2:2 (1970), pp. 56–7.
116 Philip S. Keane, 'Discernment of spirits: a theological reflection', *American Ecclesiastical Review* 168:1 (1974), p. 50.
117 In *The Angels of Darkness*, BBC Radio 3, 27 October 1975.
118 O. Cullman, *Christ and Time* (1951), p. 192.
119 O. Cullman, *The State in the New Testament* (1957), p. 102.
120 G. Vermes, *Jesus the Jew* (1973), p. 22.
121 Cited in T. S. Szasz, *The Manufacture of Madness* (1973 edn), p. 102.
122 *Love and Will* (1972 edn), p. 123.
123 Cf. Victor White, *God and the Unconscious* (1967 edn), especially Chapter 10, 'Devils and Complexes'.
124 In *The Angels of Darkness*, *op. cit.*
125 *The Month*, 'The devilish phenomenon', May 1974, p. 563.
126 MacNutt, *op. cit.*, p. 220.
127 Cf. Erich Fromm, *The Forgotten Language: An Introduction to the Understanding of Dreams, Fairy Tales and Myths* (New York, 1951).

128 Morton T. Kelsey, 'Rediscovering the priesthood through the unconscious', *Journal of Pastoral Counselling* 7:1 (1972), pp. 26–36.
129 Sheldon B. Kopp, *Guru* (1971), pp. 12–13.
130 Henry M. Pachter, *Paracelsus: Magic into Science* (New York, 1951), p. 63.
131 Comm. on Job 38:16.
132 Cited in Kallistos Ware, *The Power of the Name: The Jesus Prayer in Orthodox Spirituality* (1974), p. 17.

Chapter 4

1   *A Sleep of Prisoners*.
2   Monica Furlong, *The End of Our Exploring* (1973), p. 13.
3   *Honest to God* (1966 edn), pp. 29, 130, 30, 41, 49.
4   *Ibid.*, p. 45.
5   E. L. Mascall in *The Honest to God Debate*, ed. D. L. Edwards (1963), p. 94.
6   *Sermon* 71.
7   Cited in W. R. Inge, *Christian Mysticism* (1933), pp. 156–7.
8   *Revelations of Divine Love* 56.
9   See Vladimir Rodzianko, '*Honest to God* under the Fathers' judgment', in *Orthodoxy and the Death of God*, ed. A. M. Allchin (1971), pp. 50–6.
10 In *The Honest to God Debate* (1963), p. 195.
11 'Is mysticism normal?', *Commonweal* 51 (1949–50), p. 98, cited in J. J. Higgins, *Merton's Theology of Prayer* (1971), p. 22.
12 Rufus M. Jones, *Studies in Mystical Religion* (1909), p. xv.
13 See Geoffrey Parrinder, *Mysticism in the World's Religions* (1976), pp. 141–61.
14 *Contemplative Prayer* (1973), p. 29.
15 Thomas Merton, *Thoughts in Solitude* (1958), p. 18.
16 *Contemplative Prayer* (1973), p. 111.
17 Owen Chadwick, *Western Asceticism* (1958), p. 38.
18 Aelred Squire, *Asking the Fathers* (1973), p. 6.
19 Cited Chadwick, *op. cit.*, p. 105.
20 *Vita Antonii* 14.
21 *Conferences* 10:12.
22 *Ibid.* 10:10.
23 *Jesus Caritas* 6 (January 1961), p. 55.
24 *Letters from the Desert* (1972).
25 *Adv. Haer.* 3.20.5.
26 *Ibid.* 5, Preface.
27 *In Joannem* 32:17.
28 *De Incarnatione* 54.
29 *De Fide Orth.*, 2.12.
30 *Patrologia Graeca*, Migne, 44:1137b.
31 *The Mystical Theology of the Eastern Church* (1957), p. 39.
32 *Ibid.* p. 26.
33 *Stromata* 5.11.
34 *De Myst, Theol.* 5.
35 *Contra Eunomium* 1.373.
36 T. S. Eliot, *Four Quartets* (1944 edn), p. 29.
37 Cited in Kallistos, *op. cit.*, p. 25.

38 S. Bulgakov, *The Orthodox Church* (1935), p. 170.
39 Nicholas Zernov, *The Church of the Eastern Christians* (1942), p. 54.
40 Canon 244.
41 Rule, ch. 17.
42 *Revelations of Divine Love*, 10, 55, 11, 56.
43 *Ibid.*, 35, 37, 38, 39.
44 *Conjectures of a Guilty Bystander* (1966), p. 192.
45 *Revelations of Divine Love*, 86.
46 T. S. Eliot, *op. cit.*, p. 59.
47 *Revelations of Divine Love*, 59, 60, 61.
48 Oratio 65. See Benedicta Ward, *The Prayers and Meditations of St Anselm* (1973), pp. 141–56.
49 See Anna Maria Reynolds, 'God and the feminine', *Encounter and Exchange* 14 (1975), pp. 15–20; Eleanor McLaughlin, ' "Christ my Mother": feminine naming and metaphor in mediaeval spirituality', *Nashotah Review* 15:3 (1975), pp. 228–48.
50 *The Cloud of Unknowing* 6.
51 Cuthbert Butler, *Western Mysticism* (1926), p. lii.
52 Cited in *The Way, Supplement* 27 (Spring 1976), p. 9.
53 *Ibid.*, p. 10.
54 Joseph Veale in *ibid.*, p. 14.
55 *Exercises* 162.
56 *Director* 18.
57 *Exercises* 1. W. W. Meissner defines an 'inordinate attachment' as 'an emotional attachment, an emotional responsiveness which has escaped the effective control of ego-systems'. 'Psychological notes on the Spiritual Exercises', *Woodstock Letters* 92 (1963), pp. 349–66, and 93 (1964), pp. 165–91.
58 Gerald W. Hughes, 'The First Week and the formation of conscience', *The Way, Supplement* 24 (Spring 1975), p. 12.
59 D. Stanley, *A Modern Scriptural Approach to the Spiritual Exercises* (Chicago 1967), p. 16. On psychological aspects of Ignatian spirituality, see Ruth Tiffany Barnhouse, 'The Spiritual Exercises and psychoanalytic therapy', *The Way, Supplement* 24 (Spring 1975), pp. 74–82.
60 St Teresa, *The Way of Perfection* 17.
61 *Book of the Foundations* 5:10.
62 *Spiritual Sentences and Maxims* 57.
63 *Mansions of the Interior Castle* 4.1.7.
64 *Book of the Foundations* 5:8.
65 *The Way of Perfection*, Toledo Codex 17:6.
66 *Ibid.* 25:1.
67 *The Living Flame of Love* 3:32; *The Ascent of Mount Carmel* 3:39.
68 St Teresa, *Life* 13:15.
69 *The Ascent of Mount Carmel* 2:4.2.
70 *Spiritual Canticle* 1.11, 12.
71 Father Gabriel, *The Spiritual Director according to the Principles of St John of the Cross* (1951), p. 131.
72 See Jack Ford, *In the Steps of John Wesley: The Church of the Nazarene in Britain* (Kansas City, Nazarene Publishing House, 1968).

73 Statement drafted in Rome in September 1970 at the first informal meeting of the Secretariat with Pentecostal leaders.

74 Rodman Williams, 'Pentecostal spirituality', *One in Christ* 10:2 (1974), pp. 180–92.

75 Kilian McDonnell in *One in Christ* 7:4 (1971), p. 311.

76 Sister Rosslyn, 'Charismatic and contemplative prayer', *Encounter and Exchange* 8 (1973), pp. 4–9.

77 T. Paul Verghese, *The Freedom of Man* (1972), p. 69.

78 Cited *ibid.*, p. 69.

79 Cited in *Sobornost* 5:5 (1967), p. 318.

80 Verghese, *op cit.*, p. 55.

81 *Adv. Haer.* 5.

82 *De Incarnatione* 54.

83 *Or. 2.adv. Ar.* 21.70.

84 *De Carni Resurrectione* 8; *Adv. Marcion* 3:8.

85 *Hist. Ar.* 62.

86 *The Return of the Father* (1875), pp. 48f.

87 Lossky, *op. cit.*, pp. 65, 67.

88 Carlo Carretto, *Letters from the Desert* (1972), p. 43.

89 *Stromata* 7.

90 *Comm. on Song of Songs.*

91 *The Mystical Theology and the Celestial Hierarchies* (Godalming, Shrine of Wisdom, 1956 edn), pp. 18–19.

92 *On the Threefold Way.*

93 *Exploration into God* (1967), p. 125.

94 *IV Sent.* D.15q.4.a.1.qc.2 ad.

95 *Hugh of St Victor: Selected Spiritual Writings*, tr. A Religious of CSMV (1962), pp. 183–4.

96 *Insight* (1972), p. 3.

97 *Living Prayer* (1966), pp. 51, 52.

98 *The Ascent of Mount Carmel*, Prologue.

99 *Ibid.* 1:2.

100 *The Dark Night of the Soul* 1:14.

101 *Ibid.* 2:5.

102 *The Living Flame of Love*, 1:16, 18.

103 L. Boros, *Open Spirit* (1974), pp. 59–60.

104 Hubert Van Zeller, *Famine of the Spirit* (1950), p. 15.

105 *Ibid.*, p. 21.

106 *Conjectures of a Guilty Bystander* (1966), p. 58.

107 *The Knowledge of God and the Service of God* (1938), p. 28.

108 See Vladimir Lossky, *The Mystical Theology of the Eastern Church* (1957), pp. 23–43, and *In the Image and Likeness of God* (1974), pp. 31–48.

109 *Stromata* 5.

110 *Life of Moses.*

111 *Fifth Letter; De Myst. Theol.* 1:3.

112 *The Ascent of Mount Carmel* 1:4.

113 *The Living Flame of Love* 3:78.

114 *Ibid.* 3:49.

115 E. E. Larkin, 'The dark night of St John of the Cross', *The Way* 14:1 (1974), p. 15.
116 *The Ascent of Mount Carmel* 2:13.
117 *The Living Flame of Love* 3:31.
118 *The Dark Night of the Soul* 1:10.
119 See A. Poulain, *The Graces of Interior Prayer* (1928), pp. 178–99.
120 *Spiritual Letters of Dom John Chapman* (1969 edn), pp. 61, 317. Chapman's letters are one of the most important and most valuable sources of guidance for those beginning contemplative prayer. See particularly Appendix 1, pp. 287–321.
121 E. W. Trueman Dicken, *The Crucible of Love* (1963), p. 168.
122 *Retreats for Priests* (1962 edn), pp. 335–6.
123 Letourneau, *La méthode d'Oraison mentale du Seminaire de Saint-Sulpice* (Paris, 1903), p. 222.
124 *The Ascent of Mount Carmel* 2:18.
125 *The Living Flame of Love* 3:29.
126 *Ibid.* 3:31.
127 *Ibid.* 3:34.
128 *Ibid.* 3:38.
129 *Ibid.* 3:39.
130 *Ibid.* 3:40, 41.
131 *Ibid.* 3:46.
132 *Ibid.* 3:47.
133 *Ibid.* 3:48.
134 *Ibid.* 3:51.
135 Cited by J. Dalrymple in *Cistercian Studies* 2:1 (1967), p. 45.

Chapter 5

1 *Christian Uncertainties* (1975), p. 75.
2 Cited in Igumen Chariton of Valamo, *The Art of Prayer*, tr. E. D. Kadloubovsky and E. M. Palmer (1966), p. 63.
3 Cited in Kallistos Ware, *op. cit.*, p. 2.
4 J. Massingberd Ford, *The Pentecostal Experience* (1970), p. 3.
5 *Some Principles of Moral Theology* (1921), p. 228.
6 *The Ascent to Truth* (1951), p. 177.
7 Cited in Higgins, *op. cit.*, p. xix.
8 Thomas Merton in *Dublin Review* 223 (1949), p. 28.
9 Thomas Merton, *The New Man* (1961), p. 44.
10 *The Integration of the Personality* (1934), p. 69.
11 Cited in Kallistos Ware, 'Silence in prayer: the meaning of hesychia' in *Theology and Prayer*, ed. A. M Allchin (1975), p. 12.
12 J. Dalrymple, 'Training in the life of prayer', *Cistercian Studies* 2:1 (1967), p. 41.
13 *On Stillness and the Two Ways of Prayer* 2.
14 H. E. W. Slade, *Exploration into Contemplative Prayer* (1975), p. 11.
15 J-M. Dechanet, *Christian Yoga* (1964) and *Yoga and God* (1974); H. E. W. Slade, *op. cit.*

16 Simon Tugwell, 'The body in prayer', *Doctrine and Life* 24:2 (1974), p. 61. For these quotations see Tugwell, pp. 60–7.

17 *Meditation and the Fulness of Life* (1974).

18 *Summa Theologica* IIa IIae. q. 83 art. 13; 1. 84 art. 2.

19 Slade, *op. cit.*

20 *Yoga Sutras* 2:46–52.

21 Tugwell, *op. cit.*, p. 64.

22 *Op. cit.*, q. 83, art. 12.

23 Tugwell, *op. cit.*, p. 64.

24 See W. Samarin, *Tongues of Men and Angels* (New York 1970), pp. 227–9.

25 Eusebius, *Hist. Eccl.* 5:16f.

26 Simon Tugwell, 'The gift of tongues in the New Testament', *Expository Times* 84:5 (1973), p. 137. See the whole article, pp. 137–40.

27 U. Berlière, *L'Ascèse Bénédictine* (Paris and Maredsous 1927), ch. 7.

28 *Silent Music* (1974), p. 10.

29 *Yoga Sutras* 3.

30 *Living Prayer* (1966), pp. 51, 52.

31 W. H. Longridge, *Retreats for Priests* (1962 edn), p. 333.

32 *Ibid.*, pp. 335–6.

33 *What are These Wounds?* (1950), p. 95.

34 *Apophthegmata*, Arsenius 1, 2.

35 *Ladder of Divine Ascent* 27; Evagrius, *De Oratione* 70.

36 *Ladder* 27.

37 *Ep.* 2.

38 Tito Colliander, *The Way of the Ascetics* (1960), p. 79.

39 *Retreats Today* (1962), p. 84.

40 *Selected Letters 1896–1924*, p. 314.

41 Longridge, *op. cit.*, pp. 337–40.

42 In Owen Chadwick, *Western Asceticism* (1958), p. 207.

43 Cited in *The Art of Prayer*, *op. cit.*, p. 97.

44 *De Oratione* 44.

45 *Ibid.* 70.

46 Cited in Ware, *The Prayer of the Name*, *op. cit.*, p. 13.

47 Peter Russell, *The TM Technique* (1976), pp. 40–1.

48 *The Cloud of Unknowing*, ed. W. Johnston (New York 1973), p. 56.

49 Thomas Weide in *Journal of Transpersonal Psychology* 6:1 (1972), p. 84.

50 *The Adornment of the Spiritual Marriage* 2.

51 Carlo Carretto, *Letters from the Desert* (1972), p. 47.

52 *Silent Music* (1974), p. 59.

53 Carretto, *op. cit.*, p. 48.

54 Cited Ware, *The Prayer of the Name*, *op. cit.*, p. 11.

55 *Ladder of Divine Ascent*, 21, 27.

56 Cited Ware, *op. cit.*, p. 100.

57 In The Art of Prayer, *op. cit.*, p. 100.

58 *How the Hesychast Should Persevere in Prayer.*

Chapter 6

1 *Where the Wasteland Ends* (1972), pp. xxii-xxiii.
2 *Growth in Holiness* (1854) (1960 edn), p. 239.
3 Christian Duquoc in *Concilium* 1:7 (1971), pp. 30, 35.
4 In *Religion and Medicine: A Discussion*, ed. M. A. H. Melinsky (1970), pp. 133, 134.
5 J. E. Bamberger in *Theology and Prayer*, ed. A. M. Allchin (1975), p. 75.
6 H. J.-M. Nouwen, *Pray to Live* (1972), p. 54.
7 *The Asian Journal of Thomas Merton* (1974), p. 329.
8 *Contemplative Prayer* (1973), p. 25.
9 *Raids on the Unspeakable* (1966), p. 158.
10 Cited in *Thomas Merton, Monk: A Monastic Tribute*, ed. Patrick Hart (1975), pp. 53, 135, 183.
11 *The Face of God* (1975), p. 21.
12 Cf. P. E. T. Widdrington in *The Return of Christendom* (1922).
13 *Yes to God* (1975), pp. 28, 81.
14 *The Prison Meditations of Father Alfred Delp* (1963), p. 95.
15 Inscription on Gandhi's place of cremation at Rajghat.
16 Charles Elliott, *Inflation and the Compromised Church* (1975), p. 146.
17 'Contemplation and Resistance', *Peace News*, 18 May 1973.
18 Kahlil Gibran, *The Prophet*.

Appendix

1 Martin Thornton, *The Purple Headed Mountain* (1962), p. 17.
2 *Manual for Interior Souls* 21.
3 B. Poschmann, *Penance and the Anointing of the Sick* (1964), p. 123. See also on the history of penance, P. F. Palmer, *Sacraments and Forgiveness*, Sources of Christian Theology, Vol. 2 (1959); R. C. Mortimer, *The Origins of Private Penance in the Western Church* (1939); O. D. Watkins, *History of Penance*, 2 Vols. (1920); H. C. Lea, *A History of Auricular Confession and Indulgences in the West*, 3 Vols. (1896).
4 Ep. 168.
5 Ep. 66:2.
6 *De Spiritu Sancto* 3:18.
7 Origen, *De Oratione* 28. See N. Abeyasingha, 'Penance and the Holy Spirit', *Review for Religious* 33:3 (1974), pp. 565–72.
8 Albert Mirgeler, *Mutations of Western Christianity* (1964), p. 73.
9 Cited K. E. Kirk, *The Vision of God* (1931), p. 284. My italics.
10 J. Leclercq, F. Vandenbroucke and L. Bouyer, *The Spirituality of the Middle Ages* (1968), p. 41.
11 Council of Toledo 3, c. 11.
12 *The Babylonian Captivity of the Church*, cited Palmer, *op. cit.*, p. 228.
13 *Wesley's Works X* (1956), pp. 119f.
14 Decree on Penance (1551), chs. 6–9.
15 Discourse to the Parish Priests and Lenten Preachers of Rome, 6 February 1940.
16 See F. R. Bolton, *The Caroline Tradition in the Church of Ireland* (1958), pp. 129–38.

17 See W. Walsh, *The Secret History of the Oxford Movement* (1897), pp. 93–146.
18 J. R. W. Stott, *Confess Your Sins* (1964), p. 78.
19 *Confession and Absolution* (1960), p. vii.
20 Cf. George Bennett, *The Heart of Healing* (1971), p. 57.
21 *The Liturgy of Penance* (1966), p. 75.
22 *Penitence*, Apostolic Constitution of Pope Paul VI *Paenitemini* (Catholic Truth Society, Do 450, 1973), p. 10.
23 Christian Duquoc in *Concilium* 1:7 (1971), p. 27.
24 In C. Martin (ed.), *The Great Christian Centuries to Come* (1974) pp. 190–1. There has been little attention to such revision within Anglicanism. There is still no rite of penance in the official texts of the Church of England. Recently Anglicans in the USA, Canada and New Zealand have incorporated short forms for confession in their revised books. But only the Book of Common Prayer of the Episcopal Church of the USA has taken seriously the need for a revised rite in line with the modern Roman thinking, as well as in recognition of the fact that many people will wish to make a full confession at some crisis point. Martin Smith is correct to say that this Prayer Book has 'the strongest testimony to sacramental confession of all the prayer books in the Anglican Communion' (Martin L. Smith, *Reconciliation: preparing for confession in the Episcopal Church*, 1986, p. 121). On the background to the USA revision see Leonel L. Mitchell, 'The reconciliation of penitents', *Anglican Theological Review* 74 (1992), pp. 25–36.
25 Constitution on the Sacred Liturgy 72.
26 *Ibid.* 27.
27 J. D. Crichton, *Christian Celebration: the Sacraments* (1973).
28 On the new rites see *Penance: The New Rites* (Catholic Truth Society Do 471, 1975); *Penance: A Pastoral Presentation* (Catholic Truth Society Do 481, 1975); J. D. Crichton, *The Ministry of Reconciliation* (1974); Bruce A. Williams, 'The new rites of penance', *Homiletic and Pastoral Review* 76:1 (1975), pp. 9–22; Lionel Swain, *Words of Reconciliation* (1976); Kevin Donovan, 'The new penitential rite', *The Way* 15:4 (1975), pp. 295–302, and 16:1 (1976), pp. 57–65. More commentaries and guidelines are still appearing.
29 *Ordo paenitentiae* 4, 5 (in Crichton, *The Ministry of Reconciliation*, p. 96).
30 *Ordo* 11, Crichton, p. 100.
31 *Ordo* 22, Crichton, p. 103.
32 *Ordo* 25c, Crichton, p. 104.
33 Crichton, pp. 47–51.
34 *Ordo* 56, Crichton, p. 118.
35 Crichton, p. 62.
36 See F. J. Heggen, *Confession and the Service of Penance* (1972 edn), p. iii; J. M. Champlin, *Together in Peace* (1974), pp. 113–22.
37 Cf. Karl Rahner, *Theological Investigations* Vol. 3 (1967), p. 201.
38 Crichton, *op. cit.*, p. 7.
39 Printed in William Freburger (ed.), *Repent and Believe* (1972), p. 95.
40 See already such books as Lionel Swain, *Words of Reconciliation* (1976); Joseph M. Champlin, *Together in Peace* (1975); David Konstant, *A Penitents' Prayerbook* (1976).
41 *Principles of Christian Theology* (1966), pp. 428–9.

42 MacNutt, *op. cit.*, p. 287.
43 Crichton, *op. cit.*, p. 89.
44 *Ordo* 10a, Crichton, pp. 99–100.
45 *Penance: Commentaries on the New Rites* (1975), p. 4.
46 *Theological Investigations* Vol. 3 (1967), p. 193.
47 C. Kilmer Myers, *Light the Dark Streets* (1961), pp. 141–2.
48 *Lumen Gentium* ch. 1. para. 1.
49 Ian Ramsey in *Contact*, March 1970, p. 13.
50 Sermon 213:8.
51 Sermon 9:17.
52 Shorter Westminster Catechism, Q. 89 in T. F. Torrance, *The School of Faith* (1959), p. 275.
53 Karl Menninger, *Whatever Became of Sin?* (1975), p. 228.
54 Cf. Joseph M. Champlin, *Preparing for the New Rites of Penance* (1975).
55 Letters 41:12.
56 Alexander Schmemann, *Of Water and the Spirit* (1974), pp. 11, 12.
57 Roman Missal, Eucharistic Prayer 2.
58 See Hippolytus in Migne, *P.G.* 10:625, 628; Cyprian *Ep.* 63:11; Ambrose, *De Sacr.* 4:28, 5:17, 4:24; J. G. Davies, 'The Eucharist and the remission of sins', *Church Quarterly Review* 162 (1961), pp. 50–8.
59 *Ordo* 36.
60 José Miguez Bonino, *Revolutionary Theology Comes of Age* (1975), p. 121.
61 John Macquarrie, *The Concepts of Peace* (1973), p. 72.
62 Cited in W. A. Pantin, *The English Church in the Fourteenth Century* (1962), pp. 197, 109.
63 K. N. Ross, *Hearing Confessions* (1974), p. 59.
64 On material integrity see Bernard Haring, *Shalom. Peace. The Sacrament of Reconciliation* (1969), pp. 111–33.
65 *Ibid.*, pp. 112, 118.
66 *Confession* (1958), p. 118.
67 On the seal see E. Garth Moore, 'Should a priest tell?', *Church Times*, 6 September 1963; J. R. Lindsay, 'Privileged communications: Communications with spiritual advisers', *Northern Ireland Legal Quarterly*. May 1959; Peter Winckworth, *The Seal of the Confessional and the Law of Evidence* (1952). The only modification of the seal allowed by the Church of England is Canon 113 of 1603 which forbade a priest to disclose any details unless they involved such crimes as by the laws of the realm the minister's own life may be called in question. Lord Denning (Attorney General v. Mulholland, and Attorney General v. Foster 1963) claimed that the clergyman was not entitled to refuse to answer when directed by a judge. In fact the Canon Law is quite explicit to the contrary.
68 *Life Together* (1968), p. 94.
69 F. J. Heggen (ed.), *Children and Confession* (1969), p. 61.
70 Cf. Christiane Brusselmans, 'The catechesis of reconciliation', *The Way* 15:4 (1975), pp. 285–93.
71 Cited in *Clergy Monthly* (Delhi), February 1974, p. 88.
72 Resolution 4b cited in Michael J. Walsh, 'First confession in controversy', *The Month* 235:1277 (1974), p. 440.
73 Cited in Otto Betz (ed.), *Making Sense of Confession* (1969), pp. 79–80.

74 Heggen, *op. cit.*, p. 58. Cf. also. F. J. Buckley, *I Confess* (1972), p. 78.
75 Printed in Heggen, pp. 7–9.
76 In *The Tablet*, 11 August 1973.
77 Otto Betz in Betz, *op. cit.*, pp. 95–6, 98.
78 Kohlberg's work has been called into question in relation to women's experience by Carol Gilligan, *In a Different Voice* (1982). Gilligan's work has itself been subjected to critique by feminist writers. On the relevance of Gilligan to spiritual direction see Joann Wolski Conn, *Spirituality and Personal Maturity* (1989), pp. 37–49.
79 J. Goldbrunner cited *ibid.*, p. 101.
80 A. Snoeck, *Beichte und Psychoanalyse* (Frankfurt/Main 1958), p. 65.
81 H. B. Meyer in Betz, *op. cit.*, p. 127.
82 F. J. Heggen, *Confession and the Service of Penance* (1975 edn), p. 16.
83 F. J. Buckley, *I Confess* (1972), p. 21.
84 *Ordo* 10a.

Bibliography

Because of the vast range of relevant literature, I have only included here those books and articles which deal specifically with spiritual direction and/or with the sacrament of reconciliation, and have not included more general works on Christian spirituality.

Aelred of Rievaulx, *Spiritual Friendship*. Kalamazoo, Cistercian Publications 1974.

Joseph J. Allen, *The Inner Way: eastern spiritual direction*. New York, St Vladimir's Seminary Press 1992.

Joseph J. Allen, 'The inner way: the historical tradition of spiritual direction'. *St Vladimir's Theological Quarterly* 35 (1991), pp. 257–270.

Conrad Antonsen, 'Liturgy as a source of spiritual direction'. *Spirituality Today* 33 (1981), pp. 53–64.

'Approaches to Spiritual Direction', *The Way Supplement* 54, Autumn 1985.

The Author of *The Way, A Guide for Spiritual Directors*. London, A. R. Mowbray 1957.

Ruth Tiffany Barnhouse, 'Spiritual direction and psychotherapy', *Journal of Pastoral Care* 33 (1979), pp. 144–163.

William A. Barry, 'Spiritual direction and pastoral counselling', *Pastoral Psychology* 26 (1977), pp. 4–11.

William A. Barry, *Spiritual Direction and the Encounter with God*. New York, Paulist Press 1992.

William A. Barry and William J. Connolly, *The Practice of Spiritual Direction*. New York, Seabury Press 1982.

Benedict Baur, *Frequent Confession: its place in the spiritual life*. Dublin, Four Courts Press 1984.

J. D. Benoit, *Direction spirituelle et protestantisme, étude sur la legitimité d'une direction protestante*. Paris, Alcan 1940.

J. D. Benoit, *Calvin, directeur d'ames*. Strasbourg, Editions Oberlin 1947.

Otto Betz (ed.), *Making Sense of Confession*. Chicago, Franciscan Herald Press 1969.

F. J. Buckley SJ, *I Confess: The Sacrament of Penance Today*. Notre Dame, Ave Maria Press 1972.

Lavinia Byrne (ed.), *Traditions of Spiritual Guidance*. London, Geoffrey Chapman 1990.

Gregory I. Carlson, 'Spiritual direction and the paschal mystery'. *Review for Religious* 33 (1974), pp. 532–541.

Joseph M. Champlin, *Preparing for the New Rite of Penance*. Notre Dame, Ave Maria Press 1975.

Joseph M. Champlin, *Together in Peace*. Notre Dame, Ave Maria Press 1975.

William J. Connolly, 'Contemporary spiritual direction: scope and principles'. *Studies in the Spirituality of Jesuits* 7 (June 1975), pp. 95–124.

Catherine Cornille, *The Guru in Indian Catholicism*. Louvain, Peeters Press 1991.

Kevin E. Culligan (ed.), *Spiritual Direction: contemporary readings*. Locust Valley NY, Living Flame Press 1983.

'Direction spirituelle', *Dictionnaire de Spiritualité*. Vol. 3, Paris, Beauchesne, 1957.

Kevin Donovan SJ, 'The new penitential rites'. *The Way* 15 (1975), pp. 295–302; and 16 (1976), pp. 57–65.

Charles Hugo Doyle, *Guidance in Spiritual Direction*. Cork, Mercier Press 1958.

Martin Dudley and Geoffrey Rowell (eds.), *Confession and Absolution*. London, SPCK 1990.

Kathrine Marie Dyckmann and L. Patrick Carroll, *Inviting the Mystic, Supporting the Prophet: an introduction to spiritual direction*. New York, Paulist Press 1981.

Tilden Edwards, *Spiritual Friend*. New York, Paulist Press 1980.

John J. English SJ, *Choosing Life*. New York, Paulist Press 1978.

John J. English SJ, *Spiritual Freedom*. Guelph, Ontario, Loyola House 1975.

James C. Fenhagen, *More Than Wanderers: spiritual disciplines for Christian ministry*. New York, Seabury Press 1978.

Kathleen Fischer, *Women at the Well: feminist perspectives on spiritual direction*. London, SPCK 1989.

David L. Fleming, 'Beginning spiritual direction'. *Review for Religious* 33 (1974), pp. 546–550.

David L. Fleming, 'Models for spiritual direction'. *Review for Religious* 33 (1975), pp. 351–7.

David L. Fleming, *The Christian Ministry of Spiritual Direction*. St Louis, MO, *Review for Religious* 1988.

Victor Frankl, *The Doctor and the Soul*. New York, Random House 1973.

Forster Freeman, *Readings for Ministry Through Spiritual Direction*. Washington DC, Alban Institute 1986.

Father Gabriel ODC, *The Spiritual Director According to the Principles of St John of the Cross*. Cork, Mercier Press 1951.

Robert C. Garafalo, 'Reconciliation and celebration: a pastoral case for general absolution'. *Worship* 63 (1989), pp. 447–456.

Julia Gatta, *A Pastoral Art: spiritual guidance in the English mystics*. London, Darton, Longman and Todd 1987.

James V. Gay, 'Relationships in spiritual direction'. *Review for Religious* 38 (1979), pp. 559–565.

Carolyn Gratton, *Guidelines for Spiritual Direction*. Denville, NJ, Dimension Books 1982.

Dennis R. Graviss, *Portrait of the Spiritual Director in the Writings of St John of the Cross*. Rome, Institution Carmelitanum 1983.

Margaret Guenther, *Holy Listening: the art of spiritual direction*. London, Darton, Longman and Todd 1992.

Richard M. Gula, 'Using Scripture in prayer and spiritual direction'. *Spirituality Today* 36 (1984), pp. 292–306.

Marlene Halpin, *Imagine That! Using Phantasy in Spiritual Direction*. Dubuque, Iowa, William C. Brown Company 1982.

Bernard Haring, *Shalom, Peace: the sacrament of reconciliation*. New York, Image Books 1969.

Irenee Hausherr, *Spiritual Direction in the Early Christian East*. Kalamazoo, Cistercian Publications 1990.

Charles J. Healey, 'Thomas Merton: spiritual director'. *Cistercian Studies* 11:3 (1976), pp. 228–245.

Margaret Hebblethwaite, 'Ignatian spirituality today'. *New Blackfriars*, September 1983, pp. 365–374.

Margaret Hebblethwaite, 'Spiritual direction without the mystique'. *The Tablet*, 19 August 1989, pp. 943–5.

Monika K. Hellwig, *Sign of Reconciliation and Conversion: the sacrament of penance for our times*. Wilmington, Delaware, Michael Glazier 1982.

E. Glenn Hinson, 'Recovering the pastor's role as spiritual guide' in Gerald L. Borchart and Andrew D. Lester (eds.), *Spiritual Dimensions of Pastoral Care*. Philadelphia, Westminster Press 1985, pp. 27–41.

Thomas M. Holden, 'A therapist's view of spiritual direction'. *CTS Register* [Chicago Theological Seminary] 73 (1983), pp. 1–13.

Shirley C. Hughson, *Spiritual Guidance*. London, Mowbrays 1954.

Clark Hyde, *To Declare God's Forgiveness*. Wilton CT, Morehouse-Barlow 1984.

Damien Isabell, *The Spiritual Director: a practical guide*. Chicago, Franciscan Herald Press 1976.

Martin Israel, *The Spirit of Counsel: spiritual perspectives on the counselling process*. London, Hodder and Stoughton 1983.

Gordon Jeff, *Spiritual Direction for Every Christian*. London, SPCK 1987.

Alan Jones, *Exploring Spiritual Direction: an essay on Christian friendship*. New York, Seabury Press 1982.

Alan Jones, *What Happens in Spiritual Direction?* Cincinnati, Forward Movement Publications, undated.

Adrian van Kaam, *Dynamics of Spiritual Self-Direction*. Denville NJ, Dimension Books 1976.

Gerald E. Keefe, 'Letter to a person beginning spiritual direction'. *Review for Religious* 33 (1974), pp. 542–5.

James M. Keegan, 'Elements and dynamics of a spiritual direction practicum'. *Review for Religious* 51 (1992), pp. 34–45.

Morton T. Kelsey, *Companions on the Way: the art of spiritual guidance*. New York, Crossroad 1983.

Sheldon B. Kopp, *Guru: metaphors from a psychotherapist*. Palo Alto, Science and Behaviour Books 1971.

Jean Laplace sj, *The Direction of Conscience*. London, Geoffrey Chapman 1967.

Kenneth Leech, 'Spiritual direction and psychotherapy'. *Contact* 61 (1978), pp. 13–20.

Kenneth Leech, 'Spiritual direction and the struggle for justice', in J. E. Griffiss (ed.), *Anglican Theology and Pastoral Care*. Wilton CT, Morehouse-Barlow 1985, pp. 41–56.

Kenneth Leech, *Spirituality and Pastoral Care*. Cambridge MA, Cowley Publications 1989, Chapters 4–7.

Alice McDowell Pempel, 'The three dimensions of spiritual direction'. *Review for Religious* 40 (1981), pp. 391–402.

William McNamara, *Christian Mysticism: a psychotheology*. Chicago, Franciscan Herald Press 1981, Chapter 3, 'Soul Friending'. pp. 49–73.

Gerald E. May, *Care of Mind, Care of Spirit: psychiatric dimen-*

sions of spiritual direction. San Francisco, Harper and Row 1982.

Thomas Merton, *Spiritual Direction and Meditation*. Wheathampstead, Anthony Clarke 1975.

Thomas Merton, 'The spiritual father in the desert tradition'. *Cistercian Studies* 3 (1968), pp. 3–23.

Leonel, L. Mitchell, 'The reconciliation of penitents'. *Anglican Theological Review* 74 (1992), pp. 25–36.

August Nebe, *Luther as Spiritual Adviser*. Philadelphia 1894.

Jerome M. Neufelder and Mary C. Coelho (eds.), *Writing on Spiritual Direction by Great Christian Masters*. New York, Seabury Press 1982.

Henri J. M. Nouwen, 'Spiritual direction'. *Worship* 55 (1981), pp. 399–404.

Jim O'Connell, 'Gestalt approaches to spiritual direction'. *CTS Register* [Chicago Theological Seminary] 73 (1983), pp. 229–43.

Thomas C. Oden, *Care of Souls in the Classic Tradition*. Philadelphia, Fortress Press 1984.

Carolyn Osiek, 'The spiritual direction of thinking types'. *Review for Religious* 44:2 (1985), pp. 209–219.

M. Basil Pennington, 'The Orthodox tradition of the spiritual father and Mount Athos'. *Review for Religious* 41 (1982), pp. 610–615.

Evan Pilkington, *Spiritual Direction in the Church Today*. London, Christian Evidence Society 1980.

Bernard Pitaud, 'La direction spirituelle: propos sur un livre récent'. *Christus* 37 (1990), pp. 95–102.

Janice G. Raymond, *A Passion for Friends: towards a philosophy of female affection*. London, Women's Press 1986.

Kenneth Ross, *Hearing Confessions*. London, SPCK 1974.

Robert Rossi, 'The distinction between psychological and religious counselling'. *Review for Religious* 37 (1978), pp. 546–571.

Janet Ruffing, *Uncovering Stories of Faith: spiritual direction and narrative*. New York, Paulist Press 1989.

Sandra M. Schneiders, 'The contemporary ministry of spiritual direction'. *Chicago Studies* 15 (1976), pp. 119–135.

Sandra M. Schneiders, *Spiritual Direction: reflections on a contemporary ministry*. Chicago, National Sisters Vocation Conference 1977.

Timothy Sedgwick, 'Moral vision and spiritual direction'. *St Luke's Journal of Theology* 28:1 (1984), pp. 39–44.

Elinor Shea, 'Spiritual direction and social consciousness'. *The Way Supplement* 53 (1985), pp. 30–42.

Martin L. Smith, *Reconciliation: preparing for confession in the Episcopal Church*. London, Mowbrays 1986.

Martin L. Smith, 'The formation of spiritual directors'. *Cowley* 15 (1989), pp. 6–7.

John R. Sommerfeldt (ed.), *Abba: guides to wholeness and holiness, east and west*. Cistercian Studies 38, Kalamazoo, Cistercian Publications 1982.

Michael Stock, 'Spiritual direction from a Dominican perspective'. *Spirituality Today* 33 (1981), pp. 4–33.

Raymond Studzinski, *Spiritual Direction and Midlife Development*. Chicago, Loyola University Press 1985.

Josef Sudbrack, *Spiritual Guidance*. New York, Paulist Press 1984.

John Sullivan (ed.), *Spiritual Direction*. Carmelite Studies, Washington DC. ICS Publications, 1980.

Theological Education 24:1 (1987) and 24: Supplement 1 (1988) contain valuable articles.

Martin Thornton, *Christian Proficiency*. London, SPCK 1959.

Martin Thornton, *Spiritual Direction: a practical introduction*. London, SPCK 1984.

Max Thurian, *Confession*. London, SCM Press 1958.

Wesley D. Tracy, 'John Wesley, spiritual director: spiritual guidance in Wesley's letters'. *Wesleyan Theological Journal* 23 (1988), pp. 148–162.

Jesse M. Trotter, *Christian Wholeness: spiritual direction for today*. Wilton CT, Morehouse-Barlow 1982.

Frank Wallace, 'Spiritual direction'. *Review for Religious* 44 (1985), pp. 196–208.

Caroline White, *Christian Friendship in the Fourth Century*. Cambridge University Press 1992.

Mary Wolff-Salin, *No Other Light: points of convergence in psychology and spirituality*. New York, Crossroad 1988, Chapter 12 'Spiritual Guide or Therapist?' (pp. 135–144).

Barry A. Woodbridge, *A Guidebook for Spiritual Friends*. Nashville TN, Abingdon Press and The Upper Room 1985.

Short Index